Oscar Wilde

Rothenstein Wilde
By William Rothenstein
Willliam Andrews Clark Memorial Library

Oscar Wilde: Recent Research

A Supplement to
'Oscar Wilde Revalued'

IAN SMALL

ELT Press

UNIVERSITY OF NORTH CAROLINA AT GREENSBORO

ELT PRESS   PO Box 26170
University of North Carolina Greensboro, NC 27402–6170
E–Mail: Langenfeld@uncg.edu

NUMBER FIFTEEN : 1880–1920 BRITISH AUTHORS SERIES

ISBN 0–944318–14–2
CIP 00–133041

Distributed in Europe by COLIN SMYTHE, LTD.
P.O. Box 6   Gerrards Cross
Buckinghamshire   England SL9 8XA

TYPOGRAPHY & DESIGN

Display Type & Text Type : ITC Trump Medieval

Title-Page / Contents
Designed by Robert Langenfeld

Dust Jacket
Designed by Alison Barnes

WordPerfect 9 / CorelDraw & Corel Ventura 7.0
Printer : Thomson–Shore, Inc. Dexter, Michigan
Production Coordinators : Lee Broat & Diane Fadden

CONTENTS

Preface

IN THIS VOLUME I have tried to offer an account of recent research on Oscar Wilde since 1993 which is both complete and useful for the academic reader. In the nature of things, however, it is not comprehensive. In particular many reprints or cheap editions of individual works have been silently passed over. Some critical articles have also been omitted either because they are too slight or they contain no new information or insights. In addition I have not made any attempt to document all the general literary or cultural histories in which Wilde has been mentioned, although I have drawn attention to those where he figures prominently. There are also a number of books and articles to which I draw the reader's attention, but which unfortunately have not been available in Britain. Readers on both sides of the Atlantic might be disappointed to learn how often American books are not advertised for sale in Britain and vice versa; in addition many American periodicals are not routinely collected by British libraries.

The centenary of Wilde's death inevitably means that a number of studies advertised to appear in 2000 will be too late for me to discuss fully. I have, however, mentioned all those of which I am aware.

Ian Small
Birmingham 2000

Introduction

The study for which this volume is a supplement, *Oscar Wilde Revalued: An Essay on New Materials and Methods of Research*, was published in mid-1993. Because of the varying speed at which academic publications cross the Atlantic, however, the book's effective cut-off date for material was the end of 1992. In *Oscar Wilde Revalued* I surveyed the scholarly and critical studies on Wilde which had appeared since his death in 1900. Much of this work was not easy to find, and much of it was unknown to many of Wilde's modern readers and students; moreover it forms part of a long debate about the significance of Wilde as a twentieth-century icon. I therefore attempted to describe critical work on Wilde in terms of its relation to large trends in literary and cultural criticism, so that the reader could piece together the story of Wilde's reputation and cultural importance over the first nine decades of the last century. Any such account had of course to be value-laden, and despite my best efforts my prejudices no doubt revealed themselves. Nonetheless because of the relative paucity of good bibliographical resources at that time I felt it appropriate to attempt a descriptive rather than an evaluative account of the material I was summarizing.

A further aim of *Oscar Wilde Revalued* was to compile information about the major collections of manuscripts of Wilde's works, to list and describe them both by holding institution and by title. I also tried to indicate the depth of material about Wilde held by the major research libraries in Britain and the United States, including some of the significant letters to him, some of the significant letters about him, as well as some of the unpublished letters by him, and his contracts and connections with publishers and theatre-managers. It was clear that while most of this material was known in one way or another to some individuals in the scholarly community, its significance had been largely overlooked. I suggested that this situation was mainly due to an academic myopia—to the fact that scholars tended to "see" only that material which they expected to find, and that archival resources were typically used to confirm preexisting hypotheses about Wilde.

The nature of academic life inevitably ensures that surveys of research age quickly, and it has become increasingly clear to me that the material contained in *Oscar Wilde Revalued* needs bringing up to date. It is, however, equally clear that the methods of organization and description which I employed in that book have outlived their usefulness. The whereabouts of most of the major manuscript and archival resources for Wilde are now well-known to scholars. The new letters and manuscripts which have turned up since 1992 have been fully described in recent critical and bibliographical literature (particularly in Karl Beckson's *The Oscar Wilde Encyclopedia*, 1998). Moreover technological developments have irresistibly brought about changes in the way academic literary research is recorded. When the material contained in *Oscar Wilde Revalued* was assembled, computational bibliographies, such as that of the Modern Language Association of America, were a much less familiar resource, available only in relatively expensive formats, and then only in large research libraries. Now most subject bibliographies and the catalogues of most of the major research libraries in Europe and the United States are available online, are regularly updated, and can be accessed for a few pennies. This last fact alone would compromise an attempt simply to repeat the bibliographic formulae and ambitions of *Oscar Wilde Revalued*. This book is, then, a rather different enterprise: it is far more self-consciously evaluative than the volume for which it is a supplement.

My grounds for providing an appraisal rather than a description of recent research are in fact two-fold. If the advantage of electronic bibliographies is their comprehensiveness and the speed with which they can be updated, their disadvantage is that the sheer amount of information which they contain can be overwhelming, particularly for the scholar new to the field. For this reason, it seems to me that there is still an important role left for a deliberatively evaluative guide to research, one where the prejudices of the critic who is making the evaluations are as far as possible openly declared.

In this respect, I see the second aim of the present volume as inviting, and perhaps stimulating, critical debate. Implicit in the way I have selected and organized material is the assumption that there are clearly identifiable trends in recent Wilde research; equally implicit in my account is the assumption that some trends are more important and more valuable than others. Readers may disagree with my judgements, but I would view such disagreements in positive terms, as helping to provoke a debate about what should count as research, and particularly what should count as valuable research. As academic publications increase and as more and more material about Wilde appears, so the need to organize and judge that material becomes more pressing. The mere accumulation of new pieces of information or new opinions, without any attention to how they relate to each other, does not constitute a body of research. At its best it is a situation which produces a sense of freedom and experiment; at its worst it is a babble of competing voices which is difficult to make sense of. The aim of the current volume, then, and in contrast to my intentions for *Oscar Wilde Revalued*, is to initiate a debate about how an authoritative body of research on Wilde might be defined.

My first chapter, "Wilde in the 1990s," is closest in conception to *Oscar Wilde Revalued*, in that I attempt to trace what I see as the main directions of Wilde research over the past decade. The chapter explains and tries to justify the organizing principles of the seven chapters which follow it. Chapter 2, "Biography," is concerned with the continuing fascination with Wilde's life, and its emphasis is on how critics have moved on from dissatisfaction with Richard Ellmann's biography (1987). Chapter 3, "New Paradigms in Literary and Cultural History," is organized in terms of what I see as the three "master-narratives" or paradigms which emerged in the 1990s as ways of describing Wilde's life and work: the "gay" Wilde, the "Irish" Wilde, and "Wilde and Consumerism." The order given to these narratives is in the first instance a chronological one (the "gay" Wilde is of an older vintage than the other two). That said, my narrative will reveal both my sense that they are not of equal weight and my suspicion that some will endure better than others. Chapter 4, "Wilde the Writer," represents a different way of seeing research, in that it is organized partly generically and partly (and loosely) in terms of the various stages of Wilde's career. The structuring principle of this chapter (which in some sense could represent a further, but much less well-defined master-narrative) reflects my conviction that an important trend in research in the last decade has been an attention to what might be called the less glamorous aspects of the *oeuvre*—to the seriousness with which Wilde took his role as a poet, to the sheer amount of time he devoted to writing journalism, and to the complexities of the production and staging of the plays.

It should be acknowledged that not all of the material under review fits neatly into my categories—indeed the very fitting of it into those groupings represents a certain kind of treatment to which its authors might object. Such criticism may well be valid, in which case I readily own up to Procrustean inclinations. However, in my defence I would reply that such a treatment is an inescapable consequence of constructing any taxonomy, and claim that the benefits of such a categorization far outweigh the disadvantages which it might bring.

Chapter 5, "Critical and Introductory Studies," is devoted to works which cover the whole of Wilde's career and output: it embraces introductory accounts designed for the student reader as well as more serious or "advanced" monographs. Chapter 6, "Editions," reviews recent textual studies and editions of Wilde—of individual works, selections and collections. Many publishers have issued popular editions of the best-known works, such as *The Picture of Dorian Gray* and *The Importance of Being Earnest*. Only those which are of significance for the academic reader are mentioned. Chapter 7, "Research Resources," examines the new research resources for the study of Wilde's work which have become available over the past decade. I include information about new primary materials and about the new ways in which primary materials have been made accessible; also included are new bibliographies. Some new letters and forthcoming editions of the letters are described. Chapter 8 is a bibliography of works referred to in chapters 1 to 7; for ease of use, it is structured in two ways, alphabetically by author, and (when appropriate) in relation to individual works by Wilde.

| 1 |

Wilde in the 1990s

In *Oscar Wilde Revalued* I offered a number of predictions about the possible future directions of research and scholarship in Wilde studies. One of the interests, but also one of the disappointments, of compiling and writing the present supplement has been to discover whether these predictions have materialized and whether the trends which I described in the earlier volume have persisted during the intervening years.

Broadly speaking, in *Oscar Wilde Revalued* I identified three main avenues for possible future investigation. I described how Andrew Shelley, in a review of Richard Ellmann's biography, suggested that the reader comes to Wilde with the life already written—that Wilde's cultural prominence has been such that it is difficult to rid ourselves of preconceptions and prejudices about him. This caveat notwithstanding, my first hope about the future direction for Wilde biography was that what I called the "myth of Wilde" might be replaced by more scholarly studies based on a securer factual rather than anecdotal foundation. The second hope was that closer critical attention would be paid to the material circumstances of literary production in the 1880s and 1890s, in order that a sense of Wilde as a new type of professional writer might become more readily available to critics. My third hope—arising from the second—was that there might be more emphasis given to the textual condition of all of Wilde's *oeuvre*: that how Wilde wrote, as much as what he wrote, would become a legitimate topic for research.

Almost eight years later, we are certainly in possession of much more information about Wilde's life and work. It is now possible to see that for the twenty-five year period between its publication in 1962 and Ellmann's biography, Rupert Hart-Davis's volume of Wilde's *Letters* remained the principal source of accurate information about their author. It gave valuable and concise details about what we might call Wilde's "circle," as well as important data about the writing and publishing of the works. This said, the biographical material contained in the *Letters* is not always easy to access. In 1998 Karl Beckson published *The Oscar Wilde Encyclopedia*, a valuable resource for scholars which collects, in a much more accessible form than the *Letters* or Ellmann's biography could ever do, many of the "facts" of Wilde's writing career, including accounts of the manuscripts, particularly those of the poems. Beckson's *Encyclopedia* suggests that a different biography could now be written. The last eight years have seen the publication of a number of essays, notably those by Horst Schroeder, which continue to correct errors—either of fact or of emphasis—in Ellmann's work. Moreover a group of cultural critics, including Joseph Bristow and Alan Sinfield, have questioned the whole basis (and indeed the bias) of Ellmann's account, with its implication that Wilde and his contemporaries had, in Sinfield's words, a "concept of gayness like our own . . . lurking . . . beneath the text . . . fully formed but waiting to be unveiled."

On the other hand, it has to be acknowledged that the "myth" of Wilde as the gay martyr, which Ellmann did so much to legitimate and popularize, has persisted. It might have gathered even greater momentum. In recent studies by Gary Schmidgall, Melissa Knox, Ed Cohen, Philip Hoare, and Jonathan Fryer, Wilde is still seen as the iconic gay, a status which was confirmed by Brian Gilbert's 1997 film *Wilde*, which reconstructed (or "constructed" might be a more accurate verb) in graphic detail Wilde's sexual encounters, elements of which existed in the mind of the scriptwriter rather than in any reliable documentary evidence. It is also undeniably the case that many recent productions of Wilde's plays, as Joel H. Kaplan has shown, have traded explicitly on their audiences' advance knowledge of Wilde's gay life.

This said, it is also true that there are some new ways of understanding Wilde's biography. The most important is the idea, virtually unique to the 1990s, of Wilde the Irish nationalist. The significance which ought to be attached to Wilde's nationality and the complex difficulties in defining what that nationality actually meant to him vary between historians; but there can be little doubt that "Wilde the Irishman" (a phrase coined by Jerusha McCormack as the title for her 1998 collection of essays) has emerged as a consistent theme in many recent studies. Some critics, such as Davis Coakley, have concentrated on filling in details of Wilde's upbringing in Ireland, emphasizing the importance of the cultural life of Dublin in the mid-nineteenth century. Other accounts have traced the persistence of Ireland and of Irish issues in Wilde's understanding of himself, even after he had left his native country. Scholars have been alerted to the importance of an exiled Irishman's political agenda in works ostensibly devoted to English (or British) subjects or themes, and intended principally for English audiences. The thread of an argument which was once used consistently about the work of James Joyce—that of a complex resistance to, and an attempt to undermine, the language of the colonizing nation and its art forms—is now being applied to Wilde's writing. In the eyes of Declan Kiberd, a forceful spokesman of this new view of Wilde, this resistance can be seen in Wilde's celebration of lying, for Kiberd an unequivocally political act. For Jerusha McCormack, Wilde's attitude to Englishness is more robust and potentially more destructive: it is analogous—in her words—to "guerrilla" warfare.

It has been interesting to observe how closely the impetus of the "Irish" Wilde approximates to the mythologizing tendencies of the "gay" Wilde. The construction of both "Wildes" has to confront the problem of uneven, and sometimes contradictory evidence—which is why, of course, they become the material for myths in the first place. Both paradigms rely upon highly selective details of the life which in turn are used to instruct us in how to read the works. McCormack addresses this issue directly and in terms of a simple question: "What difference does it make to read [Wilde] as Irish?" Both myths claim to politicize the work, and both detect a deeply serious project behind the familiar figure of wit, aesthete, and dandy.

In 1992 it was just possible to detect an interest in the professional aspects of Wilde's career. Eight years later it is easy to see how that interest has sharpened and become more focused. There have been a number of studies devoted to Wilde's journalism, in particular by Josephine M. Guy, Catherine Ksinan, and John Stokes. A useful if unscientific gauge of the depth of that interest can be seen in some changes in the agendas of conferences on Wilde. The topic of the "writerly Wilde" was virtually absent from the first international conference on him held at the University of Birmingham in 1993. By contrast, one of the four colloquiums held during the first half of 1999 at the William Andrews Clark Memorial Library on *Wilde and the Culture of the Fin de Siècle* was devoted to "Wilde Writings: Attributions, Editions and Revisions." It covered the textual histories of several of Wilde's works, including his journalism, some of his poetry, *The Soul of Man*, and *Salome*. There have also been book-length studies of Wilde's revisions to his Society Comedies, and of the compositional history of *Intentions*. In addition there is a new study which examines Wilde's creativity and writing practices over the whole *oeuvre* in relation to the ways in which his works were commissioned and sold in the 1880s and 1890s.

It would be a mistake, however, to represent this last body of work as uniform; rather there are significant tensions in it. Some critics, such as Sos Eltis, see a teleological development in Wilde's *oeuvre* and a political motivation underlying his practices of composition. By contrast, other studies have emphasized the commercial basis of much of his writing, a circumstance which is not easily compatible with the idea of him being driven by a radical politics—or, for that matter, a politics of any sort, except the most loosely defined conservatism. In addition there are a number of other studies which have taken a completely different approach to understanding Wilde's writing career. Rather than attempting an explanation of his works' textual features or variants, some cultural historians have located the overall dynamic of his writing career in relation to what Regenia Gagnier has called a "market society." However, just as the significance of Wilde's revisions is disputed, so too is the precise nature of his relation to those processes of consumerism. Here the fundamental issue is whether Wilde appropriated but subverted consumerist values, or whether, from his transactions with his first publisher and his American lecture tour onwards, he was actually complicit with them.

Ironically, then, in this new work on Wilde's career as a professional writer we see a repetition of the basic tension which underlay biographical research in the 1980s and early 1990s. On the one hand, there are cultural historians who are determined to politicize Wilde's writing—to see in his work various kinds of radicalism, to understand him as a sort of meta-critic, whether of British imperialism, Victorian sexual ethics, or a market society. On the other hand, there are those "de-mythologizers" who want to see Wilde the writer as a more ordinary and pragmatic figure, and who highlight the practical details of his quotidian dealings with the culture industry, including his constant need to earn money. The tension between these two "stories" of Wilde's writing career remains unresolved.

My hopes in 1992 for a closer study of the textual condition of Wilde's works have also been partly fulfilled. Some praiseworthy new editions have appeared in the past eight years: the first volume (of nine) in the Oxford English Texts *Complete Works of Oscar Wilde, Poetry and Poems in Prose*, edited by Bobby Fong and Karl Beckson, was published in 2000. Isobel Murray's World's Classics edition of the *Poems* (which drew upon earlier research by Fong later used for the Oxford English Texts edition) makes an admirable text for students. Joseph Donohue's compendious work (compiled in part with Ruth Berggren)—*Oscar Wilde's The Importance of Being Earnest: A Reconstructive Critical Edition of the Text of the First Production, St James's Theatre, London, 1895*—was published to coincide with the centenary of the first performance of that play, and reflects a growing interest among literary and theatre historians in seeing Wilde's drama as performance texts. Merlin Holland has updated the Collins edition of the *Complete Works*, and extended the range of Wilde's *oeuvre* to cover for the first time forgotten and fugitive writing (including the unsigned journalism and reconstructions of lectures). In addition some new letters came to light during the 1990s. These have been incorporated into a revised edition of the correspondence (for Fourth Estate in Britain and Henry Holt and Co. in the United States) once again edited by Merlin Holland. Finally, there have been a number of projects aimed at making archival material more readily accessible. The most significant of these will undoubtedly be the reproduction on microfilm of *The Oscar Wilde Collection* in the William Andrews Clark Memorial Library at the University of California, Los Angeles, by Primary Source Media (of the Gale Group).

All of this activity is very welcome, and places both the scholar and the student in a much better position to study Wilde's work than they were in 1990. Unfortunately, however, alongside these scholarly projects, there has been a steady stream of inadequate and sometimes shoddy editions of Wilde's work which seem designed to trade exclusively on his name. By and large these editions have little or no textual collation, often give inaccurate or partial textual histories, and explanatory annotation of a very uneven quality. An exemplary case is the Carcanet *Selected Poems of Oscar Wilde* (published in 1992, but not discussed in *Oscar Wilde Revalued*), edited by Malcolm Hicks. As my account of Murray's 1997 edition of the *Poems* argues, much of the information for a scholarly edition of Wilde's poetry has long been in the public domain (in the form of Bobby Fong's 1978 doctoral thesis held at the University of California, Los Angeles). It is therefore hard to understand why Hicks's edition contains no textual work, little annotation and a thin introductory essay which covers very familiar ground. One is forced to the inevitable conclusion that the fact that Wilde's published works are long out of copyright licenses such a cavalier treatment. Likewise, the fact that the unpublished manuscript drafts remain in copyright, and that many have been very difficult to study, may explain why so many editions contain so little textual work. Perhaps the most positive way to view these second-rate editions is as a testimony to the enduring popularity of their author: as always, Wilde continues to move copy. A good but different example of this phenomenon has been the publication of Philip Hoare's *Wilde's Last Stand*, a book hardly about Wilde himself, and which should more properly have been entitled *The Pemberton Billing Trial*.

In *Oscar Wilde Revalued* I observed that the rehabilitation of Wilde which occurred in the 1980s had largely been produced by developments in literary and cultural theory, many of which questioned the basis of empiricist literary historiography. As a consequence, I suggested then that some of the most challenging studies of Wilde, including Regenia Gagnier's *Idylls of the Marketplace*, did not require the unearthing of much new data about Wilde's writing practices—that is, they were not in the first instance dependent upon "an accurate biography and scholarly editions" (*Oscar Wilde Revalued*, 176). Eight years later, it is surprising to see that a large number of theoretical and interpretative studies continue to be undertaken without recourse to accurate information about the textual condition of Wilde's works, or to the precise details of his biography, despite the fact that, as I have indicated, such knowledge is now much more easily available. Melissa Knox's controversial *Oscar Wilde: A Long and Lovely Suicide* (1994) is a case in point: much of the argument of the book relies on the claim, made first by Arthur Ransome and repeated most authoritatively by Richard Ellmann, that Wilde contracted syphilis as a young man. Despite the fact that a number of writers have since contested or dismissed this claim, and despite acknowledging their point that the "syphilis-thesis" is unsupported by evidence, Knox nonetheless thinks that it is sufficient simply to *state* the opposite: that "I believe that he [Ransome] was right" (xix), as though a belief, if held strongly enough, is indistinguishable from fact. Her readings of Wilde's work require that he suffered, or believed that he suffered, from syphilis; so syphilis is what he had, or believed that he had.

What seems to be a factual error of a different order occurs with Robert Tanitch's observation in *Oscar Wilde on Stage and Screen* that "at Alexander's request Wilde cut the play [*Earnest*] from four acts to three" (256). Jonathan Fryer in *André and Oscar* makes a similar claim, arguing that when Alexander "expressed the opinion that the play [i.e. *Earnest*] was too long . . . Oscar . . . had it cut from four acts to three" (105). This account of the genesis of the three-act version of the play is simply incorrect. As Russell Jackson noted in his 1980 edition, as Peter Raby described in *Modern Drama* in 1994, and as Joseph Donohue showed in painstaking detail in his 1995 edition of *Earnest*, it was Alexander who cut the text after he had dismissed Wilde from rehearsals. Of course it is true that Wilde kept faith with this decision in the sense that Leonard Smithers's 1899 book version of the play retained the three-act structure (although with many local revisions). However this is not at all the same as saying, as Tanitch and Fryer do, that Wilde was the originator of the three-act version. To dwell upon such an apparently minor error may seem nit-picking, but it is exactly these sorts of details which, taken collectively and cumulatively, feed our sense of the power-relationship between Wilde and his theatre-managers, and therefore our sense too of Wilde's oppositional relationship with the literary culture of his time. The larger and more worrying question is why such errors persist when the relevant facts can be so easily checked. In this regard, little has changed since 1992: it is as if the "stories" which critics and historians want to tell about Wilde are so compelling that they dictate in advance what is to count as evidence for them.

Most readers will hardly need reminding that the relationship between the role of evidence and the nature of literary research is a complex one. The neat paradigm shifts often taken to characterize other disciplines of knowledge seem not to occur in literary studies, in the sense that competing, often contradictory explanations of a writer and his or her work tend to co-exist rather than replace each other. This observation seems particularly true of Wilde studies over the past eight or ten years. Today it is easy to find critics writing of Wilde the Irish nationalist, Wilde the homosexual, Wilde the craftsman-writer, as well as Wilde the plagiarist. Rarely is there a sense that these different interpretations are not easily compatible with each other: or, rather, an acknowledgment of the simple truth that Wilde cannot be *all* of these things at the same time. The very fact that these contradictory "Wildes" are seen to be individually plausible and acceptable unfortunately speaks volumes about the role of evidence in research into Wilde.

A critical voice might object at this point that the nature of the reading which has to be undertaken to produce a volume such as this one has placed me in an unusual position. Covering in a relatively short period of time a large number of studies on a similar subject is almost bound to produce both weariness and querulousness. It might be thought that as a consequence I am likely to be much more alert to, but far less tolerant of, repetition and contradiction. On the other hand, it can be argued that such a reading experience does confer some distinct advantages. It is admittedly a personal view, but my suspicion is that the last eight years of research on Wilde have been marred by a variety of scholarly shortcomings. It is difficult to know which among them is the most culpable. The first, which I have alluded to already, is a cavalier attitude to certain kinds of evidence. For some critics the significance of solid but mundane facts are routinely overlooked; by contrast there has sometimes been an over-reliance on dubious or unsubstantiated evidence—occasions, for example, where reports of Wilde's activities or conversation are taken at face value. The second and related habit can be described as a highly partial attitude to what counts as relevance and therefore to what are considered relevant facts. Of course no account of Wilde can ever cover all the "facts" about him (whatever that phrase might mean). What is disturbing, though, is the sense that for some writers on Wilde counter-evidence or awkward facts tend simply to be ignored. For example, it is interesting how many accounts of Wilde's sympathies with Irish nationalism inevitably overlook his role as a Protestant landlord, one who openly lamented the low returns on family property.

Third, it is notable that a lot of what is advertised as "new research" turns out to centre on new theorizations or new interpretations of evidence which has already been in the public domain for a number of years. To take the same example as before, those essays, histories, and monographs dedicated to the "Irish" Wilde have (with some honourable exceptions) uncovered relatively little new information about his early life in Ireland, or his actual connections with the day-to-day activities of Irish nationalists. Likewise, despite all the effort which continues to be devoted to describing the "gay" Wilde, there are still many details of his sexual life which are unknown: there is no firm evidence about new lovers, about when Wilde was first initiated into homosexuality, about whether he did in fact contract syphilis, and about what his and Bosie's relationship actually amounted to in physical terms. The uncertainty about these issues continues to compromise our understanding of the larger and altogether more serious question of Wilde's own conception of his sexuality. In a similar manner, many accounts of Wilde's attitudes towards consumerism—another apparently new topic in Wilde studies—are not grounded in detailed evidence about what constituted a consumer culture in late-Victorian Britain, Ireland and the United States, nor indeed about how his works were bought and sold.

The situation I have described is perhaps the inevitable legacy of that distrust of empirical evidence associated with certain kinds of critical theory in the 1980s. It is a situation, however, which prompts a number of difficult questions. What is the status, and more importantly the value, of research which has an inconsistent relationship with empirical evidence? On what grounds is it possible to controvert the "findings" of such research? How do individual accounts relate to each other? In terms of Wilde studies, how collectively do they further our knowledge of him? At a practical level, how is the account of the "Irish" Wilde compatible with the "gay" Wilde; and how are either of these compatible with the Wilde who had to learn his living entirely by his pen? A useful project for future studies of Wilde might be an attempt to reconcile the insights generated by critical theory with the attention to secure evidence associated with traditional empiricist historiography.

| 2 |

Biography

The best recent testimony to the continuing strength of interest in Wilde's life has been the reissuing in 1997 of two early biographies by Vyvyan Holland and Sheridan Morley, both of which are of a pre-Ellmann vintage. The timing of their re-publication can perhaps be explained by the interest generated by Brian Gilbert's film *Wilde*. Both biographies claim to have been updated, but they contain little information that is new. (It is worth noting here that in 1997 Julian Mitchell's screenplay for Gilbert's film was published by Orion.)

Ellmann's biography itself is now more than thirteen years old, but it continues to dominate biographical studies, to the extent of having generated what is virtually a sub-industry of its own. Although devoted to listing conceptual shortcomings and factual errors (often of tiny detail) that industry ironically continues to ensure the pre-eminence of Ellmann's account. Given the level of dissatisfaction with his work in the scholarly community, it is perhaps surprising that a new academic biography has not been forthcoming. Actually, scholarly or academic reactions to Ellmann have been of two kinds. The first and main one, as I have indicated, has been to provide new details of Wilde's life which either contradict or amplify the story told by Ellmann. This research is scattered in specialist periodicals and has usually taken the form of short notes. Because of its dispersed nature, it will inevitably take time to filter through to critical accounts of Wilde as well as to popular biographies. Interestingly, Ellmann is still invariably the starting-point for most new lives of Wilde.

The second scholarly reaction to Ellmann has been to rethink the whole basis of what a biography should be. For the most part this sort of re-theorizing of the "story" of Wilde's life has appeared in reviews; it is, however, also implicit in some critical accounts not directly to do with biography, but which have produced interpretations of the works inconsistent with those given by Ellmann. Of particular importance too is a corpus of new historical research on homosexuality (discussed in 3. i.) which has direct implications for the ways in which Ellmann conceptualized a gay lifestyle. The only academic monograph to set out a new *sort* of life, based on entirely different premises to those of Ellmann, is Melissa Knox's controversial *Oscar Wilde: A Long and Lovely Suicide* (1994). However, as I note below, Knox's notion of evidence is derived explicitly from psychoanalysis, and it is therefore not easy to reconcile with Ellmann's basic (if occasionally flawed) empiricist historiography.

Knox apart, those biographers who have engaged directly with Ellmann have generally been non-academics and they have catered for the popular audiences who have supported the many recent and successful revivals of Wilde's plays. One consequence of this situation is that these biographies tend to contain little new factual information; in short, they simply reinterpret Ellmann's evidence, and for this reason are not, for the academic reader, as novel or as radical as their authors appear to believe. It is perhaps worth noting that the point of departure for most of these new popular biographies is almost always a desire to take issue with Ellmann's account of Wilde's homosexuality. This desire is in turn characterized by an extremism of one sort or another. Wilde either becomes "more straight" (in, for example, Joseph Pearce's *The Unmasking of Oscar Wilde* [2000]), or more extravagantly gay (as in Gary Schmidgall's *The Stranger Wilde* [1994]).

Finally, there has been a useful body of new research around the life, and this has taken a number of forms. Interest in Lady Wilde has continued, with two new studies of her life and her relationship with Wilde. There has also been a new biography of Douglas (2000) and one of Ross (by Jonathan Fryer) is in press. In contrast to recent biographies of Wilde alone, some of these works do contain significant new discoveries. There has also been a growing interest in Wilde's reputation in the years immediately following his death. These accounts generally contain little information about Wilde's own experiences, but they do inform us about the way his life contributed to early twentieth-century reactions to (and understanding of) homosexual culture.

◆ ◆ ◆

It was undoubtedly commercial considerations which in 1997 led Thames and Hudson to reprint the 1966 revision of Vyvyan Holland's 1960 biography of his father, *Oscar Wilde*. Holland's account is of course marked by a reticence understandable both in pre-Wolfenden Britain and in a son's account of his father. Nonetheless, it is worth noting that Holland's biography does contain valuable insights and some particularly striking images: of the manuscript of Max Beerbohm's "A Peep Into the Past," sketches of Sir Edward Carson, of Constance Wilde, of Robert Harborough Sherard, of the exterior of Wilde's home at 16 Tite Street, of the Kansas Opera House, and so on. Also reprinted (in 1999) was Merlin Holland's revised and corrected edition of Vyvyan Holland's 1954 autobiography, *Son of Oscar Wilde*. Merlin Holland corrects errors of fact and adds an index to his father's work, part of which describes family life in Tite Street. (For the textual importance of Vyvyan Holland's appendix on "The Unpublished Poems in Prose Told by Oscar Wilde," see sections 6. ii. and 7. i.)

Sheridan Morley's 1976 biography of Wilde was also re-issued in 1997. The bibliographical material states that it is a "new edition," although if so its bibliography and scholarship have eluded revision. Few of the sources are post-1970, and Morley even makes do without citing Hart-Davis's *Letters* (1962). The book is readable, but it is light. More than anything else, perhaps, its re-publication in paperback is once again testimony to the selling power of its subject. A much more important reprint is the issue by Dover Publications of Harford Montgomery Hyde's *The Trials of Oscar Wilde*. The reprint is an "unabridged republication of the second enlarged (1962) edition, formerly entitled *Famous Trials, Seventh Series: Oscar Wilde*" (back-cover blurb). Reprinted, too, is the foreword by Sir Travers Humphreys, who acted as "junior to Sir Edward Clarke" (7). Montgomery Hyde's book has always been an important resource, and its wider availability is to be welcomed. In "Redressing Oscar: Performance and the Trial of Oscar Wilde" (1996), David Schulz discusses the relationship of the trial to ritual and performance and the scapegoating of Wilde. Also published is a set of official documents relating to the trials and imprisonment. Entitled *Oscar Wilde: Trial and Punishment 1895–1897* (1999), the volume includes an introduction by

Michael Taylor. (See also Nancy Erber, "The French Trials of Oscar Wilde" [1996].)

Of the new popular biographies of Wilde, perhaps the most self-consciously confrontational is Gary Schmidgall's *The Stranger Wilde: Interpreting Oscar* (1994). Schmidgall's ambition is to replace what he terms "the common memory" of Wilde—that is, "Oscar the Wit and Wilde the Convict" (Schmidgall is fond of this kind of facetious word-play)—with the "stranger Wilde" of his title, a figure who is "dubious, perplexing, and inconvenient." At the "heart" of Wilde's strangeness, according to Schmidgall, is "the fact of his homosexuality" (xiv). This "fact" in itself is hardly a revelation; but Schmidgall's argument is that "the ramifications of Oscar's gay identity have not been fully and satisfyingly explored" (xv), and his biography is an attempt to correct the "discreet . . . dispensation" of an "older" generation of biographers, most particularly Richard Ellmann. Schmidgall eschews organizing Wilde's life into a straightforward chronological narrative. Instead he gives us nineteen chapters, each of which describes a discrete facet of Wilde's life or personality, and each, in Schmidgall's terms, a way of "seeing Oscar" (1). These include discussion of the representation of Wilde and the Aesthetes in *Punch*, Wilde the "fashion plate" (62), Wilde and "mothers," Wilde and Constance, Wilde and fatherhood, the childlike qualities of Wilde, and his attraction to youth (as Schmidgall puts it, Wilde the "Ass-thete," a pun which mercifully barely works in British English). There are also a series of chapters exploring aspects of the trials (one of which, for example, is devoted to the question of why Wilde did not flee Britain). Other chapters compare Wilde with contemporaries as varied as Nietzsche, George Ives, G. B. Shaw, Edward Carpenter, and Henry James. One of the central chapters, entitled "Closet Philosopher," elaborates most clearly Schmidgall's view about Wilde's sexuality—that Wilde was firmly out of sympathy with his "closeted" gay contemporaries, particularly James and Pater. It is this argument which permits Schmidgall to speculate in his penultimate chapter that, if Wilde were alive today, he would be domiciled in San Francisco, earning his living as "a splendid late-night talk-show habitué . . . a mesmerizing blend of Gore Vidal and Truman Capote" (390).

Schmidgall makes no attempt to integrate these chapters with each other, for his thesis is that in the face of the complexity of Wilde's life we should not simplify, but embrace contradiction, and enjoy the "raucous ambiguity" of Wilde's personality (16). Actually, this thesis is not at all new: the idea of Wilde, masks, and dissimulation has a long pedigree. Indeed the sense of contradiction and complexity in Schmidgall's portrait of Wilde is more a product of his book's structure than of any new information that it contains. There are also frequent if small errors of fact which remain bothersome. For example, Schmidgall talks of Aristotle's "*Nichomathean Ethics*" (304), and reports that Pater "refused" to review *Dorian Gray* because he thought it too "dangerous" (320), when in fact Pater's generally laudatory notice appeared in the *Bookman* in 1891, a detail which a glance at Beckson's *Critical Heritage* or Mason's *Bibliography* would have revealed. To British ears (and probably to those of many Americans) some of Schmidgall's slang grates. So to call Ada Leverson, one of Wilde's most loyal friends, a "handsome *bon vivant* fag hag" (292) is not only inaccurate, but also betrays a misogynist tone in Schmidgall's book. Another annoyance is the relentless interpretation of the literary works as autobiographical disclosure: there is little sense of their fictionality or artifactuality ("autobiography," Schmidgall claims, but makes no attempt to prove, "is rarely absent in his writings" [298]). Wilde's writing career and his relations with London's theatrical world are virtually absent. However the book's basic shortcoming is the failure to engage with the term "homosexual" itself. The subtleties of discrimination upon which Alan Sinfield and Joseph Bristow insist (see 3. i.) are simply not to be found. So at one point Schmidgall asks of some lines in *The Picture Of Dorian Gray*, "How, given all the novel's . . . coded and not-so-coded allusions to homosexuality, could such a statement have been read by gay readers of the time without an enormous sense of challenge and liberation?" (306). Exactly this elision of gay experience in the 1890s with that in the 1990s has been the subject of much recent theoretical writing on homosexuality.

A very different kind of popular biography is Juliet Gardner's *Oscar Wilde: A Life in Letters, Writings and Wit* (1995). In contrast to Schmidgall's work, there is not a lot of text (about 160 pages, a good half of which is illustration), and unlike some works already mentioned, it is competently written and researched. The volume is particularly good in the range and quality of its illustrations. These include, as one might anticipate, contemporary pictures of the places where Wilde lived or which he visited: Dublin, Oxford, London,

Paris, Philadelphia, San Francisco, and so on. But more unexpectedly, the volume reproduces images that are not easily accessible: a sketch of the façade of 16 Tite Street, reproductions of the title page of *Ravenna*, some of Ricketts's illustrations for *The Sphinx*, cartoons by Beerbohm of the Marquess of Queensberry, Frank Harris, and Robert Hichens (the author of *The Green Carnation*). There are, however, some weaknesses in Gardner's book which the documentary appeal of its images tends to mask. She reproduces an illustration of what she claims are "actors in *Lady Windermere's Fan*, in performance at St James's Theatre, 1892" when the photograph was one taken in a studio. There are also some errors of emphasis and some of fact: for example, the assertion that *A Woman of No Importance* "ran for 118 nights. It made its author £100 a week" (109) is inaccurate. In the main, however, the book's limitations derive from simple pressures of space. So Gardner notes that *Poems* (1881) was published "at Wilde's expense" (44). This is technically true, but the emphasis is misleading: the author does not inform us that such an arrangement was not at all unusual in nineteenth-century publishing.

A work in a similar vein to Gardner's volume is Stephen Calloway's and David Colvin's *The Exquisite Life of Oscar Wilde* (1997). Larger in size and more lavish than *Oscar Wilde: A Life in Letters, Writings and Wit*, it nevertheless disappoints. The narrative is bland, and often unsupported by evidence. The images which the book reproduces are of an excellent quality, but for a volume which is clearly intended to sell partly on its illustrations, they are few and over-familiar.

Jonathan Fryer's *André and Oscar: Gide, Wilde, and the Gay Art of Living* (1997) restricts itself to a single aspect of Wilde's biography—the friendship between Wilde and Gide—which the author rightly claims is a topic that has not been studied in any depth, perhaps because of the unreliability of the witnesses involved. The book focuses on homosexuality rather than on writing as the common ground between the two men, and uses their sexual biographies as examples of a particular kind of late nineteenth-century gay lifestyle, one which Fryer sees as explicitly international. Fryer is a journalist, and in contrast to many academic books on Wilde's sexuality, he has produced a work uncluttered with jargon and theoretical abstraction; as a result the story he tells flows easily, but it is not without its shortcomings and irritations for the researcher. Fryer provides a list of those books which he claims "were of direct use in the preparation" of his volume (239). However his text has virtually no notes and there is no attempt to source precisely any of the evidence upon which his narrative is based. As a consequence disparate kinds of evidence are conflated. So Gide's use of his own experiences in his fictional works is given the same status as properly attested documentary evidence, which in its turn is indistinguishable from anecdotal evidence. This mélange is unfortunate, given that we know that many of Wilde's contemporaries tended to mythologize his life, and that much misinformation about him appeared immediately after his death.

Wilde scholars should be reminded of the existence of Patrick Pollard's judicious *André Gide: Homosexual Moralist* (1991), and Alan Sheridan's more recent *André Gide: A Life in the Present* (1998). Sheridan describes the cultural context in France of the 1890s in which Gide experienced Wilde first as a "name" and in advance of their actual meeting. He also discusses critically Gide's (differing) recollections of that meeting. (Gide's own *Oscar Wilde* is advertised to appear in October 2000, and so unfortunately has not been examined.)

Another irritation of Fryer's work is that the actors in it are known by Christian or nicknames: Gide is André, Wilde is Oscar, Lord Alfred Douglas is Bosie, and Pierre Louÿs becomes just Pierre. Such a shorthand unfortunately gives a sense that Fryer is intimately familiar with the men involved in his story; worse, it produces a picture of nineteenth-century homosexuality in which tensions and dilemmas are intensely personal: principally they involve the guilt arising from conflicts in the relationships between married gay men, their mothers and their wives. Such an emphasis is completely at variance with most modern discussions of nineteenth-century sexuality which emphasize the importance of the political. While some readers might welcome Fryer's attention to the significance of women in the lives of Gide and Wilde, his failure to discuss the elements of power involved in nineteenth-century homosexual relationships can be disconcerting. For example, Fryer's description of Wilde's, Douglas's and Gide's trips to north Africa tends to be troped unselfconsciously in terms derived from nineteenth-century discourses—as a liberation from the stifling elements of contemporary northern European bourgeois sexual *mores*. This might well be how Gide and Wilde (as well as others such as John Addington Symonds and later E. M. Forster) saw their travels, but we might have hoped that a modern writer would maintain some sense of distance between his subjects and their representations of themselves. Other critics have seen the buying of under-age boys or vulnerable young men, many of whom were poor and did not speak English, as a form of sexual tourism, which in turn invites (or even demands) the insights of postcolonial theory to analyse it. The limitations of Fryer's approach can be seen dramatically in his description of an encounter between Gide, Paul-Albert Laurens (his travelling companion) and a young Algerian girl:

> when Paul became involved with a sixteen-year old girl called Mériem from the Oulad Nail tribe, and generously offered to share her, André seemed only too pleased to comply. . . . Mériem was like a sturdy young animal, totally without shame, in that way more like a boy than a girl. (74)

This view is presented as simple fact without any supporting evidence. That a writer might wish to interrogate the sources for such an account (to ask, for example, whether Mériem was similarly struck by Paul's generosity, and whether she would have recognized herself as "a sturdy young animal") seems lost upon Fryer. It is hard to avoid the conclusion that the narrative voice shares some of the self-deceiving attitudes to sexual predation which characterized the self-absorption of many late nineteenth-century northern European Decadent writers.

With the centenary of Wilde's death upon us, it was probably inevitable that many publishers wanted to commission new biographies. The appearance of Joseph Pearce's *The Unmasking of Oscar Wilde* at the beginning of 2000 may be one of the first of a number of such opportunist publications. Pearce's point of departure is a dissatisfaction with Ellmann's 1987 life, which (Pearce argues) "may not be a colossal lie but what emerges from his pages is not a true picture of its subject" (xv). Many critics have pointed to the frequent errors of detail in Ellmann's work; unusually, though, Pearce's quarrel is with Ellmann's interpretation of the facts he found: "as a life of Wilde [Ellmann's biography] is fairly comprehensive in facts while remaining uncomprehending of truth" (xv). Such a facile opposition between facts and truth is in itself reminiscent of the most vulgar forms of eighteenth-century historiography, that there is an inner truth which only the gifted can discern and which exists independently of empirical evidence. As Pearce puts it in his first chapter: "since the facts of

[Wilde's] life are an elaborate masquerade one must seek the truth beyond the facts" (1). More to the point, such a quaint account of truth liberates Pearce from the need to undertake new archival research, and permits him to plunder Ellmann's and Hart-Davis's material at will. For example, of the twenty-five notes for Chapter 9 ("Courting Constance"), twenty-three are references to Hart-Davis or to Ellmann (rather surprising, one might be tempted to conclude, for such an "elaborate masquerade"). So if the reader is not to find any new information about Wilde in this biography, is there anything new about Pearce's reading of his subject?

In his ambition to uncover the Wilde beneath his masks, Pearce hypothesizes a "true" Wilde and a dark angel, his "dark alter ego" (230); this alter ego is gay, transgressive, and disreputable. However Pearce swims resolutely against the tide of nearly all recent criticism by being impressed not by the *alter ego*, but its opposite: "Wilde's cynicism dances on the surface of his psyche, whereas desolation and despair lurk in the depths. The cynical shallows, the shadows of decadence, were for show, but the spiritual well was carefully concealed, smothered, shielding from public scrutiny the real Oscar Wilde" (106). Or again, apropos of *A Woman of No Importance*:

[Wilde's] higher self, emerging triumphant in his art, still clung, almost unwillingly, to the religious sensibility which had accompanied him throughout his life. His lower self, pouring forth epigrams at the dinner table or in his criticism, sought licentious liberation from the moral constraints that his higher self, the voice of conscience, sought to impose. (213)

Pearce's book is structured via a series of short chapters intermingling biography and literary criticism, in which individual works are interpreted in relation to his oddly Victorian view of the life. He tends to see Wilde's critical writings embodying the voice of the dark angel—"poisonous," he calls them. By contrast the "literary" (or fictional) works are straightforwardly moral. So, for example, in chapter 15 ("Malice through the Looking Glass") we are told of *The Picture of Dorian Gray* that "few novels have been more obviously moral in extent and intent than this cautionary tale of a soul's betrayal of itself and others" (168). In chapter 18 ("Saints and Sinners"), we learn that in *Salome* "Wilde emerges ... as a Christian moralist *par excellence*." In chapter 24 ("Out of the Depths") Pearce informs us that "*De Pro-*

fundis showed Wilde at his most honest and candid. Nowhere in its pages is there the barest hint of the disingenuous" (262). These interpretations will no doubt come as something of a surprise to most academic critics. They will be equally perplexed by the picture of Wilde as *miles Christi* which Pearce draws. For such a determinedly contrary view of Wilde to convince, Pearce needs to base his argument on much more secure, much more widely drawn evidence. He also needs a much subtler literary sensibility. The tenor of the book, and the quality of its author's interpretative imagination, are usefully captured in the following description of the relationship between Pater and Wilde: "Pater prompted the loins of Wilde's creativity, arousing the urge to probe into the lowest depths of human existence, life's lusts and not its loves. Yet Pater was too shallow to reach the heart and mind of Wilde's creativity and intellect" (38). One might object to Pearce's insensitive language when he discusses the intellectual relationship between two gay men. Equally objectionable is the gross distortion of one of the most subtle and sensitive literary minds of the late nineteenth century; Pater may have been arcane and super-sophisticated, but he was certainly never shallow.

In his aptly titled essay, "Biography and the Art of Lying" (1997), Merlin Holland discusses a number of problems in writing about Wilde's life of which writers such as Pearce and Fryer should have been aware. Holland notes that biographers have always come to Wilde's life with a certain predetermined agenda—as I have indicated, a point frequently made by reviewers of Ellmann's biography in the 1980s. Such a comment is generally true of most biographies, but Holland's thesis is that it is particularly (and often damagingly) true of the life of Wilde because it obscures the "multicoloured kaleidoscope of apparent contradictions in need not of resolution but appreciation" (16). Holland's article attempts to counter a number of especially persistent lies, including the allegation that Wilde suffered from syphilis, and Ellmann's image of a cross-dressed Wilde playing Salomé—since revealed to be a photograph of Alice Guszalewicz. (See also Melissa Knox, *Oscar Wilde: A Long and Lovely Suicide* [1994]; Merlin Holland, "Comments on Susan Balée's Review of *Oscar Wilde: A Long and Lovely Suicide*" [1996]; and Horst Schroeder, *Alice in Wildeland* [1994], all of which are discussed below). On the other hand, Holland also reminds readers that early biographies which on the surface seem least concerned with fact, and so the least objective, have the undeniable merit of being written by individuals who "knew the man in person" (8). He specifically suggests that the work of Frank Harris is "long overdue for re-evaluation" (6), a process which his introduction to a new edition of Harris's *Oscar Wilde: Including "My Memories of Oscar Wilde" by George Bernard Shaw* should help to facilitate (1997).

A work which particularly attracted Merlin Holland's displeasure was Melissa Knox's *Oscar Wilde: A Long and Lovely Suicide*; it is a difficult book to categorize because it falls uneasily between criticism and biography. Knox claims to be writing a "a pyschobiographic study of Wilde" (xi), a project which she distinguishes from "standard biography" on the grounds that it analyses the "unconscious" rather than "conscious" mind of its subject (xii). Such an ambition clearly requires a different concept of evidence from that employed by more orthodox biographers or critics. Most obviously, and by definition, there can be no direct sources of what is unconscious. Rather, for Knox, the psychoanalytic critic has to use techniques similar to those of the psychoanalyst proper: she claims to apply "psychoanalytic principles" in order to examine Wilde's writings "for the screen memories and wishes that they contain" (xv). Knox uses interpretations of literary works to reinforce her speculations about the various repressions in Wilde's psychic life, including his (alleged) erotic attraction to his sister Isola, and his (alleged) feelings of guilt (allegedly) produced by the belief that he had contracted syphilis. In chapters on *Salome*, the poetry, fiction, letters, *The Importance of Being Earnest* and *De Profundis*, Knox describes Wilde's choices about form and style in terms of psychic repressions. For example, for Knox the "rather uncommon meter" (10) of parts of Wilde's poem "Requiescat" reveals "the vision of Isola as a prostitute . . . well hidden beneath the overtly expressed sorrow" (13). Metrical tension allows Knox to identify an emotional and sexual tension: that Wilde "could not feel tenderness and lust at once" (13). She sees this pattern repeated in Wilde's relationship with Alfred Douglas.

For the non-Freudian, the logic of Knox's methodology is deeply troubling. In outline terms, her tactics are as follows: in her reading of Wilde's works she takes for granted an expressive relationship between emotion and language, one which she thinks guarantees the self-evident truth of her interpretation. In the process she ignores many of the issues with which a literary critic would be concerned:

the conventionalized and artifactual nature of literary works, as well as the self-conscious use of personas (in Wilde's case, of masks) as a literary device. The fact that Knox treats letters, plays, published and unpublished documents in more or less the same way reveals the singular nature of her understanding of literary creativity, one which pays no attention to the sophistication of the writing, nor to what philosophers call the institutional nature of art. Knox then uses her interpretations of what are often fictional, but always highly conventionalized works as evidence of feelings and desires that Wilde could not express nor even fully acknowledge. These feelings, now reified through their coded literary expression, are found in further works. There is clearly no way to break this viciously circular way of thinking, a limitation which is of enormous importance given the sensational nature of Knox's claims about Wilde's sexuality.

There are other, perhaps stronger, and more general reservations about her method. Psychoanalysis built its reputation on interview, on the disclosures, often unintended, of the speaking subject. What it means to psychoanalyse the dead is not at all clear. Neither is it clear how the highly conventionalized literary language of the 1890s corresponds to the stream of associations encouraged by the questions of the analyst. At this point the otherwise dull niceties of textual scholarship become crucially important. It is revealing that almost all of Knox's quotations from Wilde are taken from the Collins *Collected Works*; that is, in discussing the expressive qualities of Wilde's *oeuvre* she pays little attention to the different versions in which particular works exist, and to the processes of revision involved in their composition. This omission is important because drafts of, say, Wilde's poems reveal that changes to single lexical items could appear quite arbitrary. For example, in successive drafts of a poem a term is often replaced by its antonym. Here it is clear that a term is being chosen for its sound rather than its semantics. Similarly, the manuscripts of *The Sphinx* show Wilde writing lists of isolated rhyme words; so "colossal" is set against "phantasmal," and "labyrinth" alongside "hyacinth" and "plinth" (see Stuart Mason, *Bibliography of Oscar Wilde* [1914], 397). In this instance Wilde's creativity is once again being tuned to the conventional rather than to the expressive qualities of language. More importantly, if one wants to see literary works as expressive of an author's emotions, then logically the first choice of text ought to be the manuscript, as that form is least likely to be distorted by institutional censorship or revisions made in anticipation of audiences' response. Knox does list as "sources" in her bibliography manuscripts of Wilde's works held in the British Library, including those of *The Sphinx* and some of the Society Comedies, yet there is scant reference to any of this material in the body of her book. Tellingly, her chapter on *The Importance of Being Earnest* routinely quotes (as I have said) from the Collins *Collected Works*, which reprints the 1893 Bodley Head edition of *Lady Windermere's Fan* (incorporating many of George Alexander's changes), but— unusually— reproduces the four-act version of *Earnest*, which was neither published nor performed in Wilde's lifetime. This decision is particularly odd, given that we know that Wilde's initial ideas for *Lady Windermere's Fan* were, like his initial conception of *The Importance of Being Earnest*, very different from the published version. Knox gives no explanation why on one occasion she takes the final printed version of a play, and on another the manuscript/typescript version as the best evidence of Wilde's emotional state. This blindness to the significance of textual embodiments is surprising in a biographical study—it points to a damaging failure to appreciate the fact that many other agents than the author are involved in the transmission of a text. In its turn this failure fatally undermines Knox's claims for the expressivity of Wilde's work.

Susan Balée's review of Knox's *Oscar Wilde: A Long and Lovely Suicide* in *Victorian Studies* (1995) prompted an animated response from Merlin Holland (1996), who once again described the reasons for not accepting Ellmann's view that Wilde died of syphilis. Holland claimed that both "the medical and literary press have run articles supporting my view that the 'death-by-syphilis' theory is radically unsound" (539); in this he is surely correct. Holland also defends himself from allegations of unfair dealing with permissions concerning the Wilde estate, a self-justification which the vast majority of Wilde scholars who have dealt with the estate would be happy to confirm. (Another full-length account of Wilde, Barbara Belford's *Oscar Wilde: A Certain Genius*, is advertised as appearing in October 2000, too late to be read for inclusion in the present volume.)

Other critics have also been keen to winnow biographical fact from speculation. The indefatigable and scholarly Horst Schroeder (in *Alice in Wildeland* [1994]) provides information which corrects the most extraordinary error in Ellmann's biography. Schroeder tactfully prints, with the minimum of comment, the image which was re-produced on the back cover of Ellmann's first (Hamish Hamilton) edition of his biography in 1987. Schroeder simply quotes the legend from Ellmann's volume: "*Wilde in costume as Salome.*" That image had caused students of Wilde some problems, first expressed by John Stokes in the *London Review of Books* in 1992. There Stokes was em-phatic that Ellmann's picture "almost certainly isn't of Wilde," and that in the Roger Violet photo-library in Paris it "is filed with another picture, obviously of the same person and taken at the same session, labelled '*Leonora Sengera dans le rôle de Salomé à Leipzig.*'" In Ell-mann's picture, not only had Wilde contrived to grow breasts, his face (and particularly his nose) appeared to have changed shape in quite unexpected ways. Schroeder agrees with Stokes that the image is not of Wilde, but suggests it was of Alice Guszalewicz in a performance of Strauss's opera in Cologne in 1905. Schroeder traces the career of Guszalewicz and describes her performance in that production:

> Alice was costumed in a long skirt with a chevron pattern, her upper part being naked except for a richly decorated brassière. Around the ample waist of the Junoesque figure ("junonische Erscheinung") there was a gir-dle, studded with jewelled rosettes and dots. . . . Thus apparelled, Alice was an intriguing Salome, although in fairness it should be added that in the dance of the seven veils Alice was doubled by a ballet dancer, Emma Grondona (Frankfurt). (16–17)

Schroeder makes his point by printing eight further pictures of Guszalewicz, including four more of her as Salomé. Disappointingly, Schroeder omits to mention the larger implications which his re-search would support: the protean ability of Wilde's life to assume any shape which the biographer thinks appropriate. There is now what is almost a tradition of biographers of Wilde who find in his life corroboration of what they have been looking for and ignore (deliber-ately or otherwise) anything that amounts to counter-evidence. Ell-mann's biography, with its rehabilitation of syphilis, of Wilde's exploding corpse, and its "discovery" of Wilde the cross-dresser, has many examples of such a process.

Exactly this issue was the subject of my 1993 essay for the *Library Chronicle of the University of Texas*. It set out to investigate why it was the case that significant parts of the Wilde archive held at the Harry Ransom Research Center, including a number of letters, seemed to have been ignored or overlooked by Ellmann (and Hart-

Davis). I argue that this evidence pertains to the "mundane events—the 'stuff'—of 'ordinary life'" and that it presents a Wilde significantly different from the glamorous and tragic figure described by Ellmann. More precisely I suggest that the material at Texas allows us to see Wilde as a professional writer concerned with self-promotion and log-rolling. This issue is taken up in more detail in *Oscar Wilde's Profession* (2000; discussed in 5.).

In his 1997 essay, "Oscar Wilde and the Dreyfus Affair," J. Robert Maguire is also concerned with some fine details of Wilde's life. The starting-point of the complicated story which Maguire puts together is a piece by Chris Healy published within two years of Wilde's death in the English periodical *To-Day* which celebrated Wilde's key role in the freeing of the martyred French Jew, Alfred Dreyfus. Maguire finds corroboration for Healy's claim in the diaries and correspondence of Carlos Blacker, one of Wilde's oldest friends, and a trustee of Constance Wilde's marriage settlement. Drawing on court records of the case, Maguire traces the complex story of Wilde's and Blacker's involvement in the Dreyfus affair. He provides evidence that Blacker knew of Dreyfus's innocence through his friendship with Colonel Alessandro Panizzardi, the Italian military attaché who had been told that the real traitor was Esterhazy. Blacker in turn confided in two individuals, a sometime Oxford don, Frederick Cornwallis Conybeare (who published an account of the case in 1898, omitting Blacker's involvement) and Wilde. Wilde later fell out with Blacker and betrayed his confidence to Chris Healy and Roland Strong, both of whom were journalists caught up in the Dreyfus case. Healy confided his information to Emile Zola, and Strong to Esterhazy. In the body of his essay, Maguire fleshes out the details of this intriguing story through evidence derived from Blacker's papers (now privately held). For students and scholars of Wilde the account holds several areas of interest. It gives fuller details of Wilde's friendship with Blacker; it also describes Wilde's fluctuating moods and vulnerabilities following his release from prison. In addition it sheds light on the strains which the continuation of Wilde's affair with Douglas placed on his relationship with Constance.

In "Oscar Wilde: A 'Writerly' Life" (1994), Russell Jackson and I examine the similarities between what we call "Wilde's practice of local textual revision and his attempt to 'revise' or refashion his personality through the use of masks," and suggest that Wilde "construed his life in 'writerly' terms" (4). We argue that the changes in Wilde's career, his "metamorphoses," have usually been interpreted in moral terms, particularly by Ellmann, who understood Wilde's interests in masks as a desire to evade censure. Wilde's poses and his insincerity can be seen as an attempt to "present his life in terms which were appropriate to artifacts . . . as a kind of *text* . . . which he, as sole author, could control" (5); and that in trying to manipulate "the consumption of his public persona" as much as the reactions of his audiences, Wilde was required to acknowledge the power of "external and contingent forces" (5). Wilde's revisions to his works are thus best seen as responses to local circumstances and not part of an overarching artistic design—"a writerly practice analogous to the expedient self-fashioning of his life." We conclude that in order to explain both the life and the work a "modern, consumerist paradigm" is more rewarding than the "teleological narratives" of some modern scholars (10). Once more these issues are developed in Josephine Guy's and my *Oscar Wilde's Profession* (2000), where the power of those "external and contingent forces" is given much greater emphasis; so too is the agency of other professionals in shaping Wilde's public persona.

Other aspects of Wilde's life, particularly his relationship with the immediate members of his family, have been described in the last decade. Joy Melville's *Mother of Oscar: The Life of Francesca Jane Wilde* (1994) is the most substantial study to date of the relationship between Wilde and his mother, and supersedes Terence de Vere White's *The Parents of Oscar Wilde* (1967). The usual way of understanding the relationship between mother and son has been in terms of psychology, a pattern persisting even in Jonathan Fryer's study *André and Oscar* (1997), which assumes an automatic relationship between Wilde's homosexuality and a dominant maternal presence. Other critics (see Jerusha McCormack [1998; discussed in 3. iii.]) have stressed Wilde's political inheritance from his mother, and the formative role played by her participation in nationalist politics. One of the most useful features of Melville's book is the attention she gives to the less glamorous aspects of Lady Jane's life, to the way her writing career developed following the death of Sir William and her subsequent move to London. The details of Lady Jane's (and Willie Wilde's) decision to earn money by popular journalism provides a useful parallel with (and perhaps a partial explanation of) Oscar Wilde's own career in the 1880s. The transformation of the Irish nationalist poetess writing under the name of Speranza, resisting British colonialism in the 1840s, into the society columnist for the *Queen* and *Burlington Magazine*, toadying to London's "upper ten thousand" and the British aristocracy, provides an intriguing commentary on her sons' own relationships with British "polite society" in the 1880s.

Patrick M. Horan's *The Importance of Being Paradoxical: Maternal Presence in the Works of Oscar Wilde* (1997) covers some of the ground of Melville's book, although his interest is in Wilde rather than Speranza; more precisely, his concern is with the presence of Lady Wilde in Wilde's writing. The opening chapter argues for a number of intellectual similarities between mother and son—that they shared an interest in aestheticism, nationalism and feminism—as well as describing their common tendency to be attracted simultaneously by rebelliousness and orthodoxy. Separate chapters examine the mother's influence in Wilde's poetry, essays, fiction, drama and *De Profundis*. Particular emphasis is placed on Wilde's depiction of motherhood (Horan shows, for example, how the matriarchs in the Society Comedies exhibit aspects of Lady Wilde's complex personality) and his treatment of feminism. However, the last chapter is perhaps the most interesting, for it compares Wilde's mother with Douglas's (Lady Queensberry), reminding us of Wilde's conviction (described in *De Profundis*) that it was Lady Queensberry as much as anybody else who contributed to his downfall. A limitation of the study (noted by some reviewers) is Horan's reluctance to address the relationship between mothering and sexuality in both Wilde's and Douglas's life. Also published is Douglas Murray's *Bosie: A Biography of Lord Alfred Douglas* (2000), a work much more sympathetic to Douglas than Wilde. Advertised for publication in late 2000 is Jonathan Fryer's *Robbie Ross: Oscar Wilde's Last True Friend*.

María Pilar Pulido's essay, "Lady Wilde 'Speranza': A Woman of Great Importance" (1994), covers ground already familiar from, and explored with greater sophistication in, a number of recent biographical and critical studies. Also published is Joan Schenkar, *Truly Wilde: The Unsettling Story of Dolly Wilde, Oscar's Unusual Niece* (2000), which documents the unconventional life of Willie and Lily Wilde's daughter, Dolly.

A small detail of Wilde's life attracts the interest of Francis O'Gorman who throws new light on the possible meeting between Ruskin,

Wilde and Lillie Langtry. In "Ruskin, Wilde, and Lillie Langtry" (1997) O'Gorman notes John Unrau's claim (made in *Notes and Queries*, August 1982) that biographers have never indicated a source for the account of this meeting, and points out that it almost certainly derives from Langtry herself (Lady de Bathe) in *The Days I Knew* (n.d. [1925], 150). In passing O'Gorman notes inaccuracies in Ellmann's account of the meeting in his biography.

An even slighter detail is the subject of John Scarry's brief note, "A Correction for Richard Ellmann's *Oscar Wilde*" (1993), in which he points out that the actress Mary Anderson (for whom Wilde wrote *The Duchess of Padua*) was born in Sacramento, California, and not, as Ellmann claimed, in Kentucky. However, how Anderson's place of birth affected Wilde's relationship with her is still not entirely clear.

Masolino D'Amico's short essay, "Oscar Wilde in Naples" (1994), describes the reactions to Wilde's residence in the town by local newspapers, focusing in particular on the "sloppy reporting" (78) of Matilde Serao for a Neapolitan daily newspaper, *Il Mattino*. D'Amico describes Serao's report as "a small masterpiece of professional sloth" (77). Disappointingly D'Amico fails to register the wider political implications of Wilde's choice of domicile (see Joseph Baylen and Robert L. McBath, "A Note on Oscar Wilde, Alfred Douglas and Lord Rosebery, 1897" [1985]).

In "Wilde's Dark Angel and the Spell of Decadent Catholicism" (1994), Ronald Schuchard attempts to document the history of Wilde's engagement with Roman Catholicism which he sees as a "refuge from a frightening sensuality" (371). Schuchard begins with an account of David Hunter Blair's unsuccessful efforts to "bring Wilde safely into the fold" and proceeds to discuss the influence on Wilde in the 1880s of "pre-conversion decadents" (such as J.-K. Huysmans and Barbey d'Aurevilly) as well as Verlaine and Baudelaire. In a manner not dissimilar to Joseph Pearce's *The Unmasking of Oscar Wilde* (2000; discussed above), Schuchard describes Wilde's emotional life in terms of "an insidious sensual-spiritual affliction of the soul" in which his attraction to aestheticism is merely "a plaster for an ailing Catholic consciousness" (376). This argument is used to explore a number of Wilde's works which Schuchard interprets as expressing Wilde's "devouring sin [of] lust" and his "fear of damnation that underlies an excess of sensual pleasure" (384–85). Far from being an impulse, Wilde's "deathbed" conversion, according to Schuchard, was the culmination of a "long-repressed desire to be received into the Church" which had been successfully hidden from Wilde's friends by his "aesthetic mask" (388). Schuchard concludes: "beneath the glittering *carnaval* [sic] of the Happy Prince of Aesthetes was the *danse macabre* of the decadent Catholic" (392). Schuchard's essay should perhaps be read beside Owen Dudley Edwards's "Impressions of an Irish Sphinx" (discussed in 3. ii.) which draws attention to the importance of Wilde's Protestant heritage.

The crassly punning title of Philip Hoare's *Wilde's Last Stand* (1977) is misleading on a number of counts. In the first place the book is not really about Wilde himself, but rather about the Pemberton Billing libel trial (and the events leading up to it) which took place eighteen years after Wilde's death. Second, the Pemberton Billing trial was not of course the last word on Wilde's homosexuality. Hoare justifies his use of Wilde's name in his title on the grounds that the occasion of the trial was a production of *Salome*, and the terms in which the trial was conducted were dictated by the homophobia which was legitimated (and perhaps encouraged) by Wilde's conviction in 1895. Furthermore many of Wilde's acquaintances were drawn into the case; they included Lord Alfred Douglas (who gave evidence for Pemberton Billing), Robert Ross, and Christopher Sclater Millard (Stuart Mason). Furthermore a junior counsel from Wilde's trial, Sir Travers Humphreys, was appearing for the prosecution (that is, for the libelled Maud Allen, the actress who had played Salome). Another element of continuity was the suspicion of sexual corruption in high places (so the rumours about Rosebery in the 1890s found their equivalent in rumours about Asquith in 1918; Asquith moreover was on Pemberton Billing's list of 47,000 homosexuals). On the other hand, and as Hoare's narrative makes clear, there were many profound discontinuities between the two periods, not the least of which was the fact that Britain was at war. As a consequence the stakes were much higher: sexual corruption was seen to produce a vulnerability to treason, an issue which was clearly not pressing in 1895.

Some of Hoare's material has been covered already, in particular by Michael Kettle (1977) and William Tydeman and Steven Price (1996; see 4. iv.). A problem for any historian wishing to document these events is the absence of a full and accurate transcript of the trial itself. Hoare (like Kettle) relies on the *Verbatim Report* published by Pemberton Billing's Vigilante Society, supplemented by press reports. The provisional nature of this evidence is not aided by Hoare's copious but undifferentiated use of quotation and citation. Although quotation is sourced at the end of the book, it is done so in a manner which makes it difficult to distinguish easily between material derived from court reports, newspaper articles, memoirs of the participants, and the work of other modern historians. Hoare's eschewal of the conventions of academic footnotes certainly makes for a lively and entertaining read, but it does tend to elide the kinds of distinctions insisted upon by other cultural historians—that discourses about sexuality are very closely tied to their time. So, for example, talking about "Urnings" in 1918 may not have had the same resonance as it did in the 1890s. The principal value of Hoare's book to the Wilde scholar is in explaining why his reputation as a writer suffered in the way that it did and for as long as it did.

Another book which trades on Wilde's name, although in manner far removed from that of Hoare, is John Stokes's *Oscar Wilde: Myths, Miracles, and Imitations* (1996). The basis of Stokes's book is a series of essays published between the early 1980s and the early 1990s, all revised and expanded. In addition he includes a paper given at the 1993 conference on Wilde at the University of Birmingham. Stokes's study is "about" Wilde only in the sense that Wilde is the loosely connecting theme between different subjects. These include an account of a circus trick ("The Magic Ball") which figures in a number of *fin-de- siècle* "miracle" stories, some of which may have been generated by Wilde; an essay on James H. Wilson's (unsuccessful) attempts to publish a pamphlet criticizing the operations of British justice in Wilde's trials; an account of the diaries of George Ives (see *Oscar Wilde Revalued*, 21); a discussion of late nineteenth-century re-interpretations of Romanticism, particularly by Arthur Symons; a comparison of the aesthetics of Beardsley and of Alfred Jarry, "a mixture of the graceful and the grotesque with more than a hint of the erotic" (110), which links both men to Wilde. Wilde's visits to Dieppe provide the occasion for a detailed description of the French coastal resort and its attractions for late nineteenth-century British travellers and artists. The final chapter, "Wilde Interpretations" reproduces the arguments of Stokes's 1994 essay (with the same title) in *Modern Drama* (discussed in 4. iv.).

The subject of Rod Boroughs's meticulous detective work in his essay, "Oscar Wilde's Translation of Petronius: The Story of a Literary Hoax" (1995), is the history of the publication by Charles Carrington in Paris in 1902 of an English translation, allegedly by Oscar Wilde, of the *Satyricon* of Petronius. Burroughs argues that it is tempting to see Carrington's attribution of the translation as a "clever, if tasteless publicity stunt"—that is, as an attempt to exploit the "notoriety" of Wilde's name to "underscore the homosexual themes" in the work (18–19). He also suggests that Carrington may "have counted on his customers' awareness of Wilde's public references to Petronius" and may also have hoped that "the ascription would gain some credibility from the fact that [Wilde] had studied the classics" (21). However, Burroughs goes on to stress that there was a great deal more to the hoax. He presents evidence that Wilde and Carrington knew each other in Paris in 1898, and that the publisher may have at one point secured Wilde's agreement to produce a translation. Moreover, it was entirely in Carrington's character, Burroughs comments, to refuse "to be put off by the inconvenient death of his commissioned translator" (25). In the last sections of his essay, Burroughs traces Robert Ross's vigorous attempt to expose Carrington's forgery, which in turn was part of a larger campaign to suppress Carrington's pirated editions of Wilde's works. Burroughs also suggests that the real translator of Carrington's edition of the *Satyricon* was Alfred Richard Allinson, almost certainly a party to the forgery.

Roy Rosenstein's ambition in "Re(Dis)covering Wilde for Latin America: Martí, Darío, Borges, Lispector" (1994) is to describe Wilde's reputation in Latin America; indeed he claims that it was "among a handful of Hispanics" that Wilde "may well have found . . . his first, most devoted, and most diverse readership abroad" (349). Rosenstein substantiates his argument by examining Wilde's importance for the Cuban critic and journalist, José Martí, the Nicaraguan poet, Rubén Darío, the Argentinian writer of fiction, Jorge Luis Borges, and the Brazilian writer, Clarice Lispector. It is worth noting that Rosenstein's essay eschews discussing "borrowings or influence" in favour of looking more generally at the "respect" afforded to Wilde among this group of writers (357).

Fictional works which take Wilde as their subject may, I suppose, also be loosely identified under the title of posthumous reputation. See Stefan Rudnicki's *Wilde: the Novel of the Screenplay of Julian*

Mitchell (1997); Thomas Kilroy's *The Secret Fall of Constance Wilde* (1997; see also 3. ii.); C. Robert Holloway's *The Unauthorized Letters of Oscar Wilde* (1998); Jeremy Reed's *Dorian: A Sequel to Dorian Gray* (2000); and Clare [Blossom] Elfman's *The Case of the Pederast's Wife: A Novel* (2000). Finally, a measure of how Wilde's name is still traded in ways that are reminiscent of the publicity surrounding the trials is to be seen in his inclusion in *Going Down: Lip Service from Great Writers* (1998), an (unexamined) anthology of writing on oral sex.

| 3 |

New Paradigms in Cultural & Literary History

I observed in *Oscar Wilde Revalued* that the reassessment of Wilde's reputation in the 1970s and 1980s owed a great deal to the insights generated by the explicit critical theorizing of those decades. This use of theory has continued but with some significant qualifications. Broadly speaking, where theorizing had its most dramatic impact on Wilde criticism in the 1980s was in gender studies and queer theory. In brief, these hypothesized the existence of sub-textual meanings which permitted Wilde to be seen as a subversive and politicized writer. During the 1990s this way of reading Wilde's *oeuvre* has continued, but it has also been subject to some interesting criticism by cultural historians who have tried to introduce a greater degree of historical sensitivity and specificity to our understanding of homosexuality. The central concern of much commentary written in the 1980s was to see in Wilde the paradigmatic example of the modern homosexual and to stress continuities between gay experience in the late nineteenth and late twentieth centuries. More recently a number of historians have insisted on difference rather than continuity, and on the cultural specificity of sexual identities. More particularly, it has been claimed that before Wilde's trials, transgression, effeminacy and homosexuality were not necessarily qualities closely identified with each other, and that the general public did not necessarily perceive Wilde's sexuality to be threatening. As Alan Sinfield trenchantly points out, such a view has important implications for critics who wish to see homoerotic sub-texts in Wilde's pre-trial works. More generally, this body of research may require us to re-think the politics of Wilde's writing, and to be much more cautious about labelling him as a "subversive" voice. That said, it is worth noting that many critics, particularly Gary Schmidgall in *The Stranger Wilde* (discussed in 2. i.), continue to insist on reading the whole of Wilde's life in terms of an explicit gay politics.

It is tempting to observe that the "Irish" Wilde and the "consumerist" Wilde which appeared in the 1990s are broadly comparable to the "gay" Wilde of the 1980s, in so far as they are ways of understanding his work which have been generated by abstract political and cultural theorizing. So the general insights from postcolonial theory have been used to re-describe the power relationships between Wilde and British cultural institutions, and Wilde's Irish nationality has been invoked to identify in his work an oppositional politics analogous to those attributed to the gay man. This area of research is relatively new, and whether its insights will be underwritten by sustained evidence is something of an open question. Similarly, the figure of Wilde described by theorists of commodity culture is (with a few noteworthy exceptions) still largely an abstraction; it has been argued that the hypothesizing of a late nineteenth-century consumerism is itself more a product of abstract reasoning than of empirical research. More specifically, the way in which commodity culture is said (at a theoretical level) to "work" has yet to be confirmed by detailed evidence about how markets really behaved in the late nineteenth century. What empirical research that has been undertaken suggests that there may be mismatches between actual markets and what theorists have termed a "market society." Once again, if our present understanding of consumerism in the nineteenth century turns out to be ill-founded or insecure, then clearly it will be necessary to rethink our contemporary picture of Wilde as a media personality and critic of consumerism.

This brief overview discloses my reservations about the durability of all three recent paradigms of Wilde. Nonetheless it would be ungenerous not to acknowledge that the past decade has witnessed the emergence of a number of exciting new ways of thinking about Wilde, and these in turn have happily led us away from the polarities which traditionally dogged critical writing about him—the wit set against the gay martyr, or the dilettante opposed to the political icon.

3. i. *The Gay Wilde*

Ed Cohen's *Talk on the Wilde Side: Toward a Genealogy of a Discourse on Male Sexualities* was published in 1993, and was thus unfortunately too late to be discussed in any detail in *Oscar Wilde Revalued*. It has proved to be one of the most significant books published on Wilde in recent years. Cohen begins by taking issue with Harford Montgomery Hyde's account of the trials (see 2. i.) which, he notes, were based principally on newspaper reports, and not trial transcripts. The comment is perhaps a little unfair to the later editions of Hyde's work, where he points out that:

> the official Court shorthand-writers and compilers of the *Central Criminal Court Sessions Papers*, who might have been expected to present the facts objectively, declined to print the proceedings of the trials on the ground that the details disclosed by them were "unfit for publication" (*Sessions Papers*, cxxi, 531–32). . . . [S]ustained by the recent Obscene Publications Act, I have been enabled to reproduce some portions of the evidence verbatim which discretion obliged me to paraphrase in the earlier [1948] edition. . . . Secondly . . . the official Home Office and Prison Commission Papers relating to Wilde's conviction and imprisonment were made available to me without restriction. (Hyde, 1962, 20–22)

The reliability or otherwise of Hyde notwithstanding, *Talk on the Wilde Side* documents what Cohen calls a moment in late nineteenth-century social and legal history when Wilde became "the paradigmatic example for an emerging public definition of a new 'type' of male sexual actor: 'the homosexual'" (2). Cohen's project is to reinterpret "the (con)textual nexus from which the prevailing narratives about Wilde's 'tragedy' . . . emerged" and "to elucidate the ways in which Wilde became a crucial figure both for what it meant to be an 'English homosexual' at the end of the nineteenth century and for how 'English homosexuality' has subsequently come to be figured in this [i.e., the twentieth] one" (3). Cohen describes the origin of the term "homosexual" as a way of "marking out the boundaries of sexual and gender norms" (10) and goes on to suggest that the label itself still retains its "normalizing function" in contemporary America (11). This thesis is thoroughly documented, but it is not at all dry;

moreover Cohen gives the reader a sense of the importance of his subject by tying it to his own experiences. His overall argument is that
the term "homosexual" was defined in relation to "middle-class
standards for male propriety," when those standards themselves were
codified in terms of "acceptable public representation" (212).

In common with many other cultural historians, Cohen sees the
term "homosexuality" emerging "under the mark of pathology and
powerlessness" (18). However his ambition in the first section of his
book is not to focus on homosexuality as a category of "deviance,"
but rather on the "normative male gender and ('hetero')sexuality"
which constituted the background "against which 'the homosexual'
could appear" (14). The first three chapters of Cohen's study thus
sketch in the normative concept of "'healthy'" middle-class masculinity against which Wilde's "otherness" would later be defined and
judged. The second section of the book concentrates on Wilde's trials
and conviction, and argues that they "played no small part in crystal-
lizing the concept of 'male homosexuality' in the Victorian sexual
imagination." Cohen begins this section by examining what he
terms "the shift" from sodomy (a "law against specific, transgressive
acts") to gross indecency ("a new secular, criminal injunction against
specific sexual *relations* between men" [102]). Subsequent chapters
examine the way in which newspapers represented Wilde during his
trials. Here it is Cohen's claim that Wilde himself—that is, descriptions and representations of his actual body—became a "metonym"
(209) for criminalized sexual practices that could not be specified in
print, and in this way Wilde himself later came to stand as the arche-
typal homosexual.

Looking back at Cohen's thesis from the vantage point of a new
century, it is easy to see how much it owes to the work of an earlier
group of historians of gender, such as Jeffrey Weeks, Peter Gay and
Eve Kosofsky Sedgwick. Its legacy for more recent research is perhaps
best seen in two later works. The first is Philip Hoare's *Wilde's Last
Stand* (see 2. ii.). Like Cohen, Hoare is interested in Wilde as a cultural icon, rather than as the author of particular works—that is, he is
interested in the meanings for the twentieth century generated by the
scandal associated with and evoked by Wilde's name. This said, Cohen's focus on 1895—the date of the trials—as the moment when homosexuality became defined in the public domain, chimes usefully
with recent ways of thinking about Wilde's sexuality in relation to

his literary output. Here it has been suggested that to read works such as *The Picture of Dorian Gray* or the Society Comedies as covert articulations of Wilde's homosexuality might be anachronistic. It is precisely this proposition which has been the point of departure for two important recent critiques of how we read Wilde's work in relation to his sexuality, those by Alan Sinfield and Joseph Bristow, discussed below.

A further book to follow Cohen's lead is Michael S. Foldy's *The Trials of Oscar Wilde: Deviance, Morality, and Late-Victorian Society* (1997). As his title suggests, Foldy's aim is to re-examine the cultural contexts of Wilde's trials, using a variety of methodologies, including (perhaps controversially) psychoanalysis. The first part of the book gives a description of the trials which largely relies on press reports. Like Cohen, Foldy is interested in the role the press played in establishing a climate of opinion which helped to secure a conviction. He also shows that there was an awareness of the power of the press at the time and that a few commentators (such as the conservative Robert Buchanan) protested at Wilde's treatment. It is perhaps worth observing that both Foldy and Cohen tend to gloss over the uncomfortable fact that Wilde was guilty, and admitted as much in *De Profundis*. In accounts such as theirs there is often a conflation of two quite distinct issues: a dissatisfaction with British laws about homosexuality at the time, and an unease with legal processes, such as miscarriages of justice.

Much of the basic source material of Foldy's book has of course been known for some time. As a consequence, the newness of his account exists in his interpretation of those sources. On some occasions there is a suspicion that Foldy's desire to be original leads him to make speculations which his material will not necessarily support. For example, he attempts to substantiate the suspicion that Wilde's conviction (and later the surveillance of him in Posillipo, described by Joseph Baylen and Robert L. McBath [1985]) was part of a larger strategy designed to protect the reputations of British political figures, particularly Lord Rosebery. In the absence of new hard evidence (which in the nature of things will now be very elusive) Foldy uses arguments from psychoanalysis to suggest that Rosebery's mental state implicated him in Wilde's case. As in Melissa Knox's *Oscar Wilde: A Long and Lovely Suicide* (1994; see 2. i.) such an approach certainly produces a provocative argument, but it is one which requires more concrete evidence in order to convince entirely.

In contrast to Foldy's thesis, what impresses in Alan Sinfield's *The Wilde Century* (1994) is the careful use of detailed historical evidence, and the sense of theoretical sophistication which guides his research. Like many historians of gay culture, Sinfield wants to place Wilde in the context of a history of homosexuality, of what he calls in the book's subtitle, the "queer moment." Like Ed Cohen, he also sees Wilde's trials as a turning point in that history. However, the originality of Sinfield's argument lies in his proposition that before his trials, Wilde's "effeminacy" was not seen as queer; as he puts it, "homosexuality was *not* manifest from Wilde's style" (1). Sinfield substantiates this claim by means of a detailed history of what he calls the complex "uses of effeminacy," from Shakespeare to present-day queer politics; he stresses that prior to 1895, "although there was a tendency to perceive same-sex passion as effeminate, effeminacy still did not necessarily signal same-sex passion" (45). His larger point is that even though the categories of masculine and feminine may have become more fixed during the course of the nineteenth century, "it was not settled which persons and practices, and in what terms, were to be identified through that binary structure" (45). Put another way, "social behaviour was defining, and sexual practice was secondary" (46). Sinfield also discusses representations of masculinity in the nineteenth century—arguing that what he terms "manliness" and "effeminacy" could be markers of class rather than sexual difference: or, more precisely, the link between effeminacy and an aristocratic "leisure-class" functioned to exonerate "the Wildean dandy" from "looking like a queer" (71). Such an argument leads Sinfield to be very cautious about interpreting pre-trials works in terms of homoerotic sub-texts. Discussing, for example, the question of Dorian Gray's "vices," he argues that the novel "should be viewed not as the cunning masking of an already-known queerness, but as reaching out towards formulations of same-sex experience that were . . . as yet nameless" (102–103).

Sinfield goes on to discuss the trials themselves, arguing (once more in a manner similar to that of Ed Cohen) that they marked the moment when "the image of the queer cohered" because "the leisured, effeminate, aesthetic dandy was discovered in same-sex practices, underwritten by money, with lower-class boys" (121). As a result, dandyism "forfeited the protection from same-sex imputations that the image of general dissoluteness had afforded. The leisure-class man . . . was the sodomite" (122). The final chapters of Sinfield's book explore the consequence of this process of redefinition through the twentieth century. Written in an accessible style, he succeeds in showing the relevance of Wilde for modern cultural concerns, yet at the same time maintaining a due sense of historical distance.

In "'Effeminacy' and 'Femininity': Sexual Politics in Wilde's Comedies" (1994), Sinfield concentrates more on the implications of the general thesis of *The Wilde Century* for interpreting Wilde's *oeuvre*. He offers some salutary observations on various deconstructionist projects which read for "significant" silences in particular works. Such silences, he suggests, are "likely to be read as a deafening roar about homosexuality" (34). Sinfield questions many recent accounts of the plays which purport to "discover" gay sub-texts by connecting, say, "Earnest" with "Urning" and "uraniste," and which speculate over the possible double meanings of "Bunburying." Sinfield finds no historical evidence to support such interpretations, and cautions us against the doxography at work in such reading practices; in a passage already partly quoted, he notes:

> We need to recover the initial perceptions of Wilde, and of his dandy characters—before the notoriety of the trials. It is a mistake to suppose that Wilde and his audiences "really" had a concept of gayness like our own, but kept it behind a mask; that it is lurking, therefore, beneath the text—as if it were a statue under a sheet, fully formed but waiting to be unveiled. The modern idea of the homosexual was in the process of being constituted—largely . . . through the figure of Wilde himself. (35)

Sinfield argues that in the nineteenth century the dandy was understood to be a heterosexual figure, and points out that "for the most part, Wilde's dandies are heterosexually passionate, and/or philanderers"; he goes on to suggest that "dandy effeminacy signalled class, far more than sexuality" (38). Sinfield also discusses Wilde's representation of Society women. Using the insights of cultural historians such as Leonore Davidoff (*The Best Circles* [1973]) and Geoffrey Best (*Mid-Victorian Britain: 1851–75* [1979]), he sees the "frivolous and knowing stance of the dandified, feminine woman . . . as . . . an affront to middle-class ideas of womanliness as the effeminate dandy was to ideas of manliness" (44). As a consequence "in the plays, Wilde undermines the earnest woman, and empowers the correlate of the effeminate man—the boldly feminine woman" (45).

A further work in the same series as the *Wilde Century* is Joseph Bristow's *Effeminate England: Homoerotic Writing after 1885* (1995), which examines how a number of gay writers have explored questions of gender and identity, and the relationships between two sorts of culture, homosexual and heterosexual. Bristow focuses on the development of the stereotypical effeminate homosexual since the 1885 Labouchère Amendment. As well as detailed discussions of E. M. Forster and Ronald Firbank, there is a chapter devoted to Wilde.

Bristow pursues the issue of Wilde's homosexuality in a later essay in *The Cambridge Companion to Oscar Wilde* (1997). In "'A complex multiform creature': Wilde's sexual identities," he identifies a paradox in current debates about Wilde's homosexuality. For Bristow the very acceptability of this topic, and the fact that "gay-affirmative" readings have now become mainstream, have produced distortions of their own. He suggests that there is more than a suspicion that some of the more programmatic sub-textual readings of Wilde's works—those "critical methods that would reduce each and every moment of suggestive obliquity in Wilde's writings to an undeniable instance of homophile intensity" (196)—might simply be "mistaken" (197). The issue for Bristow is what the term "homosexual" actually means when it is applied to Wilde's life and to his sense of his own sexuality. Bristow contrasts the arguments of Alan Sinfield with those of Gary Schmidgall, siding with the former; he suggests that there is little evidence that before the trials either Wilde or his works were seen as "queer" (200), or that the attitude towards him was one of that "scandalised disgust" (201) which emerged during the course of the trials.

Bristow goes on to discuss two works which modern critics have consistently wanted to read in homoerotic terms: "The Portrait of Mr W. H." and *The Picture of Dorian Gray*. In these two pieces, same-sex desire possesses, according to Bristow, both "notorious invisibility . . . yet unwavering implication" (204). He acknowledges that "The Portrait of Mr W. H." is "fascinated" with "male friendship," but resists the idea (put forward by Lawrence Danson in "Oscar Wilde, W. H., and the Unspoken Name of Love" [1991]) that the story "revealed Wilde's political resistance to the hetero-normative imperatives that increasingly demanded that all men should conform to the needs of the nuclear family" (208). Bristow voices similar doubts about readings in which "same-sex desire" is assumed to lie "at the root of Dorian's crimes" in *The Picture of Dorian Gray* (211). He concludes his essay with some perceptive comments about the Society Comedies. Acknowledging that the plays see married life as inhibiting "the kind of friendship that promises to harmonise the soul and body" (215), he is nonetheless cautious about equating this critique of marriage with a celebration of same-sex desire, a conclusion which is at one with those of Sinfield in his *Modern Drama* essay and in *The Wilde Century* (1994). The Bunburyist, Bristow reminds the reader, was never "at any point the 'homosexual' that Wilde, in our confused modern age, was for decades thought to embody" (215).

In "Ada Leverson's Wild(e) *Yellow Book* Stories" (1999), William M. Harrison takes his cue from the arguments of Cohen and Sinfield, that Wilde's trials "marked the beginning of a new socially recognized male homosexual identity" (21). He examines two short stories contributed to *The Yellow Book* by Leverson. The first, entitled "Suggestion," was published during Wilde's trial in April 1895; the second, which appeared some months later in January 1896, was called "The Quest for Sorrow." Both feature the affairs of Cecil "Cissy" Carrington, described by Harrison as "a foppish, dandified Wildean character" (21). Through a close textual analysis of the two stories and of the cultural context in which they appeared, Harrison argues that they can be seen to "parallel the change in the social-cultural reading of the Wilde figure. Leverson develops her depiction of Cissy from an effeminate and ironic character to one who appears more openly disruptive of the heterosexual cultural order: Cissy becomes a figure we may read more strongly as 'queer'" (21). Harrison concludes that Leverson's stories have "merit" because she is "sympathetic" (27) in the ways she represents the changes brought about by Wilde's trials; Cissy Carrington, according to Harrison, is simply "a character free to be 'queer'" (27–28).

Like Sinfield and Bristow, Linda Dowling's concern in her study, *Hellenism and Homosexuality in Victorian Oxford* (1994), is with the conceptualization of the homosexual. Controversially, she argues that the modern construction of homosexuality as a "positive social identity" was made possible by what she terms "Oxford Hellenism" and the "Oxford University reform movement." Dowling proposes that by trying to establish in Hellenism "a ground of transcendent value alternative to Christian theology," reformers such as Benjamin Jowett unintentionally created a means by which figures like Pater and Wilde could develop "a homosexual counterdiscourse able to justify male love in ideal or transcendental terms: the 'spiritual procreancy' associated specifically with Plato's *Symposium* and more generally with ancient Greece itself" (xiii). In a detailed and elegantly written account, Dowling traces the cultural anxieties (specifically about masculinity) underlying the Oxford reform movement, and the role played by a re-defined classical studies in a programme for national renewal: "liberal reformers . . . would thus seek in the study of Greek culture nothing less than the surety for England's future life as a nation" (xiv).

Much of this ground, as Dowling herself acknowledges, had already been covered by historians such as Richard Jenkyns. Dowling's emphasis, though, is on the way this project could be given a new inflection by Oxford aesthetes such as Pater, J. A. Symonds and Wilde in order to extend the idea of a liberal education to legitimate male-male relationships. Dowling places great emphasis on the function of the (one-to-one) Oxford tutorial in fostering new forms of male intimacy. She also stresses the gradual way in which "a new system of values and attitudes . . . having in common their relation to the inchoate counterdiscourse of 'homosexuality,'" came to be possible (132). In common with many other critics, Dowling sees Wilde's trial in 1895 as curtailing any possibility that Oxford Hellenism might have redefined male love "as the agent of personal and cultural transformation" (141). Dowling's account is original, but it has been subject to criticism. A number of gay critics have objected to her separation of the conceptualization of homosexuality from its practices; for example, as early as 1990, critics such as Richard Dellamora suggested that it is the ways in which homosexuality is experienced—that is, how desire finds its physical expression—which determines the ways it is understood. Other critics have objected to what they see as the elitist tendency of Dowling's historiography—that it equates the cultural and social diversity of Britain with Oxford. In terms specific to Wilde, it assumes that Wilde's undergraduate career had more influence on his sexuality than his later experiences in London's gay subculture, or his trips to north Africa with Douglas.

Denis Donoghue's essay, "The Oxford of Pater, Hopkins, and Wilde" (1994), covers some of the same ground as Dowling's *Hellenism and Homosexuality* and reaches some similar conclusions. Donoghue, for example, sees all three figures sharing an antinomianism which opposed what he terms the "official culture" of Oxford, "diversely represented . . . by Arnold, Jowett, and Ruskin, [and] predicated upon common sense, realism, and the definition of reality in civic and social terms"; he also describes "the Oxford of Pater, Hopkins, and Wilde" as "a homosocial sanctuary" (112–13). Donoghue's larger argument, however, involves picking a fight with something of a straw man. He draws attention to the relationship between Wilde, Pater, and Hopkins chiefly in order to contest the history of modernism drawn up by *Scrutiny* and the Leavises: a straw man because that history, which included Hopkins but excluded the "feminine" impressionism of his two contemporaries, has been thoroughly discredited for forty years or so.

Jeff Nunokawa's study, *Oscar Wilde* (1994), which appeared as part of the Lives of Notable Gay Men and Lesbians series, gives an account of Wilde's biography and his writing which, as the title of the series suggests, emphasises the centrality of his sexuality and the homophobia of the society which brought about his downfall. The target readership of the series appears to be the student reader (Nunokawa's book includes, for example, such basic information as a chronology, a list of further reading and a bibliography of Wilde's books). However the reader who requires this sort of detail may be deterred by the theoretical sophistication and dense argument of some parts of the book.

In contrast to the emphasis on the history of social and cultural institutions in the work of Cohen, Sinfield, Bristow and Dowling, Claude J. Summers's *Gay Fictions, Wilde to Stonewall: Studies in a Male Homosexual Literary Tradition* (1990, but unfortunately overlooked in *Oscar Wilde Revalued*) relies on close readings of the work of gay writers. He chooses texts on the grounds that they typify a particular tradition of representing gay men in Anglo-American literature. It is worth noting here a marked contrast between this interest and that of historians of homosexuality who have tended to emphasize the importance of *local* factors (such as, for example, the role which Dowling gives to pedagogic practice in Victorian Oxford in defining a concept of the homosexual in Britain). Summers interprets Wilde's writing in terms of a general pattern of gay *bildungsromans* in which the protagonists' struggle to come to terms with their sexuality involves overcoming a cultural homophobia which had been internalized. Summers concentrates on "The Portrait of Mr W. H.," *The Picture of Dorian Gray*, and *De Profundis*. In the first two works selfhood is seen by Summers as divided, a feature which is attributed to Wilde's own ambivalence about his sexuality. By contrast, he sees *De Profundis* as a document which testifies to Wilde's acceptance of that sexuality, and which posits a complex but unified notion of selfhood. This last work is for Summers the most important, because it links Wilde to E. M. Forster and thus to a tradition of twentieth-century gay fiction. Indeed Summers argues that *De Profundis* was a direct influence on Forster's *Maurice*. Summers's book is self-consciously propagandizing, in the manner of Richard Dellamora (in, for example, *Masculine Desire* [1990]). Some critics, notably perhaps Michael R. Doylen, whose account of *De Profundis* is described below, will be in sympathy with this enthusiasm; by contrast, others (such as Sinfield and Bristow, discussed above) have argued that we should resist the temptation to read Wilde's pre-trial works as inevitable expressions of a homosexual identity.

A different and—for the most part—less convincing reaction to the popularity of homoerotic readings of Wilde is to be found in Barri J. Gold's essay, "The Domination of *Dorian Gray*." Gold traces a "narrative of erotic domination," which, it is claimed, "is largely indifferent to the question of gendered object choice" (27). The essay explores the range of erotic relationships depicted in the novel, including those between Sybil Vane and Dorian, Basil Hallward and Dorian, and Lord Henry Wotton and Dorian, arguing that "the text reveals the investment in (gender) fluidity, in role-playing, and in mutual reproduction which grounds the desire for domination." Gold concludes, a little obscurely perhaps, with the assertion that "*Dorian Gray* thus complicates the traditional picture of s/m . . . and begins to suggest its potential as a social, political and critical practice. Erotic domination emerges as a practice which may subvert the same discursive constructs through which it is articulated" (30). It is worth noting that domination linked to non-gendered object choices is also a feature of *Teleny*, of which there have been three new editions recently: by Wordsworth Editions, which does not specify an author, by the Gay Sunshine Press and by Prowler Press. These last two attribute authorship (albeit tentatively). The introduction to the Prowler Press edition by John McCrae is even-handed and to be recommended.

Michael R. Doylen begins his essay "Oscar Wilde's *De Profundis*: Homosexual Self-Fashioning on the Other Side of Scandal" (1999) with the observation that although *De Profundis* "is the only major prose work that Wilde wrote on the other side of the scandals prompted by his 1895 trials," it "has received little serious consideration from scholars in gay male studies" (547). Doylen rejects the idea that *De Profundis* is a summing up, the *terminus ad quem* of Wilde's life, representing his "sincere contrition" and capitulation to bourgeois ethics; he argues instead (and explicitly against commentators such as Jonathan Dollimore) that the letter signals "new directions of Wildean self-fashioning" (547). Doylen points out that some of Wilde's contemporaries, particularly George Bernard Shaw and Max Beerbohm, as well as some modern critics, such as Joseph Butwin and Regenia Gagnier, recognize the importance of "self-invention" in the work, a theme which Doylen sees operating "as the means by which Wilde strives to interrupt his interpellation as 'sexual pervert' by Victorian medical and legal institutions." For Doylen, Wilde's "social marginalization as 'sexual pervert'" provides him with the opportunity "to fashion a new self" (550). Doylen explores his thesis by adapting elements of Foucault's late writings, particularly the idea of "homosexual *askêsis*," which "names a technology of self-stylization whereby gay men and lesbians might eventually move beyond the limiting view of sexuality as containing the truth of the self," and which recommends the "conceptualization of 'the self as a work of art' as the basis of a modern ethics addressed specifically to sexually deviant populations" (551).

In the body of his essay, Doylen concentrates on the differences between Wilde's pre-prison letters to Douglas and the way in which Douglas is described in *De Profundis*—on how the "'dearest of created things'" becomes in the prison letter "the embodiment of all the negatively charged terms of [Wilde's] aesthetic principles" (555). However, he goes on to argue that in "reassessing his past relationship with Douglas, Wilde does not repudiate his perverse passions *per see*, but he does submit his previous *expression* of those passions to an ethical analysis that he had formulated in his earlier writings and now extends in new directions" (558). That new ethics encompassed, according to Doylen, "humility" and the elevation of sorrow "to the status of an aesthetic principle" (558); more importantly, it also involved "not obedience to social norms . . . but voluntary submission to precepts formulated by the self in relation to the self" (558). Doylen concludes that Wilde's concern in *De Profundis* with "the ethical subject"—what Doylen terms a "depth model of subjectivity"—is "perfectly consistent with representations of selfhood in his earlier writings" because when Wilde wrote of a "deep self" he always distinguished it from the "'authentic, sincere subject' of bourgeois humanism." For Doylen, the Wildean self in *De Profundis*, as in the rest of the *oeuvre*, is always "decentred" (559). Doylen's argument is complex and not always easy to follow. Moreover, his emphasis on the antinomian qualities of *De Profundis* are not perhaps as novel as he supposes. *De Profundis* may not have figured centrally in what he terms "gay male studies," but its anti-bourgeois tenor has been identified in the work of many other literary historians. (Doylen's essay can usefully be read alongside Oliver Buckton's account of the confessional qualities of *De Profundis* in Dellamora's anthology *Victorian Sexual Dissidence* [1999]).

Another piece which concentrates on elaborating a gay reading of a single work by Wilde is Christopher Craft's chapter on *The Importance of Being Earnest* in *Another Kind of Love: Male Homosexual Desire in English Discourse, 1850–1920* (1994). The overall theme of the book is to pursue what Craft terms a "homosexual thematics" (xiv) in a range of late nineteenth- and early twentieth-century texts by authors such as Tennyson, Bram Stoker and D. H. Lawrence. The chapter on *Earnest* begins with an account of a case-study in Havelock Ellis's *Sexual Inversion* in which Wilde appeared in a dream and "perpetrated *fellatio*" on the disgusted dreamer (110). Craft uses this detail to elaborate the distinctiveness of Wilde's understanding of sexuality: "writing against all essentialist notions of being, inverted or otherwise, Wilde refuses to identify subjectivity and sexuality, insisting on the irreducible difference between." Craft goes on: "what Wilde seeks in desire is . . . the vertigo of substitution and repetition" (110). In a dense, witty, but sometimes impenetrable essay, Craft develops this idea in relation to *Earnest*: a good example of his rhetorical strategies and style is his observation that "in the revolving door of Wildean desire, the counters of comedic representation are disclosed as formal cyphers, the arbitrarily empowered terms whose distribution schedules and enforces heterosexual diegesis" (111). Much of Craft's essay is devoted to elucidating the significance of the name Bunbury; according to Craft, it "operates within the heterosexual order as its hidden but irreducible supplement . . . the homosexual 'excess' that it refuses to embrace but to which it continuously alludes" (117). Craft goes on to give seven gay meanings for the name Bunbury and a list of what he terms "demonstrative exempla" in which he claims to show evidence to underwrite gay interpretations of the play. It is worth repeating that Craft's proselytizing gay reading of the play has been resisted by other scholars, most notably Joseph Bristow. It is also worth noting that Craft's reading demonstrates a cavalier attitude to the textual condition of the play. His evidence draws from both the three- and four-act versions of *Earnest*; but in a revealing footnote he confesses he does so "without worrying the issue of textual authority" (214). In an essay which relies so heavily on speculation about authorial intention in order to identify Wilde's alleged sub-texts, such details cannot be dismissed so lightly.

The issue of Wilde's sexuality is also addressed (if obliquely so) in the first two chapters of Richard Dellamora's *Apocalyptic Overtures: Sexual Politics and the Sense of An Ending* (1994). Chapter one is an extended engagement with Neil Bartlett's *Who Was That Man?* Dellamora is less interested in the historical details of Wilde's life than in Bartlett's use of them in relation to the AIDS crisis of the 1980s and 1990s, and the way in which it problematized the gay "sociality" of the 1970s (33). Wilde also makes a brief appearance in the second chapter as a representative (along with Walter Pater) of a "counterdiscourse" to what Dellamora terms "Dorianism," defined as "the institution of pederasty as it existed in the army of ancient Sparta" (44). Dellamora reads *The Picture of Dorian Gray* as a satire on "male culture, especially as it existed at Oxford" (60). This material is covered in much more detail, but with a different interpretation, in Dowling (see above).

3. ii. *The Irish Wilde*

In his foreword to Davis Coakley's *Oscar Wilde: The Importance of Being Irish* (1994), Merlin Holland observes that "there is one area of study that has been almost entirely neglected—the lifelong effect on Wilde of his Irish background" (ix). This topic became the concern of a number of critics during the course of the 1990s, beginning with the work of Coakley himself. His book researches the background of Wilde's upbringing in Ireland. (Part of it is rehearsed in a short piece entitled "The Neglected Years: Wilde in Dublin" in C. George Sandulescu's collection, *Rediscovering Oscar Wilde* [1994].) *Oscar Wilde: The Importance of Being Irish* comprises a series of brief chapters, the first of which examine the lives of Wilde's parents and give details about the family homes in Westland Row and Merrion Square. The social and cultural milieu of the Wilde family, including Speranza's salons and the Mary Travers scandal, are given particular attention. Coakley also describes Wilde's education at the Portora Royal School and Trinity College, Dublin. In addition he examines the physical spaces in which Wilde's upbringing took place, paying attention to the nature of Victorian Dublin and the importance to the Wilde family of their fishing lodges in the west of Ireland. Coakley's closing chapters look at Wilde's involvement with Irish-American culture during the lecture tour and his final visits to Dublin after he had settled in London. In addition Coakley's volume contains a number of interesting images, particularly those of contemporary Dublin, of the places where Wilde was educated, and of the family properties in the west.

Coakley claims that his book "demonstrates unequivocally that Wilde's formative years in Ireland left a significant imprint on his writing" (3). Certainly he provides a great deal of new and useful information about the details of Wilde's life in Ireland; however the connections which are made between the life and the *oeuvre* tend to be brief and occasionally simplistic; often they beg important questions about the nature of influence and cultural transfer. For example, Coakley's account of the cultural prestige of a Merrion Square address is used to illuminate the exchange between Lady Bracknell and Jack in *The Importance of Being Earnest* about the significance of a good London address. Coakley fails to explain how this metamorphosis took place—to explain in what precise ways Wilde's theatrical satire of London snobbery derives from his childhood experience of living at a "snobbish" Dublin address. Put more generally, what precise mechanisms transformed a member of one elite into a critic of another. Coakley's study provides useful and often fascinating information, but it does require a more sophisticated account of the relationship between social, political and cultural phenomena.

In his study, *The Thief of Reason: Oscar Wilde and Modern Ireland* (1995), Richard Pine acknowledges that Coakley's book covers some of what he calls "the same terrain" as his own, but not "in such depth" (xii); in fact Coakley's book came to press too late to be given any extended discussion by Pine. In contrast to Coakley, Pine is more interested in the specificities of Wilde's literary work and in theorizing what it meant for him to be Irish. Pine's book represents a revision of his earlier 1983 biographical study *Oscar Wilde* (see *Oscar Wilde Revalued*, 2–3), but it relies upon a proposition which is not at all easy to understand. Pine's basic thesis is that "being Irish ... is quite different from that of being English and French"; he argues that "for the Irishman ... the social construction of reality is in fact 'unreal' because he cannot subscribe to its rules and its canon" (2–3). Pine takes to task a number of earlier biographers and critics of Wilde (particularly Norbert Kohl, Richard Ellmann and me) for not attending either to Wilde's Irishness or to the particularities of Irish nationalism.

Pine's opening chapter tries to "*divine*" rather than "*define*" Irishness (23) by discussing the views of contemporaries such as Matthew Arnold, and then Ernest Renan and Bishop Berkeley. He suggests four elements central to the Irish mind: "*vagueness*," "the idea of *discontinuity*," "the *icon* or mythopoeic *image*," and the "*fable*" (41), and that Irishness can "be seen as a decadent frame of mind" (44). Pine's second chapter gives a brief social history of Irish nationalism, followed by a discussion of Irishness in the fiction of Sydney Owenson, Sheridan LeFanu, Samuel Ferguson and Charles Maturin; he also examines the *Nation* and the *Dublin University Magazine* and the careers of Wilde's parents. Pine then focuses more closely on Wilde's biography. He uses the work of the modern American sociologist Irving Goffman to explain Wilde as someone for whom "acceptance is craved, yet disclosure is still feared, unless both can be achieved on the deviant's terms rather than those of society" (35). In a manner not dissimilar to the drift of Christopher Craft's thesis in *Another Kind of Love* (1994; discussed in 3. i.), Pine argues that Wilde's life and work can be understood in terms of finding "a middle path ... which is neither a compromise nor an accommodation ... but a new element, creating a 'third meaning' which was the 'deep central emotion' of his Irishness, his homosexuality and his sense of the intellectual mission of the critic" (111). Chapters 4 to 6 explore how this idea of a "third meaning" (or perhaps a third way?) is exemplified in Wilde's writing.

The final chapters return to biography and to Wilde's influence on modernism. Pine looks at "three interrelated aspects of the manner in which Wilde lived openly and covertly within English society—as an Irishman, in social contradistinction; as an artist, in aesthetic revolt; and as a homosexual" (316). He also compares Wilde to Yeats and to modernists such as Joyce, Borges, Barthes and Genet. (One might enquire at this point how an Irish nationalism, which Pine earlier argued is unique, can so easily find analogues in twentieth-century Argentinian and French culture.) Pine's concluding claim for his book is the hope that he has established "how far Wilde's Irishness has become—however subliminally—a genre for our own time" (380).

Pine's book self-consciously and often aggressively wants to establish a new agenda for Wilde studies in which his Irishness must be foregrounded. This is an understandable ambition, for Wilde's nationality had been a neglected topic. Nevertheless I have reservations about some elements of his thesis, particularly his basic assumption that there is an automatic congruence between national difference, sexual difference and artistic difference. It could be argued that some aspects of English culture, such as Oxford and the West End theatre, have historically been more tolerant of certain forms of difference than their Irish counterparts. There are also difficulties with his claim about the uniqueness and elusiveness of Irish nationalism (too complex, it seems, to be grasped by German, American or English critics).

The mainly Irish contributors to Jerusha McCormack's 1998 collection, *Wilde the Irishman*, demonstrate the influence of Pine's way of thinking, but also, inadvertently, some of its limitations. McCormack's volume had a wider remit than the traditional academic monograph, for her contributors include not only literary critics and historians, but also actors, poets, novelists, and dramatists. The resulting mixture produces a wide variety of responses to Wilde "the Irishman," but not surprisingly these do not coalesce into a particularly coherent or compelling portrait of their subject.

McCormack's short introduction, "The Irish Wilde," claims that the answer to the question which her volume poses—"Who is Oscar Wilde?"—is an "oxymoron": Wilde, she argues, desired to "have it every way," for he chose to be "both Irish and British" (1). McCormack goes on to suggest that her collection testifies to "the complexity of being Irish," that to be Irish was to have "multiple, and divided, loyalties ... to inhabit a space where contraries meet and are transvalued into something else, a something which by definition escapes definition: to be in a provisional and mutating stage, not a recognized state but a state of mind" (3). This stress on the flexible and protean qualities of Irishness might seem to undermine the whole purpose of McCormack's project, for it suggests that her subject-matter—the issue of "what it means to be Irish"—is simply intractable, and possibly unknowable. Put another way, if it *is* the case that Irishness "is something which by definition escapes definition," then it is difficult to see how it would be possible to answer McCormack's question "what difference does it make to read [Wilde] as Irish?" with any clarity or usefulness (3). Happily, the majority of McCormack's contributors are much more confident than she is of the possibility of pinning down the precise qualities and experiences which define Wilde's sense of his Irish identity.

The piece which opens the volume is a reprint of Declan Kiberd's "Oscar Wilde: The Artist as Irishman," which first appeared in his 1995 *Inventing Ireland*. The remit of that book was, in Kiberd's own words, "to trace the links between high art and popular expression in the decades before and after independence, and to situate revered masterpieces in the wider social context out of which they came" (1996 edn., 3). In a broadly chronological narrative Kiberd interspersed analysis of Irish political and cultural history with detailed commentary on what he called "major texts" (3). Interestingly, Wilde figures as the first writer of the "Irish *risorgimento*" which Kiberd attempts to document. As with the work of Coakley and Pine, Kiberd's ambition is to redescribe Wilde as a writer with avowedly anticolonial concerns: he was, according to Kiberd, "the first intellectual from Ireland who proceeded to London with the aim of dismantling its imperial ideology from within its own structures" (32). Kiberd's chapter on Wilde intermingles biography with analyses of the literary works, arguing, for example, that "the politics and psychology of [*The Importance Of Being Earnest*] are quintessentially republican: Bunbury must not be interred in England but in Paris, home of European radicals and Fenian exiles" (46). Kiberd's reassessment of Wilde is lively and contentious, if occasionally tendentious.

Given that Kiberd's work was one of those instrumental in establishing the Irish Wilde as a new area of interest, it is understandable that McCormack chose it in order to set the tone and agenda of her volume. On the other hand, it might have been helpful to have been provided with a more up-to-date piece in order to see how Kiberd's views had developed in response to other, more recent work in the field. (See, for example, Kiberd's contribution to *The Cambridge Companion*, "Oscar Wilde: the resurgence of lying" [1997; discussed in 4. iv.], which develops ideas from his earlier work in relation to Wilde's plays.)

Kiberd's essay in *Wilde the Irishman* is followed by a contribution from the Yeats scholar, Deirdre Toomey, on "The Story-Teller at Fault: Oscar Wilde and Irish Orality." (Toomey's essay is a later but scarcely changed version of her contribution to *Rediscovering Oscar Wilde* [1994], "The Story-teller at Fault.") Her argument is that there are certain features of Wilde's written texts, such as his use of stereotypes and plagiarism, which are often judged as "cardinal sins." Yet they can be revalued once we understand them as "typical of the oral mode" (28). Orality in its turn is seen by Toomey to be of particular value in Irish culture: she goes as far as to claim that Ireland possessed "the most oral culture in Western Europe" (25). It is not immediately obvious how such a claim could ever be proved; and even if it were true, then the most likely explanation would implicate social conditions, as banal even as low levels of literacy. Toomey's argument proceeds by comparing features of Wilde's written texts, including the "The Soul of Man Under Socialism" and "The Critic as Artist," with lengthy discussions of what she terms his "oral tales." There is an obvious methodological problem with this strategy in that in order to be studied the oral tales must have been written down, and in that process of inscription what distinguishes them from written texts is immediately lost. More to the point, the recording of Wilde's "oral tales" was not undertaken by Wilde himself, so we cannot be sure of their provenance—few other scholars are convinced that they are by Wilde alone. Toomey acknowledges these difficulties, but seems largely untroubled by them: for example, she notes that one of Wilde's "most popular oral tales, 'The Poet,' survives in many accounts," but then gives a long quotation from what she describes as a "full version" (32) published by Charles Ricketts in 1932. One wonders how Toomey is confident that this is a "full version" if she knows nothing of the original. Moreover, her claim that Ricketts "acknowledges having heard it many times" (32) is not a very adequate guarantee of authenticity (neither, it might be said, is the testimony of André Gide, whose recollections form the basis of Toomey's suggestion that "writing bored" Wilde [25]).

Such reservations make it difficult to know how to treat Toomey's conclusion that "'The Poet'" with its "richly classicized tale," its "*l'art pour l'art*" aesthetic and its centaur from the Olympia pediment, is an Irish folk tale inverted, the product of the dying oral culture to which Wilde was tied by . . . the culture of those who listened to spoken tales" (35). Furthermore her comments are not easy to reconcile with new evidence about the provenance of "The Poet" given by Fong and Beckson in the section "Questionable Texts" in *The Poems and Poems in Prose* (2000). Fong and Beckson note that the tale recorded by Wilde's auditors is quite different from the text of a surviving autograph manuscript fragment of the tale. (See also Stokes, *Myths, Miracles, and Imitations*, 1996; and sections 6. ii. and 7. i. below.) It is also worth noting that the Wilde drawn by Toomey does not square with the figure identified by text-editors, that writer who spent such time and effort in polishing his writing. Nor does the Wilde of her essay chime with the man in *De Profundis* who lamented the dispersal of the *éditions de luxe* in his library. Most importantly, though, Toomey seems unaware that some Wildean aphorisms, which she sees as "typical of the oral mode," were first carefully worked out on paper: their spontaneity, that is, was a contrivance achieved by a *writer*, rather than the product of the skills of a raconteur.

Angel Bourke's essay in McCormack's collection, "Hunting Out the Fairies: E. F. Benson, Oscar Wilde and the Burning of Bridget Cleary," also focuses on what some might consider a rather esoteric subject. Her argument is that an article written by E. F. Benson in 1895 on the trial of nine people for the murder of a Tipperary woman, Bridget Cleary, "reads like a masked or coded commentary on Wilde's fate" (36). Bourke goes on: "it is as though the space consciously left blank for Oscar Wilde has been occupied by Bridget Cleary. . . . Wittingly or unwittingly . . . Benson has given us a refracted picture of Oscar as Irishman, as story-teller and as misunderstood victim" (38). Bourke's unsureness about Benson's intentions is revealing: it tends to undermine the significance of her evidence, certainly as it pertains to Wilde's predicament in 1895. Her account ends up resorting to the familiar historical parlour-game of "what if": so, she asks, "What would Oscar Wilde have made of the story of Bridget Cleary?" She then answers her own speculation with the observation that "Wilde's Irish background would have given him an understanding of the transactions between the lives lived by rural people and the oral fictions they told" (43). The fact that in his writing Wilde showed absolutely no interest in rural life (except, perhaps, occasionally to disparage it) preferring instead the rich and decadent salons of the metropolis, makes Bourke's question rather redundant. Her account of Benson's essay, and the "largely invisible" image of Wilde which "floats between [its] lines" (46), is certainly inventive, but it adds nothing concrete to our understanding of Wilde's own attitude to his Irish identity.

Owen Dudley Edwards's contribution to *Wilde the Irishman*, "Impressions of an Irish Sphinx," is aptly titled, for rather than present any particular thesis about Wilde's Irishness, it instead takes the form of a series of musings on certain themes in and features of Wilde's writing and personality, and their relationship to his upbringing in an Irish Protestant family in a Catholic country, a topic on which he spoke in the 1997 University of Birmingham conference on Wilde. So, for example, Edwards examines the persistence of the idea of betrayal in Wilde's *oeuvre,* and wonders whether it originates in some particular treachery during his school days at the Irish Protestant school, Portora, or whether it was simply "the inevitable outcome of the very conditions of Wilde's childhood in Ireland" (49). Another and more arresting of Edwards's interests is Wilde's arrogant self-confidence, and apparent disregard for public opinion—attributes which he again sees as quintessential characteristics of the Irish Protestant who "was answerable to nobody" (50). A further feature of Wilde's work illuminated by his family's religion is what Edwards terms an "evangelical strain." He identifies its presence in Wilde's parents when they wrote on the Irish famine, and argues that it "works its way out in Wilde" by a tendency "to evangelize from platform and proscenium in place of pulpit" (55). Dudley Edwards also discusses the familiar idea of Wilde as a good "talker," a quality which this time he attributes to the "*seanchaí,* story-teller or folk-raconteur" of the "Irish Catholic peasant society" (57). Other topics which interest Edwards include the impact on Wilde's creativity of his relationship with his sister Isola (although he mentions none of the sexual dynamics identified by Melissa Knox; see 2. i.), the "obliteration" of Ireland in the syllabuses at both Portora and Trinity College, Dublin. (For a larger account of the Trinity literature syllabus, see Aileen Douglas and Ian Campbell Ross, "Singularity and the Syllabus" in *Locating Swift* [1998]). Unlike some of the contributors to McCormack's collection, Dudley Edwards has no particular axe to grind, and his essay provides a useful reminder of what Wilde acquired from both a Protestant and Catholic heritage.

In "Venus in Blue Jeans: Oscar Wilde, Jesse James, Crime and Fame," Fintan O'Toole reexamines Wilde's lecture tour of America in order to see how his experience of the "American frontier" (81) shaped his subsequent career. O'Toole begins by drawing attention to parallels between the "apotheosis" of Jesse James (which followed his death in 1882) and the "fate" which would eventually befall Wilde (71). O'Toole suggests that Wilde would have found much with which to identify in James's life: typical of O'Toole's humour and flippancy is the comment that "Wilde may have shot from the lip rather than from the hip, and his duels may have been conducted across a dinner table, rather than at high noon on a dusty and deserted Main Street, but his public persona had all the hauteur and recklessness of the outlaw" (75). O'Toole acknowledges that his account of Wilde's attraction to "outlaw life," and thus to the "'barbarism' of the Wild West" is not one easily reconciled with the "official narrative" of his lecture tour in which he "arrived with the mission of civilizing America" (73). However, O'Toole goes on to argue that the contradiction can be explained in terms of Wilde's Irishness—of what it meant to be an Irishman in late nineteenth-century America. He argues that "British colonial language" used the "savagery of Indian tribes as a convenient analogue for the native Irish" (77). By contrast, in America the "wild Irish" could be re-characterized as "cowboys"; as "Indian killers and clearers of the wilderness," the Irish were "the mythic outlaws" (78). According to O'Toole, the Irishman as outlaw is a figure of profound "ambivalence": outlaws are "the killers and the victims, the civilizers and the wild men, the good guys and the bad guys . . . insiders and outsiders" (78). Furthermore, O'Toole argues, there is a deep sense of "theatricality" and "self-dramatization" involved in being an (Irish) outlaw: it means "playing the white man and remembering the savage native that is left behind" (79). O'Toole claims that these ambivalent images were "enormously influential" in the development of "global consumer culture." But they were also "close to the centre of Wilde's career" (79). He concludes with the suggestion that Wilde's appropriation of them in order "to be criminal and saint, artist and outlaw," and to "have it every way" (80) helps explain the particular quality of his fame, both today and in the 1890s.

At this point it is perhaps worth noting that Sandra Siegel's essay, "Oscar Wilde's Gift and Oxford's 'Coarse Impertinence,'" which appeared in a different collection of essays (*Ideology and Ireland in the Nineteenth Century* [1998]), also attempts to make connections between Wilde's American lecture tour and other moments in his career. Moreover, as in O'Toole's piece, the point of connection is once more Wilde's identity as an Irishman. Unlike O'Toole, however, Siegel's essay looks backwards rather than forwards. She argues that certain comments in Wilde's lectures, which argued for Irish independence and castigated British attempts to govern that country, can be traced back to the Oxford Union's refusal the previous year to accept the gift of his volume, *Poems* (1881). Siegel admits that there is "no extant evidence" to connect these events; nevertheless she insists that merely to "introduce into view Wilde's reading of Anglo-Irish relations" is sufficient to "claim that his affective memory recalled that earlier encounter" (78). Of course the problem with this logic, as O'Toole's essay demonstrates, is that there is more than one way to interpret Wilde's "reading of Anglo-Irish relations." Significantly O'Toole and Siegel seem to understand the notion of the political in completely different (and incompatible) ways. For O'Toole, the idea of "self-dramatization" is a defining element in the way Wilde articulates his sense of Irishness; it is the peculiar form of the "outlaw" politics which he appropriates from America. But for Siegel this self-same quality is inimical to comprehending Wilde's nationalist sympathies, because to focus on "self-dramatization," Siegel argues, is to "obscure that larger encounter between Ireland and England" (78). The tensions between O'Toole's and Siegel's accounts are perhaps best understood in terms of the larger problems posed by inadequate and often unreliable evidence. Much of our knowledge of Wilde's American lecture tour—and indeed of the content of his lectures—is not first-hand. We have to rely on contemporary reporting of Wilde's activities, and in turn this tends to come from figures who were anything but disinterested. For this reason accounts of Wilde's American experience tend to suffer from the same speculative quality as accounts of his oral tales.

Some of the themes of O'Toole's piece are echoed in the punning title of Jerusha McCormack's own contribution to *Wilde the Irishman*: "The Wilde Irishman: Oscar as Aesthete and Anarchist." McCormack's discursive method, with its interweaving of details from Irish history with commentary on Wilde's biography and literary works, is similar to that of Owen Dudley Edwards. She too tries to show the subtle ways in which Ireland and Irish issues are present throughout the *oeuvre*, although for McCormack the refracting lens is not religion, but Wilde's interest in the dandy. It is a phenomenon which she reinterprets in explicitly political terms, for the dandy is simply an "*agent provocateur*" (85). Her general thesis is that Wilde's dandy is a "terrorist by another name" (85). McCormack pursues this argument by first attempting to connect Wilde's interest in Nihilism in *Vera* with "his experience as the son of an Irish landlord" (84); so she sees Prince Paul, with his "ironical and self-cancelling wit," as "an honorary Irishman" (88). McCormack then muses on why the polemic of "The Soul of Man Under Socialism" was not taken as "sedition" (86). Noting that the piece appeared in the same issue of the *Fortnightly* as Grant Allen's "The Celt in English Art," McCormack speculates that "on this occasion" the typical English characterization of the Celt (that is, for her purposes, the views of the ever reliable but overworked Arnold) as undisciplined and anarchical may have acted "against readers taking [*The Soul of Man*] in earnest." Wilde, as an Irish artist addressing an England audience, could only be seen as a "provocateur"—that is, as a dandy, rather than revolutionary (87). McCormack goes on to see *An Ideal Husband* as rewriting "Parnell's fate as comedy" (90), and she notes that Parnell/Chiltern is rescued not by political action, but (once again) by the dandy "with the power of exposing empire-speak so as to reveal its forked tongue and the actual spiritual anarchy on which it rests" (91). McCormack's essay concludes with a reiteration of her overall thesis: that Wilde's dandyism should be "interpreted in terms of protest and provocation and even in terms of larger political dissent" (94). McCormack's contribution to the 1993 Monaco conference on Wilde, "The Once and Future Dandy," pursued a similar theme by comparing Wilde's dandyism with Gandhi's political career see 4. vi.), a comparison which might strike some readers as far-fetched.

McCormack's two essays, which tend to strain the usual understanding of terms such as "dissent" and "sedition," should perhaps be read alongside Stephen Calloway's "Wilde and the Dandyism of the Senses" (1997) and earlier studies of the dandy, particularly by Sima Godfrey, described in *Oscar Wilde Revalued*. Calloway's piece offers a more traditional view of dandyism as an aesthetic (rather than political) experience, one which looks back to, and is derived from, the languid narcissism and "obsession with manners, style and *ton*" of Regency England (36).

Jerusha McCormack's essay for *The Cambridge Companion to Oscar Wilde*, "Wilde's Fiction(s)" (1997), is on a theme similar to that pursued in her piece for her own collection, *Wilde the Irishman*. It is a series of observations on the fiction seen through the lens of Wilde's Irish identity. For McCormack Wilde's career can be plotted in terms of "counterspeech," an activity generated by his precarious position within a "colonial regime" (97), a paradigm which in turn recalls the central argument of Declan Kiberd in *Inventing Ireland*. For McCormack, Wilde's linguistic and writerly methods were "strictly those of guerrilla warfare. Camouflaging his own attack in the language of the enemy, he blew it up" (99). McCormack thus reads Wilde's fiction in terms of an extended engagement with the idea of empire. So, for example, "The Young King" is not "an anodyne Sunday-school fantasy," but is rather a "bitter satire" on "London's obscene luxury," seen from the perspective of "post-Famine Ireland" (104). (Conveniently perhaps, McCormack has less to say about Wilde's frequent and pointed comments about the poverty of London's "sunless lanes": that the facticity and ubiquity of poverty, rather than its nationality, might be his real concern, one structured perhaps by stories and recollections of the Famine, but not—as Dudley Edwards has argued—necessarily restricted to it.) Likewise in "The Portrait of Mr W. H." Willie Hughes's "chameleon-like personality" makes him "incorrigibly Celtic" (110). This line of argument is extended to *The Picture of Dorian Gray* which, in McCormack's view, "in deconstructing itself . . . is released back into the indeterminacy of an oral tradition" (114)—that is, back into an alignment with Irish culture and mythology. McCormack's desire to reclaim the "Irishness" of Wilde's work is, as I have said, of a piece with her anthology *Wilde the Irishman*. While the ambitions of that project are important and wholly admirable, they can sometimes result in over-programmatic readings which distort the fluidity and complexity of Wilde's relationship with British culture. More precisely, they tend to marginalize the importance of other pressures and imperatives, including the simple commercial need to sell books to an English readership, an imperative which modern commentators might deprecate, but one which affected all writers in the British Isles in the 1890s. Moreover, McCormack's extended metaphor of Wilde's writing as "guerrilla warfare" obscures the uncomfortable fact that the last ten years of his life were spent (literally) sleeping with the enemy.

W. J. McCormack's short essay in *Wilde the Irishman*, "Wilde and Parnell" (1998), plots developments in Wilde's career in the 1880s and early 1890s against key events in Parnell's life. McCormack does not claim that the lives of these two men ran in "parallel" (98); indeed he acknowledges that "no neat correlation of Parnellite and Wildean chronologies can be tabulated" (99). McCormack's strategy is more subtle and speculative than such "mechanical" mapping: he points only to certain "affinities" between the two men, in the hope of determining "the degree and nature of Wilde's unquestionable awareness of Parnell's fate" (99–100). McCormack notes, for example, that Wilde's preoccupation with suicide and forgery in "The Portrait of Mr W. H." coincides with the suicide (in 1889) of Richard Pigott, who had been exposed as the forger of a series of letters allegedly written by Parnell. McCormack also sees similarities in the divorce case which eventually forced Parnell's resignation from the Irish party and controversies surrounding the Lippincott *Dorian Gray*: "the common denominator," he argues, "was the recurrent and pervasive Victorian phenomenon of a double life" (99). McCormack goes on to speculate that Wilde's revisions to his novel—what McCormack calls its "intensification" (101)—may have been informed, at least in part, by Wilde's response to the Parnell crisis. In a similar way, McCormack wonders whether memories of Parnell's "self-destructive hubris" (102) also informed the writing of *Earnest*—in particular, the omission of the Gribsby episode. "In cutting the scene," McCormack argues, "Wilde not only improved the dramatic structure of the play, he also avoided a public preview of his own fate" (102). There is a problem with this line of argument, one already mentioned and one which a more careful editor of the volume in which McCormack's essay appeared should have picked up. It is of course the fact that it was George Alexander (and not Wilde) who originally cut the scene. Given what we know about Alexander's hostility to a four-act farce (described fully by Donohue in his 1995 edition of *Earnest*; 6. ii.), it is very hard to believe that Alexander had Parnell in mind. McCormack's essay is suggestive, but like many pieces in *The Irish Wilde*, it provides insufficient evidence to substantiate its concluding proposition: that we should "recognize in Charles Stewart Parnell an objective correlative whose career Wilde observed and suppressed" (102).

For the Wilde scholar, the title of Bernard O'Donoghue's essay, "The Journey to Reading Gaol: Sacrifice and Scapegoats in Irish Literature," is rather misleading: not only is Wilde's prison poem never mentioned, but his long prison-letter, *De Profundis*, merits only two brief sentences. O'Donoghue's interest is much more in Irish literature in general, than in Wilde's particular contribution to it. O'Donoghue begins by acknowledging that sacrifice is an idea which "pervades the Irish cultural tradition," but he claims that it has been understood "too simply" (103). He distinguishes three distinct senses of the term: "self-sacrifice" (such as "hunger-striking"), "ritual sacrifice" (which entails "violence towards other people or creatures"), and a "symbolic sense of the term," derived from Christianity (105). O'Donoghue then traces these meanings in works by a wide variety of Irish writers. Unfortunately, and as I have hinted, his comments on Wilde are both sparse and brief; moreover, they are also not particularly original. So few readers will be surprised to learn that Wilde's idea of sacrifice is generally "a sentimental Christian one" (109)—he tells us frequently enough himself in *De Profundis*. The limitation of Wilde's work for O'Donoghue is summed up in his dismissive judgement of *De Profundis*, that it refuses to "share Heaney's 'understanding' of a barbarous revenge, as the only way of appeasing guilt" (112). Such a comment seems a little unfair: to accuse a nineteenth-century writer of failing to anticipate a twentieth-century counterpart is to construct an idea of tradition with absolutely no sensitivity to historicity.

At first glance John Wilson Foster's contribution to *The Irish Wilde*, "Against Nature? Science and Oscar Wilde," is also something of a puzzle, as its subject-matter does not seem very closely related to Wilde's Irishness. Foster's starting-point is the "surprising" (116) discovery that despite his aesthete's rejection of nature, Wilde took a deep interest and pleasure in science. So, for example, Foster notes that while an undergraduate at Oxford, Wilde "read assiduously" (116) the work of figures such as Huxley, Tyndall and Spencer. In an argument which parallels the case made by Philip E. Smith and Michael S. Helfand in their 1989 edition of the *Oxford Notebooks*, Foster goes on to explain Wilde's ideas about individualism and self-realization in terms of his reading of contemporary evolutionary science, particularly the work of Darwin and William Kingdon Clifford. Of Wilde's literary works, the one which most interests Foster is *The Picture of Dorian Gray*, in part because it seems to be so hostile to nature (and thus by implication, to science). For Foster, however, the scientific and the aesthetic are not mutually opposed in the novel. For example, Foster views Dorian's mania for collecting, classifying and cataloguing objects as reminiscent of the fundamental activities of the natural scientist. Foster argues that in that novel "the artistic connoisseur and the scientific collector meet in taxonomy and nomenclature" (117). Foster claims that Wilde's interest in heredity and pathology in *Dorian Gray* and *De Profundis* are also derived from contemporary science, particularly the work of Henry Buckle and Cesare Lombroso. Foster's general conclusion, then, is that science is not "dispatched" by Wilde the aesthete; rather, it is "translated" (124). The "Irish" element of Foster's argument appears only briefly and rather tangentially in his claim that Wilde's "interest in science, including evolutionary theory, an admiration for Darwin, a respect for the nature of things and the honouring of self-realization . . . all distinguish [him] from Yeats" (124). This observation in turn prompts Foster to argue that Wilde's work should be enlisted in any attempt to recuperate "natural history and nature writing in Irish culture, or in late-Victorian literary history" (124). This hint that Wilde's interest in science and nature places him in both Irish *and* British literary traditions suggests a complexity to the relationship between science and nationalism which Foster's essay unfortunately does not pursue. (See also Foster's piece of the same title in *University of Texas Quarterly* in 1993.)

The second section of *Wilde the Irishman* is entitled "Continuities." The emphasis appears to be on the relevance of Wilde to Irish culture in the present day. However, in contrast to the first section, a number of the pieces make little attempt to address directly the Irish theme which is supposed to define the volume. Paula Murphy, in "A

Statue of Oscar Wilde for Dublin," writes on the commemoration of Wilde by a sculpture by Danny Osborne commissioned by Guinness Ireland and erected in Merrion Square in October 1997. A short piece by Frank McGuinness, "The Spirit of Play in *De Profundis*," reflects on the "theatricality" (145) which helps to keep that work alive for modern readers. In "Ellmann's Wilde," Derek Mahon revisits the limitations of Ellmann's biography, arguing that we do need another biography, for "Wilde still needs explaining" (147), a view which many critics would undoubtedly share. Alan Stanford in "Acting Wilde" draws on his own experiences (as both director and actor) to explain the differences between the ways English and Irish audiences respond to Wilde's drama. Surprisingly, perhaps, Stanford claims that it is *Irish* audiences who "have never really understood Wilde," because they "fail to grasp that Wilde wrote as an Irishman and what he wrote were savage satires on the war games of English society," a judgement which some may think rather overstates the issues involved (152).

Victoria White's "Women of No Importance: Misogyny in the Work of Oscar Wilde" takes its cue from some of the speculations about Wilde's sexuality offered by Melissa Knox in *Oscar Wilde: A Long and Lovely Suicide* (2. i.). White argues that the "mature, sexually active, reproductive woman" has "no place in Wilde's cosmology" (160)—a circumstance which she believes is explained not by a misogyny produced by Wilde's desire for men, but rather by his attraction to sexually immature bodies. Wilde, she reminds the reader, "did not sleep with children, but he did sleep with boys in their teens. He is one of the greatest writers for children who had an unhealthy obsession with youth, a club he shares with Lewis Carroll and J. M. Barrie" (164). The title of Thomas Kilroy's *"The Secret Fall of Constance Wilde* (An Excerpt from a New Play)" is self-explanatory. It takes the form of an (of course imagined) post-prison dialogue between Wilde and Constance about their children and their memories of their marriage (see also 2. ii.). It is followed by another piece of creative writing, a short poem in Irish by Gabriel Rosenstock (accompanied by a translation by Noel Griffin). The anthology closes with Seamus Heaney's address on the occasion of the dedication of a memorial panel to Wilde's memory in the east window of Poets' Corner in Westminster Abbey, 14 February 1995.

For students of Wilde, McCormack's volume is likely to be one of their first encounters with the topic of the "Irish Wilde." In this respect it is disappointing that the essays it contains are so varied in their quality. A further disappointment is the whole issue of evidence which I broached in the introduction to the present volume. Many of the essays are highly speculative and seem to strain to make connections. It is perhaps revealing that in a number of the pieces the "Irish dimension" (for the want of a better term) seems rather gratuitously tacked on. For example, what of any real substance do we learn specifically about Irishness from Yeats's and Wilde's opposed attitudes to science? It is also worth noting that Wilde's *oeuvre* is treated very unevenly. Perhaps the most glaring omission is the lack of attention given to the early poems, many of which were published in Irish periodicals. (For an account of the relationship between the early poetry and Wilde's nationalism, one at odds with the tenor of many essays in *Wilde the Irishman*, see Nick Frankel, "'Ave Imperatrix': Oscar Wilde and the Poetry of Englishness" [1997], 4. i.). These—admittedly large—reservations aside, McCormack's volume has the merit of pointing to a number of new avenues of research. At the very least the diversity of the essays in her collection demonstrates that there is a lot of work to be done before we can satisfactorily answer the question which opens her collection: "what difference does it make to read [Wilde] as Irish?"

A further attempt to situate Wilde's work in relation to Irish literary and cultural traditions is Vicki Mahaffey's *States of Desire: Wilde, Yeats, Joyce, and the Irish Experiment* (1998). The "experiment" of Mahaffey's title is a linguistic one; her argument is that the three writers in question "use language to riddle or puncture the everyday idols that dominate private and public life. Their demanding practice of writing trains receptive readers to develop a more flexible politics and a more complex and vibrant mode of perception and interaction" (4). More precisely, Mahaffey sees this form of experimental or "subversive" (13) reading as an alternative to "futile resistance to colonial domination by Britain" (11). She argues further that such a development occurred specifically in Ireland because of its "highly literate culture . . . that values language as a repository of local customs and traditions" (11). The long introductory chapter of Mahaffey's book is a dense theoretical elaboration of her idea of experimental reading which draws explicitly upon the work of Giles

Deleuze and Félix Guattari; it pays particular attention to their elaboration of Freud's concept of oedipal desire. In an argument which is often difficult to follow, and even more difficult to summarize, Mahaffey attempts to show how "all three writers [are] torn between a possessive desire that their culture endorses and the experimental desire that drives their writing" (31). The long chapter devoted to Wilde ranges widely across the *oeuvre*. It has three large ambitions: to examine Wilde's reputation; to show how he was brought "down" by "the crude representations of him" (40); and thereby to explain "exactly how dangerous a confusion between life and textuality can be" (40). It is worth observing that many of these issues have been covered by earlier cultural historians; moreover there are few new facts about Wilde's Irishness (and the notes contain a number of errors). The value of Mahaffey's account will depend upon the readiness of the reader to accept its elaborate theoretical superstructure.

The issue of Wilde's Irish nationality was also broached by Warwick Gould in his contribution to the 1993 Monaco international conference on Wilde. In "'The Crucifixion of the Outcasts': Yeats and Wilde in the Nineties," Gould argues for the importance of Wilde for Yeats's retrospective understanding of the 1890s as "tragic," and for Yeats's theory of masks. Gould draws attention to the fact that Yeats's interest in Wilde was not in his homosexuality but as "an Irish hero" (168), an identity which Gould uses to remind his reader of the prejudices against Wilde in Britain and of Wilde's position as "a scandal to orthodox publishing" (179). He shows how both Wilde and Yeats were rejected by Macmillan, a decision which Gould in turn attributes to the firm's "studied prejudice against Irish writing" (172). Scholars of Wilde will be particularly interested in the appendix to Gould's essay which prints two readers' reports from the Macmillan archive rejecting *The Happy Prince* and a collection of essays (which almost certainly became *Intentions*).

Neil Sammells's concern with Wilde's nationality in "Rediscovering the Irish Wilde" (1994) leads him to examine the editorial principles underlying *The Field Day Anthology of Irish Writing* (1991), a work which at the time of its publication provoked a lively debate about what constituted an Irish literary tradition. Sammells draws attention to the contradictory and uneasy attempts by the various editors to assess the nature of Wilde's achievement. Sammells himself suggests that "the key" to the "Irish Wilde" is "a function of *dif-*

ference . . . [He] expresses himself in a series of subversive literary strategies and a distinctive wit" (365). Sammells goes on to list examples of these subversive textual strategies in a number of Wilde's works, concluding (unremarkably) that "the Irish Wilde is defined both by and against the English Wilde" (369).

Michael Stanley's *Famous Dubliners* (1996) aims to "give a concise but comprehensive biography of each of the Dubliners named" (9)—that is, Yeats, Joyce, Swift, Wolfe Tone, Wilde and Edward Carson. The chapter on Wilde gives basic and not always accurate biographical information, interspersed with some brief excerpts from the works. The bibliography is short and most of the works cited are now very dated. Stanley was clearly constrained by the form of his book, but there are many better introductory studies to Wilde available (see, in particular, 5.); certainly there are better accounts of Wilde's nationality. Another work of similar value is Don L. F. Nilsen's *Humor in Irish Literature: A Reference Guide* (1996). Nilsen covers works from the sixteenth to the late twentieth century and includes not only what he terms "Anglo-Irish" and "Gaelic Irish" (1) but also first-generation Irish expatriates born in Britain and the United States. Such a large remit unsurprisingly gives Wilde, probably the prime candidate for such a study, only a few pages (81–89). Nilsen gives a brief and untheorized account of Wilde's humour and the range of its subjects, and follows this with some examples. In addition there is a bibliography of criticism with an emphasis on work dealing with his humour. A book which came too late to include in *Oscar Wilde Revalued*, but which perhaps anticipated some of the recent concerns with Wilde's nationalism, was David A. Upchurch's monograph *Wilde's Use of Irish Celtic Elements in "The Picture of Dorian Gray"* (1992).

3. iii.   *Wilde & Consumerism*

Regenia Gagnier's 1992 essay "On the Insatiability of Human Wants: Economic and Aesthetic Man" in *Victorian Studies* set a pattern for a number of her essays over the following years. She argued that changes in late nineteenth-century economics (that is, the "marginal revolution" of the 1870s, and the supersession of classical political economy) "closely parallel [the] late-Victorian shift from normative to formal aesthetics" (126). More precisely, Gagnier attempted "to show how [William Stanley] Jevons, the mathematical economist, and Pater, the donnish aesthete, converge in their promotion of subjectivism, individualism, passive consumption, and ultimately formalism" (145). According to Gagnier, Pater's "rational aesthetic man . . . sounds much like rational economic man" (147). In later work Gagnier again uses this thesis about the "convergence" of "economic" and "aesthetic" man in the last third of the nineteenth century in order to explore the relationship of late nineteenth-century literary culture to consumerism—to what she calls a "market society." Wilde figures prominently in a number of these essays. For example, in "Aesthetics and Economics in *A Florentine Tragedy*" (1994), Gagnier applies her ideas about "economic" and "aesthetic" man to Wilde's play. Much of the piece recapitulates the earlier essay in *Victorian Studies*; the new material, that on *A Florentine Tragedy* itself, amounts to less than a third of the whole piece—only about a thousand words. This imbalance oddly undermines her claims, for it prompts one to question the utility of a paradigm which requires so much elaboration of its own premises but which by the same token seems to provide so little new explanation of, or insights into, the texts to which it is applied. There is more than a suspicion that critical interpretation of this sort does not require such a complex or complicated theoretical superstructure. Comments such as "the play acts out the subtle workings of markets: goods markets, art markets, and marriage markets" (80) are neither novel, nor are they particularly illuminated by the specificities of late nineteenth-century marginal utility theory. After all, it is possible to find a very similar theme—the idea that "nothing has value until it is given a price of the market" (71)—in authors as varied as Ben Jonson and Jane Austen.

Gagnier continued to rehearse her ideas about late nineteenth-century economics and aesthetics in a number of further pieces, including "Is Market Society the *Fin* of History?" (1995) and "Wilde and the Victorians" (1997). Again there is significant overlap between both these pieces and the earlier essays. "Is Market Society the *Fin* of History?" uses the same thesis (and often takes complete sentences) from the *Victorian Studies* essay to discuss a different work by Wilde: on this occasion *Salome* is analysed in terms of "the formal theory of rational choice" (305). Gagnier's argument is that although Wilde "was tempted by the individualism, subjectivism, anarchy, even the consumerism central to *fin-de-siècle* aesthetics and economics . . . he never entirely abandoned his commitment to the more substantive value of the earlier Victorians" (305). In "Wilde and the Victorians" in *The Cambridge Companion to Oscar Wilde* (1997), the scope is broader, for Gagnier attempts to locate Wilde's *oeuvre* in relation to what she terms the "modernity and postmodernity of the Victorians," qualities exhibited in concerns about "bread, knowledge and freedom" (20). The section on "Bread" reprises her ideas about late nineteenth-century economic theory, this time in order to suggest that Wilde "interrogated the modern and Victorian dilemma between personal individuation and social good" (24). The section on "Knowledge," which restates ideas first expressed in *Idylls of the Marketplace* (1986), looks briefly at the relationship between Victorian liberalism (particularly that theorized by John Stuart Mill) and Wilde. Here Gagnier claims that Wilde's views about freedom and individuality were complicated (and compromised) by his participation in a "consumer society" (26). The final section on "Freedom" looks at Wilde in relation to Ruskin and Morris, asserting that Wilde's "progressive aesthetics" has outlasted the influence of the other two writers because "it is more assimilable to market values" (31). (It might be worth noting here that celebrations, and an exhibition, of Ruskin's work in Britain in the spring of 2000, and the general revival of interest in the PreRaphaelites, tends to throw doubt on the validity of such a conclusion.)

A further piece by Gagnier on these themes was entitled "Production, Reproduction, and Pleasure in Victorian Aesthetics and Economics" and appeared in a collection called *Victorian Sexual Dissidence*, edited by Richard Dellamora (1999). Once again there is overlap with the earlier essays. Gagnier's most recent reiteration of these ideas appears in "The Law of Progress and the Ironies of Individualism in the Nineteenth Century" (2000)—an essay which does not directly discuss Wilde—and in her forthcoming book, *The Insatiability of Human Wants: Economics and Aesthetics in Market Society* (2000).

Gagnier's focus on the relationships between the discourses of late nineteenth-century economics and aesthetics is clearly an attempt to extend beyond the case of Wilde the work on consumerism first developed in *Idylls of the Marketplace* (1986). At the time, that book was influential, not least because it was a welcome reminder to critics that literary works (particularly plays) were and are also commodities. It paved the way for a new understanding of Wilde's relationship with changes in late nineteenth-century literary culture. On the other hand, some reviewers expressed reservations about the kind of theorizing which was being put forward. More particularly, *Idylls of the Marketplace* was criticized for the unevenness of its empirical research. For example, in 1988 Joseph Donohue (in "Recent Studies of Oscar Wilde") rebutted some of Gagnier's assumptions about the class composition of the audiences of Wilde's plays, particularly of *The Importance Of Being Earnest.* (More recent research on the composition of music hall audiences in Britain has since confirmed Donohue's suggestions.)

Reservations about the empirical basis of Gagnier's theorization of consumerism, and about her interpretations of source material, have also been voiced about her later essays. In "Aesthetics, Economics and Commodity Culture: Theorizing Value in late Nineteenth-Century Britain" (1999), Josephine M. Guy has questioned the basic interpretation of Jevons's marginal utility theory which underlies Gagnier's account of the relationship between late nineteenth-century economic and aesthetic theories. Earlier, in "The Economies of Taste: Literary Markets and Literary Value in the Late Nineteenth Century" (1996), I argued that an attention to market ideology is not always compatible with an examination of actual market conditions. I then used examples from Wilde's *oeuvre* to show how these different ways of understanding the economic dimension of his work produced very different readings of it. For example, in Gagnier's argument, Wilde's emphasis on individualism and subjectivity appears to align him with the theorization of individual preference found in some parts of contemporary economic doctrines; by contrast, those same concerns place him in opposition to a market understood—as a publisher might have done—in terms of the social relations of taste. Similarly, more recent empirical research by Josephine M. Guy and me into Wilde's *actual* commerce with a market society—the ways in which he sold his books, the amounts of money he earned from his writing, and so on—compromises Gagnier's proposition that Wilde in some sense was able to engage critically with (or to subvert) consumerism. In "How Many Bags of 'Red Gold'?" (1999) and *Oscar Wilde's Profession* (2000), discussed in 4. iv. and 5. respectively, we argue that Wilde was deeply complicit with (and in no position to resist) the consumerism of the late nineteenth-century culture industry.

In this sense, the ideas in Gagnier's latest publications, despite (or perhaps because of) the elements of repetition or reiteration which they contain, have proved to be less persuasive than *Idylls of the Marketplace*. It is worth noting too that the last fifteen years have seen a blossoming of empirical research by historians such as John Sutherland, Simon Eliot, and Peter D. McDonald into the specific details of the careers of a whole range of late nineteenth-century writers and their day-to-day commerce with the late nineteenth-century book trade. The implications of this research for the highly abstract accounts of the literary market given by critics such as Gagnier, as well as Norman Feltes (1993), Jeff Nunokawa (see below), Patrick Brantlinger (1996), and Jonathan Freedman (1990) has yet to be fully appreciated.

Finally I confess to an admittedly personal complaint: Gagnier's thesis about late nineteenth-century economics and aesthetics recapitulates (but with little acknowledgement) many of the topics, labels and many of the minor writers to which I drew attention in a series of much earlier essays from the late 1970s onwards, and which were brought together in *Conditions for Criticism* (1991). This recognition of the importance of William Stanley Jevons, Herbert Spencer, Alexander Bain, Bernard Bosanquet, and the popularizing role of Grant Allen (in, for example, *Physiological Aesthetics* [1877]) in understanding the language and conceptual basis of late nineteenth-century aesthetics, predates Gagnier's work by some years, yet her essays consistently present this body of ideas as principally her own—a circumstance to which I drew attention in "The Economies of Taste" (1996).

A difficult essay which appears to plough the same furrow as Gagnier (but which interestingly does not acknowledge her work) is Carolyn Lesjak's "Utopia, Use, and the Everyday: Oscar Wilde and a New Economy of Pleasure" (2000). Using the insights of a range of modern theorists—not all of whom would be comfortable bedfellows, and who include Herbert Marcuse, Frederic Jameson, Michel de Certeau, and Theodor Adorno—Lesjak argues for a new understanding of Wilde's concept of pleasure and labour, one which places him "in the company of [William] Morris" (181). Such an eclectic range of authorities does not make for an easily accessible argument nor (given the convolutions of Lesjak's style) a particularly easy read. She suggests that for Wilde "pleasure is something to be worked at and worked for." Such an interpretation, however, only becomes possible once the reader performs "two important theoretical shifts."

The first involves showing "how the notion of pleasure in [Wilde's] texts dovetails with notions of use versus exchange value"; the second requires the uncoupling of "the concept of pleasure from sexuality *per se*" and the linking of it instead "to a more expansive notion of use." These theoretical shifts in turn "excavate the space for a more complex and variegated understanding of pleasure" (180). At this point, Lesjak's failure to define her economic terminology (particularly as it might have been understood by nineteenth-century thinkers) makes her argument unclear. Nevertheless she goes on to explore her ideas by looking first at Wilde's American lectures. In them, she argues, "need becomes indistinguishable from taste" and "luxury is reinvented as use" (183). Lesjak then moves to a discussion of *The Picture of Dorian Gray*, which she sees as being concerned with a particular notion of collecting (strangely, perhaps) predicated on the "nonidentical" nature of objects (185). Thus Lesjak can claim that "the very *form* of collecting serves both as a recognition of the temptation of commodity fetishism and as a resistance to it"; collected objects, that is, possess "an amateur value but no use-value" (186). (John Wilson Foster's account of collecting in *Dorian Gray*, "Against Nature? Science and Oscar Wilde," in *Wilde the Irishman* [1998], is almost totally at odds with that of Lesjak, for Foster talks of Wilde's engagement in his novel with the scientist-collector and with nineteenth-century science's obsession with taxonomies; see 3. ii.). Lesjak proceeds to discuss Wilde's ideas about work and pleasure in "The Soul of Man Under Socialism" and *De Profundis*, arguing that he is "best situated within a particular strand of Marxism, a utopianism whose basis lies not in valorizing labor . . . but in a *liberation from labor*" (195). Lesjak concludes by suggesting that Wilde's "'new Individualism' is . . . best understood as a . . . recognition that neither ascetic rejections of consumption nor productivist conceptions about work, technology, and efficiency are the answer" (200–201). Lesjak's piece is not easy to summarize, and she seems to ignore the fact that one of Wilde's constant concerns was entertainment: her over-use of famously difficult twentieth-century Marxist critics to understand

Wilde's interest in the links between pleasure and politics calls to mind the proverb about sledgehammers and peanuts.

Altogether more interesting is Jeff Nunokawa's elegantly written "The Importance Of Being Bored: The Dividends of Ennui in *The Picture of Dorian Gray*" (1996). Nunokawa observes that in the novel "long stretches of the story are almost unbearably uninteresting." He goes on to connect this effect with the treatment of boredom in the narrative: "the ennui it induces mirrors the ennui it describes" (357), a state which is imaged in "the diagnostic vocabulary of bodily fatigue" (359). Nunokawa suggests that ennui contrasts with, but is related to states of desire: "they are actually the same body in different lights" (360), and the physical "weariness that underwrites the recession of desire in Wilde's novel casts in the gravest light the glib comfort with which his dandy greets it" (361). Nunokawa goes on to analyse Wilde's representation of passion in the light of this dualism: "extending beyond both sanctioned and scandalous species of sexual passion, the desires that Lord Henry encourages include as well the upmarket varieties of consumer demand" (366). Using the insights of Rachel Bowlby (in *Shopping with Freud* [1993]) into the relationships established in the novel between beauty, fashion and pleasure, Nunokawa relates the novel's central themes to late nineteenth-century consumerism:

> The general proliferation of desire that [Lord Henry] encourages functions more broadly to support the increasingly specialized market for commodities that evolved in the second half of the nineteenth century. . . . The ephemerality of individual desires heralded in *Dorian Gray* can thus be read as the subjective correlative of the obsolescence built into the objects that the dandy prefers[,] . . . such as the cigarettes . . . whose "chief charm" is that they "don't last." (366)

Nunokawa's essay concludes by noting that there is one form of desire in the novel which appears to escape from the inevitable boredom induced by commodity culture—what Wilde famously called "the love that dare not speak its name." That is, an enduring spiritualized (rather than decaying bodily) form of homosexual passion. As Nunokawa puts it: "the desire that . . . dares not assume bodily shape is congratulated as the one that transcends bodily exhaustion" (368). Yet there is a "catch," for what prompted desire in the first place is "the youthful body" (368). Nunokawa's is one of the most subtle and sug-

gestive attempts to connect consumerist ideology with the specificities of homosexual desire, and how both could be and were
represented in the 1890s.

In his essay, "Wilde and the Dandyism of the Senses" (1997), Stephen Calloway also addresses the topic of consumerism, but in a
rather more oblique manner, via the topic of the Aesthetes' interest
in the Dandyism of the Regency period; in so doing Calloway addresses another and neglected subject—what he calls Wilde's "own
visual taste" (39). He attempts to document Wilde's "actual personal
artistic predilections" in three areas: "in his dress, his interiors and in
the appearance of his published books" (39–40). Despite the often
celebrated modernity of Wilde's house in Tite Street, and his boasting
about his own collection of art-objects, in Calloway's view Wilde
lacked sophistication in matters of taste. Wilde, he argues, "seems
never to have developed much of a connoisseur eye for quality in . . .
individual works of art" (49). Calloway goes on to suggest that Wilde's "splendour . . . was a splendour of phrases, not of visual effects; a
richness of word-pictures rather than of objects" (50). The exception
to this pattern was Wilde's decisions about book design. Here, Calloway claims, his "discrimination was extraordinary . . . his judgement
. . . remarkably astute" (50). It is perhaps worth making two comments about Calloway's account. First he has little to say about the
way the limits to Wilde's financial resources constrained his taste.
Likewise, the book-designs which Calloway admires unreservedly
were often chosen for material as much as aesthetic reasons; moreover Wilde's agency in these decisions was not a straightforward matter: often publishers like John Lane (of the Bodley Head) paid the
piper, and so insisted upon calling the tune.

Calloway's essay can usefully be read alongside Charlotte Gere
with Lesley Hoskins, *The House Beautiful: Oscar Wilde and the Aesthetic Interior* (2000), a lavish volume published to accompany an exhibition of the same name at the Geffrye Museum, London (from July
2000 to January 2001). In the first five chapters, Gere attempts to
trace the influence of Wilde and the Aesthetic Movement on the
decorative arts. She looks at the artists, architects and designers with
whom Wilde associated and the interiors which he admired, showing
how his ideas on art and interior decoration were disseminated
through his lectures and through the drawing rooms of London's social elite. A chapter is devoted to Wilde's own house, 16 (now 33) Tite

Street. Interestingly Gere suggests that Wilde's "ambitions for his house and his search for originality caused him to break a number of the decorative conventions which he was still publicly and emphatically peddling in his lectures" (102). The final chapter, which is written by Lesley Hoskins, looks at the popular expression of the Aesthetic Movement in the decorations to be found in the ordinary middle-class home, as well as in the numerous contemporary pamphlets and magazines on interior design. *The House Beautiful* is very handsomely produced with an abundance of interesting illustrations, many of which will be new to the reader. It gives a sense of tangibility to those objects of desire to which late Victorian middle-class metropolitan consumers aspired. The book's weakness lies in the text, which contains a number of factual errors relating to details of Wilde's life; but the occasional lapse does not does detract from its value as a visual resource.

Another a book very relevant to Calloway's essay is Nicholas Frankel's *Oscar Wilde's Decorated Books* (2000). Taking his cue from the work Jerome J. McGann and D. F. McKenzie, Frankel examines the textual embodiments of a number of Wilde's works, drawing attention to the ways in which their decorative devices were central to Wilde's understanding of his own writings as well as to what Frankel calls his "aesthetic theory of language." The first half of Frankel's book examines the textual history of *Poems* (this is a reworking of his essay "Ave Imperatrix," discussed in 4. i.), and *Salome*, which Frankel understands as a "field of social differences working in contestation with one another" (49). The four chapters of the second section examine the designs and production values of four of Wilde's books—*Intentions*, *Poems* (1892), *The Picture of Dorian Gray* and *The Sphinx*—with the aim of demonstrating how the "the book [works] as a visual device for a textual performance" (177). Frankel's study undoubtedly addresses an important topic, and given the rarity of first editions of Wilde's books, many readers will find the information about their decorative qualities, together with his book's illustrations very useful—although some of those illustrations fail to capture their subjects' sumptuousness. By contrast, Frankel's overall thesis may be less convincing, and for a number of reasons. The most obvious is the fact that it does not encompass the whole of Wilde's *oeuvre*. In particular, he unaccountably omits to discuss *A House of Pomegranates*, a work whose illustrations caused considerable controversy, in part because of their poor technical quality, but most importantly because of the perceived mismatch between them and the text. A second limitation is Frankel's restricted understanding of materiality. In particular he pays relatively little attention to the extent to which the economics of book production in the 1890s determined design-choices. Finally there are some bibliographical errors and lacunae, disappointing in a study informed by editorial and bibliographical theory. For example, by compressing the complexities of Wilde's negotiations with John Lane (at the Bodley Head) over the publication in Britain of the French version of *Salomé*, Frankel seriously misrepresents the power-relationship between author and publisher.

Finally it is worth noting that Calloway's piece bears some similarities to Rhonda Garelick's study of the dandy in *Rising Star: Dandyism, Gender and Performance in the Fin de Siècle* (1998). Garelick's ambitions are much wider-ranging than those of Calloway, for she attempts to give a detailed history of dandyism from its origins in Regency England through to modern film and pop icons. Wilde scholars will be most interested in her lengthy discussion of *Salome*, although they may be surprised that scant attention is paid to the much more obvious dandy-figures in *The Picture of Dorian Gray* and the Society Comedies. Indeed the presence of female dandies in these last works tends to compromise Garelick's overall thesis about the ways in which the dandy is gendered. Garelick's study in turn can profitably be read in conjunction with Michael Patrick Gillespie's 1993 essay "From Beau Brummell to Lady Bracknell: Reviewing the Dandy in *The Importance of Being Earnest.*"

| 4 |

Wilde the Writer

A notable feature of some research on Wilde in the 1990s was an attention to the way he wrote—to his writing practices. This development might have a straightforward pragmatic explanation, insofar as information about Wilde's drafts and typescripts is now much more easily available than it was prior to 1980. It might also, however, have drawn strength from a larger and equally recent interest in the history of the book, in itself propelled by the theoretical work of Jerome J. McGann and D. F. McKenzie as well as the empirical findings of historians such as Simon Eliot and John Sutherland. An interest in the textual condition of Wilde's work is, of course, a central concern of the Oxford English Texts *Complete Works* of Wilde, the first volume of which appeared in 2000 (see 6. i.). By the middle of the present decade, well over half of the edition should be published. More importantly, perhaps, the volumes which will appear next, the fiction, criticism and *De Profundis*, cover precisely those works which have received little or no editorial treatment to date. One clear benefit of the OET edition will be a much more thorough account of Wilde's sources. Throughout the 1990s, scholars have continued to turn up (albeit in a piecemeal way) new allusions, quotations and influences; these, however, need systematic collation if they are to feed into critical judgements.

As I noted in *Oscar Wilde Revalued*, Wilde's career as a poet suffered a great neglect for most of the twentieth century. Almost for the first time, the 1990s saw a number of serious attempts to reassess the place of poetry in Wilde's *oeuvre*. They were helped by the appearance of the first adequate popular edition (edited by Isobel Murray, 1997) and will be helped in the future by the first full scholarly edition (edited by Bobby Fong and Karl Beckson, 2000). As the poetry becomes more widely read, it will inevitably attract more critical interest. Wilde's criticism, however, has generated relatively little discussion: it still tends to be described in terms of the way it illuminates other aspects of the *oeuvre*. The only significant exception to this pattern is Lawrence Danson's book-length study of *Intentions*; although elegantly and wittily written, Danson's thesis does not offer any radical or fundamental re-conceptualization of his subject. Such a treatment might well have to wait for a textual description of *Intentions* which connects it more directly with contemporary journalism. Such a state of affairs might not be too far off, for the subject of Wilde's journalism (one conspicuously absent from research in the 1980s) has been a notable sub-area of recent interest. John Stokes's pioneering work has been supplemented by a number of competing accounts, many of which concentrate on Wilde's stint as editor of *Woman's World* in the late 1880s.

Despite these welcome developments, the main focus of attention on Wilde's writing practices continues to be *The Picture of Dorian Gray* and the drama. It is interesting that almost every account of the novel in the 1990s has tended to follow the well-worn path of identifying new sources or generating new interpretations of what is seen to be an inherently plural novel. It has been something of a surprise to note how little critical disquiet has been expressed over the incompatibility of some of these readings; in this respect more attention to what is meant by the concept of the plural or polyvocal text would be welcome. In contrast to the fiction there have been new lines of research in the drama. Much more attention has been given to the plays as part of the history of performance—to understanding them as theatrical experience, rather than simply assimilating them into a general literary history. There has also been a critical use of textual scholarship to try to understand better the politics of Wilde's plays. Of particular note has been a virtual explosion of interest in *Salome*, a work which was seen in the 1970s and 1980s as the anomaly in Wilde's dramatic output.

4. i. The Poet

In "'Ave Imperatrix': Oscar Wilde and the Poetry of Englishness" (1997), Nick Frankel pertinently observes that "the role of poetry in shaping [Wilde's] life remains poorly understood" (117). In attempting to adjust this imbalance, Frankel begins with a detailed account of the numbers of poems which Wilde published in periodicals prior to 1881. He argues that they can be "split into an English and an Irish half," a split which is "all the more striking for the fact that [the] Irish publications occurred while [Wilde] was a student at Oxford." Frankel further comments that Wilde's speech became "more English" at the very time when he "identified his poetry exclusively with Irish journals" (119). Frankel explores these tensions in relation to questions about Wilde's national identity. In a study which combines critical sensitivity with a detailed knowledge of the textual condition of many of the early (and neglected) poems, Frankel argues that Wilde's poetry represents an "equivocal embrace of the idea of 'Englishness'" (126), when "Englishness" is defined in relation to Matthew Arnold's "program for cultural and national renewal through poetry, with Wordsworth and Keats in the phalanx" (127–28). Frankel goes on to suggests that Arnold's writings allow us to reassess the significance of Wilde's poetry, and in particular to "cast the issues of Wilde's Romanticism and plagiarism in a new light" (128).

Frankel re-examines the Oxford Union affair (see also Sandra Siegel, "Oscar Wilde's Gift and Oxford's 'Coarse Impertinence,'" 3.ii.), and the generally hostile reception which Wilde's *Poems* (1881) received from English critics. He argues that Wilde's poetry posed a threat to the "hegemonic idea of 'English literature'" (129), and that English critics applied the critical language of Aestheticism to Wilde's poetry "as a way of reifying the sanctity of an English canon whose monopoly on originality . . . Wilde's essentially classical skills at imitation threatened to violate" (130). Frankel ends his essay with some brief observations about the reception of Wilde's poems in the United States, claiming that their "Englishness" was much "clearer to American eyes": that "*Poems* came to represent an English aesthetic—finally English Aestheticism" (131). However Frankel also notes that America paradoxically "granted Wilde the necessary space also to recover his Irishness," for he took the opportunity to lecture on Irish poetry (132). Frankel sees no necessary contradiction here, observing that "as much as Wilde's lecture attempts to recover a suppressed Irish tradition, it also articulates the ideological rationale for [Wilde's] own cultivation of an 'English' aesthetic" (133). The serious attention which Frankel gives to the early poetry is welcome, and the sophistication with which he discusses the complexities of Wilde's national identity can be useful read alongside the essays in Jerusha McCormack's *Wilde the Irishman* (1998; see 3.ii.). On the other hand, it could be argued that in reconstructing the cultural milieu in which Wilde's poetry was written and the politics underlying its reception, Frankel overestimates the value of some of the early poems. It is also worth noting that Wilde's conception of himself as a poet can be glimpsed in a recently discovered scrap-book put together by him in the mid- to late-1870s; see Fong and Beckson, 2000 and 7. i.

In "Wilde as Poet" (1997), Bobby Fong and Karl Beckson also attempt to reassess the worth of Wilde's poetry, drawing attention to its variety of themes and styles. They discuss Wilde's use of Italian subjects, of pastoral themes and settings, the influence of PreRaphaelite poetry, and his representation of some contemporary political concerns (particularly in the poems on the Balkans crisis). They also describe the better-known influence of "avant-garde impulses" (64), such as French Impressionism and French literary Decadence. They conclude with the fairly conventional judgement that *The Ballad of Reading Gaol* is Wilde's most significant achievement and that "its force remains undisputed" (67). The essay should be read in conjunction with Fong's and Beckson's edition of the poems and its introductory essays (see 6. ii.).

In "'A very curious construction': masculinity and the poetry of A. E. Housman and Oscar Wilde" (1995), Ruth Robbins contrasts Wilde's *The Sphinx* (strangely given here as "The Sphynx," a manuscript spelling of the title which does not occur in the first edition, nor in the text printed by Robert Ross, from which Robbins claims to quote) with Housmans's *A Shropshire Lad* (1896) (equally strangely, here just *Shropshire Lad*); the essay concludes with an account of Wilde's response to "both his own disgrace, and to Housman's poetry"—that is, *The Ballad of Reading Gaol* (here more strangely still, dated as "1897"). Robbins, like many other commentators, sees Wilde's trials as a cultural watershed, and the poetry of Wilde and Housman "may be seen as different but comparable models for the construction of masculinity in the run up to and the aftermath of the events of April and May 1895" (138). She describes the attention paid to Wilde's writing during the first trial, commenting that by the 1890s "masculine language practices" possessed a "quality of restraint" (142), while by contrast, "an effeminate use of language would be one which preferred the phatic to the functional" (143). For Robbins, in *The Sphinx* the linguistic and the phatic become uppermost: "the only outlet for ... desire is linguistic. ... [T]he poem is insisting only on the pleasure of words ... to which extent, the poem is ... phatic" (145). Robbins goes on to contrast Wilde's poem with some of the lyrics of *A Shropshire Lad*, which are marked by "restraint, and this may be one reason why his poetry would not have landed [Housman] in court" (148). (Of course Wilde was not actually being tried for the content of his writing.) She goes on to suggest that one of Wilde's models for *The Ballad of Reading Gaol* was *A Shropshire Lad*—although "Wilde is not entirely successful in his adoption of Housman's poetic technique; he finds it impossible to capture the other man's restraint in his own poem" (154). Robbins's understanding of the significance of Wilde's trials for discourses about desire is entirely familiar (as she acknowledges) from the work of Ed Cohen; her assumptions about Housmans's attitude towards his own sexuality, and his role in providing a model for Wilde are new, but will perhaps be contested.

Norman Page's detective work in his essay "Decoding *The Ballad of Reading Gaol*" (1994) centres on a brief rehearsal of the biographical background to the poem and a slightly longer discussion of what he terms its "alien poetic genre and style" (311). Page's argument is that although deriving from "the most intense experience of Wilde's life," the work is nevertheless "a very literary poem, almost a pastiche" (308). Page compares *Reading Gaol* to Christopher Isherwood's *Goodbye to Berlin*, another piece in which "painful autobiographical material is transformed and objectified" (310).

Another discussion of *Reading Gaol* is to be found in Karen Alkalay-Gut's "The Thing he Loves: Murder as Aesthetic Experience in *The Ballad of Reading Gaol*" (1997). Alkalay-Gut attempts to shed light on the "incongruities, inconsistencies, and distortions" which characterize the poem by clarifying its "foundations and methods"—a task which in turn "present[s] for discussion some social and critical issues often elided in the same manner as in the poem" (349–50). Alkalay-Gut begins by examining the "very thorough" (350) way in which Wilde transforms his source, the hanging of trooper Charles Thomas Wooldridge in Reading Gaol. She stresses Wilde's use of the passive tense to describe the murder and the way he ignores Wooldridge's victim, tactics which allow blame to be shifted to the institution, so that the "real victim" becomes the murderer (352). Alkalay-Gut claims that the dehumanization of Wooldridge's wife is "not an assertion of misogyny" because "even while he erases the real victim of the crime, Wilde perceives the very root of his misconduct in the sad human tendency to negate the other" (354). For Alkalay-Gut this "paradox" is central to the poem, and the rest of her essay is devoted to an exploration of it. Her reading of *The Ballad of Reading Gaol* posits what she terms a "non-literal" or symbolic interpretation, one which co-exists uneasily with its elements of realism; these two sorts of meaning in turn echo Wilde's central preoccupation in the poem: "it is precisely the relation between reality and symbol, and the necessity for considering them together in the real world that Wilde wishes to examine" (358).

Unfortunately not noticed in *Oscar Wilde Revalued* was Margueritte Murphy's *A Tradition of Subversion: The Prose Poem in English from Wilde to Ashberry* (1992) which in keeping with many monographs in the early 1990s emphasizes the oppositional elements in Wilde's work.

4. ii. The Journalist

John Stokes continues his long-standing interest in late nineteenth-century periodical culture in his 1997 essay, "Wilde the Journalist." He focuses on Wilde's lesser-known and often anonymous work written in the early and mid-1880s—that is, before the famous pieces of journalism put together in *Intentions*. Stokes acknowledges the problems in identifying the extent of Wilde's unsigned journalism. It is worth reiterating that Christopher Millard's [Stuart Mason] annotations to his proof copy of the *Bibliography of Oscar Wilde*, now in the Clark Library, identify Wilde as the author of more pieces than the published version of his bibliography does; see also Oskar Wellens (1994, discussed below). Stokes suggests that issues of attribution are made difficult because of the "complicated life that Wilde lives in the columns of newsprint," that he "both reveals and disguises himself" (77). Stokes's thesis is that Wilde's journalism is characterized by a "duality" in which Wilde is both "oracle and echo" (77) and that his work is marked by frequent changes of mind and a "play of moods" (78). Despite this reassessment of the early journalism, Stokes's concluding judgement of it is uncontroversial:

that when Wilde was "finally in a position to give up journalism he did so quite easily, turning to genres where he could be more forthcoming about deception" (78). Stokes's argument ought to be read in conjunction with the stronger claims made for Wilde's journalism, especially by critics such as Catherine Ksinan (1998, discussed below), and those who argue for continuities between the journalism and the later work (such as Guy [1998], and Guy and Small (2000); see 6. i.).

Wilde and one of his periodical titles, *Woman's World*, figure in Laurel Brake's *Subjugated Knowledges: Journalism, Gender and Literature in the Nineteenth Century* (1994). Brake's subject is the changing nature of print culture in the last decades of the nineteenth century, and in particular the tensions produced by "the attempt to create a clear-cut dichotomy between literature and journalism" (xii). Brake describes Wilde's involvement with that changing journalist culture and his ambitions as he collected some of his periodical pieces in *Intentions*: "Wilde excluded and never reprinted in his lifetime ... numerous reviews and articles from the daily *Pall Mall Gazette*, the *Court and Society Review*, *Queen*, and *The Speaker*. He constructs himself in *Intentions* as the irreverent and youthful upstart who takes on and displaces the aging gurus" (68).

One of the few essays concentrating exclusively on Wilde's journalism is Catherine Ksinan's "Wilde as Editor of *Woman's World*: Fighting a Dull Slumber in Stale Certitudes" (1998). Ksinan examines Wilde's work at Cassell and Co. as editor of that magazine, her overall argument being that "Wilde's labours for and with women have been disconcertingly ignored by criticism ... [and] his temper and talents as an editor seriously overlooked." For Ksinan, an investigation into what she calls "the Cassell era" throws "fresh light on Wilde the thinker, writer, critic, *and* woman's advocate" (410). Her account begins with an examination of the *Lady's World*, the magazine which Wilde transformed into the *Woman's World*. She comments on Wilde's success in "coaxing talented women writers and thinkers to contribute to the new magazine," particularly those in "elite circles" (414); but she also acknowledges that he "was not entirely successful in excising trivia and nonsense from his magazine" (415). Ksinan attributes this imbalance not to Wilde's "failure as an editor" but rather to "market-driven concessions," and it was this need to compromise which probably led to his "boredom" (415). Ksinan goes on to give detailed discussions of contributions to the *Woman's World* by the feminist Millicent Garrett Fawcett, the conservative Lucy Garnett, and Lady Wilde; she also examines Wilde's own column, "Literary and Other Notes." Ksinan observes that while his writing could be "sophisticated and serious" (422), it was also witty. She concludes by asking the reader to recognize Wilde as one of the very few "public male" feminists, a position which, she argues, "would be fully productive in [his] later dramatic sketches of women" (424). Ksinan attempts to give a balanced account of the *Woman's World*, acknowledging both its weaknesses and strengths. Less judicious perhaps is her assessment of Wilde as a proto-feminist. Other critics (most notably Kerry Powell in *Women and the Victorian Theatre* [1997]; discussed in 4. iv.) have come to the opposite conclusion, that Wilde's apparent commitment to feminism was only ever opportunist, and that in his actual dealings with women (including his wife) he was anything but even-handed. Moreover attitudes to women in Wilde's drama are not consistent, and tend to trade upon generic Victorian stereotypes of sinfulness and repentance.

Stephanie Green's topic in "Oscar Wilde's *The Woman's World*" (1997) is also that magazine's feminist sympathies. Green sees the *Woman's World* as "proto-feminist" (103), but not consistently nor coherently so. Nevertheless she notes what she terms "the conservative shift in the magazine's content" (106) following Wilde's departure, and interprets this move as a response to "public anxiety about reformulations of social roles for women" (106), in which the *Woman's World* was implicated. Like Ksinan, Green bases her argument on a detailed examination of selected contributions to the magazine, noting in particular that Wilde's representation of women in his "Literary Notes" is "often contradictory"—that Wilde could be "arch and patronizing" while at the same time (in his editorial policy) enabling women's voices "to be heard" (108). Green also places the *Woman's World* in relation to other contemporary magazines (including the *Savoy* and the *Yellow Book*), as well as comparing it with Wilde's representation of women in his later works. Green concludes with the comment that the *Woman's World* was "an exquisite paradox. . . . It proved that women could be intelligent and successful, showed them freedom and adventure and then told them that their highest duty was to stay at home" (112).

In her essay "The *Woman's World*: Oscar Wilde as Editor" (1997), Anya Clayworth also argues for a reassessment of Wilde's career as a journalist, seeing it as a central moment when "Wilde learned the skill of writing to public demand" (85). His time working for the *Pall Mall Gazette*, the *Saturday Review* and the *Dramatic Review* helped Wilde to develop that skill, but he was then always under the "guidance of an editor" (85). It is here, according to Clayworth, that Wilde's time at the *Woman's World* becomes important: with "Wilde in the editorial role, his influence on the magazine in response to the changing market for women's magazines is easily identifiable . . . [it is] a significant indicator of a change in his writing tactics to one of actively addressing and manipulating the markets for literature" (85). Clayworth details those changes and she suggests that it was Wilde's status as a "celebrity" which led Cassell to employ him. Like Stephanie Green, she notes that women's magazines were beginning to discuss issues of public policy, such as the future of education for women, and that Wilde could attract the kind of contributor who would bring in a new type of reader. Clayworth also discusses the significance of Wilde's decision to change the title of the magazine from *Lady's World* to *Woman's World*, examining what the terms "lady" and "woman" might have suggested to a contemporary reader. Clayworth, however, resists the temptation to see in Wilde's actions an explicitly political motive: "it is possible to argue that Wilde's motive was . . . calculated and . . . cynical" (89). Clayworth goes on to argue that the failure of the *Woman's World* was in part due misjudgements on Wilde's part—he failed to assess properly the appeal of his magazine and overestimated the number of buyers it would attract. Nonetheless, his experience as an editor, according to Clayworth, "laid the foundation for enduring success" (98).

In "A Hitherto Unnoticed Review by Wilde" (1994), Oskar Wellens reports on the "marked file" of the *Athenaeum*, housed in the Library of the City University, London, in which "successive editors or their assistants identified each anonymous contribution." In addition to Wilde's anonymous review (4 September 1880) of R. C. Jebb's essay on Greek history for the *Encyclopaedia Britannica*, Wellens notes that the file identifies Wilde as the author of the anonymous review of John Addington Symonds's *Sketches and Studies in Italy* (1879) which appeared in the *Athenaeum* (no. 2694 [June 1879], 754–55).

4. iii. *The Critic*

In "Wilde in Arden, or the Masks of Truth" (1994), Lawrence Danson examines Wilde's essay "Shakespeare and Stage Costume," a piece which was later revised to become "The Truth of Masks" in *Intentions*. (While Danson may be aware of it, he does not mention the fact that "Shakespeare and Stage Costume," published in the *Nineteenth Century* in May 1885, was itself the reworking of another essay, "Shakespeare on Scenery," published in the *Dramatic Review* in March 1885.) Danson locates Wilde's arguments—and particularly his revisions—in relation to contemporary debates about archaeological realism in the theatre (associated particularly with E. W. Godwin), and to the production in Coombe Park of *As You Like It* about which Wilde wrote in the *Dramatic Review* later in 1885. Danson suggests that Wilde describes the production via a series of allusions to Gautier's *Mademoiselle de Maupin*. These in turn allow him to endorse the "realism" of the Godwinian staging while at the same time detecting "a prolonged erotics of illusion" associated with Gautier's aesthetic (24). Danson ends his piece with some brief comments about how Wilde's own plays were influenced by these opposing ideas; not surprisingly, he sees *The Importance of Being Earnest* as a place where "the famous distinction between Illusion and Reality dissolves" (31).

In a further piece, "Wilde as Critic and Theorist" (1997), Danson reexamines *Intentions*. He argues that the admiration of modern critics for the essays' purported radical and innovative elements was not one shared by Wilde's contemporaries for whom the work provoked a "strong sense of *déjà vu*" (82). Danson argues rather flatly that the "best way to understand Wilde's intentions . . . is to locate them in the context of the times" (81); in his essay that context amounts to Wilde's use of Pater and Arnold, his hostility towards realism, and his use of Chuang-Tzu. Danson's concluding "conspectus" stresses the "performative qualities" in Wilde's piece and acknowledges an "inconsistency" which "allowed him the virtue of insincerity" (94)—qualities which Danson sees exemplified in "The Soul of Man Under Socialism" (an essay which Wilde once thought of including in *Intentions*). Portions of Danson's 1994 essay are reprinted as his chapter on "The Truth of Masks" in his book *Wilde's Intentions: The Artist in his Criticism* (1997). Likewise his 1997 piece presents in summary form the thesis of that book (see 5.).

In "A Printing Error in 'The Soul of Man Under Socialism'" (1996), Horst Schroeder corrects one of the mistakes in *Oscar Wilde Revalued*. He points out that a letter from Wilde to an unidentified correspondent which I printed (28) was to Frank Harris, not John Morley, and goes on to describe how the error to which the letter refers remained uncorrected in Arthur Lee Humphreys's edition of the essay in 1895. Schroeder also points out that the error persisted in Ross's edition and in modern collections: "the paragraph rearrangement, requested by Wilde in his letter of the beginning of 1891, is still a desideratum" (51). It is interesting, however, that Schroeder overlooks the significance of his observation—that it is strong evidence that Wilde had little or nothing to do with Humphreys's book edition of his essay.

Elsewhere Robert J. G. Lange makes a correction to the claim made by Horst Schroeder in his *Oscar Wilde, "The Portrait of Mr W. H."—Its Composition, Publication and Reception* (1984) that there were no publications of the longer book-length version of *The Portrait of Mr W. H.* in the years between Mitchell Kennerley's limited edition of 1921 and Vyvyan Holland's Methuen edition of 1958. Lange observes that Ian Fletcher and John Stokes claimed the existence of a 1923 Doubleday Page edition which was "several times" reprinted, but notes that they give no further details. His "page by page" (202) comparison of the Kennerley and Doubleday Page editions show them to be "identical." Lange also observes that the book-length text of *The Portrait of Mr W. H.* was republished in 1927 in volume 6 of *The Complete Works of Oscar Wilde* by William H. Wise & Company.

4. iv.   The Dramatist

In *Oscar Wilde Revalued*, I noted that the 1970s and 1980s saw several book-length studies of Wilde's dramatic output. Surprisingly, perhaps, the 1990s have seen only one major study since Kerry Powell's *Oscar Wilde and the Theatre of the 1890s* (1990)—Sos Eltis's *Revising Wilde* (1996), which examines the composition of Wilde's Society Comedies and *Vera*. Her declared ambition is to discuss Wilde's plays in relation to what she terms "the radical Wilde who attacked Victorian society in 'The Soul of Man Under Socialism,' mocked moral seriousness in 'The Decay of Lying,' and outraged conventional sexual and social codes in *The Picture of Dorian Gray"* (4). Although her analysis concentrates on the drama, implicit in her thesis is an idea of Wilde as a "revolutionary" (5) writer. Consequently her book is described alongside other full-length studies of the whole career in chapter 5.

Although John Russell Stephens's *The Profession of the Playwright* (1992) is not devoted to Wilde, it nevertheless provides one of the most useful commentaries on the milieu in which he worked in the early 1890s. Stephens gives a thorough account of the professionalization of dramatic authorship in the nineteenth century, covering such topics as the funding and management of theatres, copyright legislation, changes in the ways dramatists were paid, piracy and plagiarism, and changes in the ways play-texts were published, culminating in the phenomenon of published reading-texts of plays which emerged in the 1890s. Stephens's study is full of useful details of the careers of an impressive range of nineteenth-century playwrights, from the familiar—such as Wilde, Shaw, Jones and Pinero—to the barely remembered, such as Charles Dance and Catherine Ann Crowe. In the process he gives the reader a salutary reminder of the size of the nineteenth-century theatre industry and thus the attractions of theatrical writing for the professional author, circumstances which help to explain Wilde's decision to persist with the genre after his failures in the early 1880s.

Theatre historians have often observed that research into nineteenth-century theatrical culture is hindered by the absence of documentation. As a result hard information about the commercial details of individual theatres and specific shows, as well as about the relative success of particular playwrights, is not always accessible. Stephens goes some way to rectifying this situation, because he does include abundant details of contracts and earnings which allow the careers of different dramatists to be usefully compared. Unfortunately, however, in the case of Wilde, his information is not always correct. Stephens bases his calculations of Wilde's royalties on the evidence of early historians and biographers (such as Hesketh Pearson), thus perpetuating the myth that Wilde was among the highest dramatic earners (in Stephens's phrase, "at the very top of the market" [79]). In fact archival evidence in the Clark Library about the returns of particular plays and testimony from Lewis Waller to Wilde's bankruptcy hearing (details of which are now in the Public Record Office) force us to modify this judgement substantially (see Guy and Small, 1999 and 2000; see also Holland's new edition of the *Letters* [2000]; see in addition 3. iii, 5. and 7. ii.) In this respect the use of Stephens's book for the Wilde scholar or critic is not so much in what he tells us about Wilde himself, but how he fills in details of the cultural milieu in which Wilde worked.

In a very odd essay, entitled "Oscar Wilde as a Modern Dramatist and Actor" (1994), Jacques de Langlade attempts to reassert the "modernity" of Wilde, an ambition which is rather compromised by his conclusion that "the playwright, so successful in his time, is presently almost ignored" (248). He does qualify this claim by suggesting that the greatest neglect of Wilde is in France. His piece, though, merely discloses de Langlade's ignorance of British theatrical culture in the 1990s; the essays which are discussed below reveal the depth of that ignorance.

The focus of Peter Raby's essay "Wilde and European Theatre" (1994) is the relationship between Wilde and Ibsen, although he also mentions Scribe, Sardou and Chekhov. Raby also briefly surveys modern stagings of Wilde's plays (by Philip Prowse, Peter Hall, Nicholas Hytner, and Steven Berkoff) observing, as several other theatre historians have done, that the works continue to startle, with a content which is "disturbingly contemporary" (329). Raby goes on to suggest that it is only with "the passage of time" that the theatre has "found the confidence to give full realisation to Wilde's originality, to prise him loose from an inward-looking Englishness of reference and presentation, and to place him within the wider frame of a European perspective" (337).

In "The Truth About *Vera*" (1993) George Rowell describes the "brief and inglorious" (94) early stage history of that play. Rowell dismisses the proposition (made by, among others, Richard Ellmann) that the assassination of Alexander II was the "grounds for withdrawal" for *Vera* (95). Rowell points out that eight months had elapsed since Alexander's death, and that it was Wilde, and not the management of the Adelphi Theatre, who was responsible for the play's withdrawal. Rowell claims that Wilde had approached the actress Mrs Bernard Beere and "may also have sought her good offices for the use of the Adelphi" for a matinée for *Vera* (98). He further suggests that Wilde was unable to find the financial backing to stage that matinée—"his own resources were already stretched by such undertakings as the private publication of *Vera* and the *Poems*, and he had looked to the production of the play as an item of income, not outlay" (99). Rowell muses on whether the production of *Vera* ever got as far as casting or rehearsal; nevertheless, its "positive outcome" (100) for Wilde was his sustained friendship with "Bernie" Beere, for whom he was to create the role of Mrs Arbuthnot in *A Woman of No Importance* over a decade later.

Kerry Powell's "Oscar Wilde, Elizabeth Robins, and the Theatre of the Future" (1994), fleshes out the poorly documented friendship between the Irish playwright and the Boston actress. "Ellmann's account of their relationship is typical," claims Powell—that Wilde was Robins's "benevolent pilot through theatrical shoals." Powell, extending and adapting Ellmann's nautical metaphor, suggests that this "conceals the more complicated truth—not only that he steered her onto those shoals instead of through them, but that in the end Robins sought to become Wilde's pilot to what she thought of as the Theatre of the Future" (220). Powell's essay then documents the development of Robins's career and the emergence of what he calls her "feminist criticism of Victorian theatre" and "Wilde's relationship to it" (221)—how she envisaged that Wilde would become a "key figure in her campaign" for a "Joint Management" theatre (226). However, the Wilde whom Powell describes is, in his transactions with Robins, a man of bad faith. He never "followed through on his good intentions" to support her, and in the event was a playwright working with, rather than against, the commercial values of the contemporary theatrical establishment. Powell's judgement of this abortive collaboration reinforces the sense of Wilde's conservatism and commercialism which some other critics have described:

> Perhaps only half-facetiously, Wilde once described his aim in writing a play as making "a lot of red gold" . . . More than Robins, certainly, he entered into the economy of the theatre as it was, working within the established framework rather than against it . . . the "red gold" came to Wilde as it came to other successful playwrights of this period, and when Robins saw him for the last time he seemed marred by gain and overconsumption. (234–35)

Powell's essay is reproduced with some alterations and additions as Chapter 7 in his 1997 monograph on *Women and Victorian Theatre*. The principal subject of this book is obviously not Wilde, but Powell's interpretation of Wilde's relationship with Robins is a key piece of evidence in his overall thesis about what he sees as systematic discrimination against women by late nineteenth-century theatrical institutions. Powell's use of feminist theory, as well as some of his evidence (including that concerning Wilde), has been disputed. For example, J. P. Wearing has noted that "Wilde is blamed for giving Robins misleading advice, although what he seems to have done is advise her that real, tangible success was to be found only at the major commercial venues—advice that Wilde himself followed." (See Wearing, "Women in Victorian Theatre" [1999], 232.)

Some of the evidence for Powell's account of Robins relationship with Wilde is to be found in Robins's own memoir, written (according to Powell) "perhaps around 1950" and entitled "Oscar Wilde: An Appreciation." The manuscript, which is held in the Fales Library of New York University, was edited and annotated by Powell for a piece in *Nineteenth Century Theatre* (1993). Two biographies of Robins, also mentioning her relationship with Wilde, are Joanne E. Gates, *Elizabeth Robins, 1862–1952: Actress, Novelist, Feminist* (1994) and Angela V. John, *Elizabeth Robins: Staging a Life, 1862–1952* (1995).

Powell pursues his interest in Wilde's relationship with feminist politics in the theatre in a further essay, "A verdict of death: Oscar Wilde, actresses and Victorian women" (1997). As the title suggests, Powell's theme is Wilde's attitudes towards actresses. He examines Wilde's commerce with Sarah Bernhardt, Ellen Terry, Elizabeth Robins and Eleanor Calhoun; he also looks at the portrayal of the actress (Sibyl Vane) in *The Picture of Dorian Gray*. As in his other pieces, Powell maintains that Wilde pursued a largely conventional line both in his actual relations with particular actresses, and in his fictional representation of the actress-type. Wilde, Powell argues, is "held captive by [a] deeply engrained Victorian habit of conceiving the performing woman as being outside the boundaries of gender, health and even human life itself. Whether consciously or not, [*The Picture of Dorian Gray*] followed the Victorian strategy of neutralising power when a woman held it, of rationalising a strong voice when it happened to be female and compelled men to silence" (192). As Wearing hints in his review of *Women and Victorian Theatre*, it has long been

recognized that Wilde's feminist sympathies had an element of opportunism to them, and we should perhaps not be surprised to find an
equal opportunism in his dealings with actresses. Moreover, it may
be that Wilde was not exercising any particular prejudice against
women on the stage: he looked to his own advantage in most, if not all
of his dealings with other professionals, in both the theatrical and the
publishing worlds.

Powell's fascination with Wilde's tense relationship with late-
Victorian feminism is also the subject of his contribution to the 1993
Monaco Wilde conference, "Wilde & Two Women: Unpublished Accounts by Elizabeth Robins & Blanche Crackanthorpe." Focusing on
unpublished correspondence between Robins and Crackanthorpe (in
the Fales Library) and once again on Robins's unpublished memoir of
Wilde, Powell shows how these "advanced" women "talked and ago-
nized over Wilde at the time of his public disgrace" (313). As in the
rest of Powell's recent research, the Wilde who emerges from this evidence is not a particularly admirable figure: on this occasion it is Wilde's treatment of Constance which most dismays the two worthy
feminists.

Like Powell, Richard Dellamora's contribution to the 1994 *Modern Drama* special issue, "Oscar Wilde, Social Purity, and *An Ideal
Husband*," also concentrates on Wilde's attitudes towards women
and female emancipation. Dellamora is interested in an ambivalence
in contemporary feminist writing (particularly by Mona Caird) on
women's place in a market economy, and therefore on the relationship between economic and sexual liberation. For Dellamora, it is a
slightly later writer, Walter Lippmann, who best understood that dilemma, for he "identifies the tension between self-development and
the demand for [sexual] purity as a leading problematic within contemporary feminist politics" (124). Dellamora proceeds to examine
Wilde's political polemic (particularly in "The Soul of Man Under Socialism") in relation to these gender concerns, claiming that Wilde's
politics are an "intermediate" position between Shaw's "feminine
norm of 'will'" and Lippmann's more modern insights. Dellamora
then examines *An Ideal Husband* in relation to this political debate,
arguing that in the play "female insistence on purity occurs at the
price of extinguishing individuality" (127), and that the comedy
"opens onto possibilities of pleasure and connection unacknowledged in either aristocratic or middle-class British culture" (135).

Much of Dellamora's analysis turns on a novel interpretation of the symbolism of Mrs Cheveley's brooch/bracelet which he sees as signifying "an exfoliating variety of possibilities that may be summed, in Shaw's phrase, 'the third sex'" (133). The soundness of Dellamora's overall thesis aside, the thematic significance which he attaches to the brooch/bracelet device is not easy to square with the history of the play's composition: according to Wilde's own testimony (the truth of which is borne out by the surviving typescripts of the play) the brooch/bracelet was not added until within ten days of the first performance—a circumstance which strongly suggests that for Wilde it was not intrinsic to his conception of the play or its politics. In some ways, Dellamora's argument shares the same political ambition (and thus some of the same limitations) of Powell's accounts. The problem is that of doxography identified by Alan Sinfield; or, as J. P. Wearing puts it, it is reading and judging works of the past in terms of "today's . . . ideological ideal" in which "there is little sense of the objectivity for which traditional research has striven" (Wearing, "Women in Victorian Theatre" [1999], 229). Dellamora's account (and perhaps those by Powell) are usefully read alongside the work of Sinfield and Bristow, both of whom—as I suggested in earlier chapters—raise profound doubts about the kinds of subversive meanings it is legitimate to read into Wilde's Society Comedies, and so into his intentions for them.

In contrast to Dellamora's concern to explain the politics of Wilde's drama in relation to nineteenth-century intellectual culture, a number of other commentators in the 1990s focused on how those politics were expressed in the staging of his plays—on how they worked (and continue to work) as performance. For example, the 1994 special number of *Modern Drama* devoted to Wilde prints a conversation between Joel Kaplan and Philip Prowse about Prowse's staging of Wilde's Society Comedies at the Citizens Theatre in Glasgow (*A Woman of No Importance*, 1984; *An Ideal Husband*, 1986; *Lady Windermere's Fan*, 1988). Kaplan also discussed Prowse's productions in a paper given at the 1993 Monaco conference entitled "Wilde in the Gorbals: Society Drama and Citizens Theatre." In his *Modern Drama* interview, Kaplan reports that the attraction of his first production was, for Prowse, its combination of "studied artificialities" and "heightened realism" (194), in which the social distinctions between characters are vital. So the position of Gerald Arbuthnot in

A Woman of No Importance—"educated as a gentleman, even though he is only a bank clerk"—is one of "the problems of doing the play. The exact social niceties between the characters are crucial. In an increasingly classless society young actors find it difficult to comprehend the structures, and when they do comprehend them they tend to dismiss them as unimportant. Of course they are to them, but not to the characters involved" (199).

Prowse and Kaplan go on to discuss the differences between modern conceptions of feminism and what Prowse calls Wilde's "prefeminism" ("the issues Wilde raises haven't really changed a great deal in the last hundred years" [200]), and how Prowse, by allowing Mrs Allonby to witness the action at the end of Act III, makes her a kind of commentator on the play. In both Kaplan's and Prowse's view, *An Ideal Husband* is an altogether darker play, and that darkness is produced, for Prowse, by the move from the country to the town; it is a play "concerned with politicians" (201). The need to make that world available to modern theatre-goers—to find a modern equivalent for audiences who are "unschooled in the social dynamics of Wilde's world"—explains Prowse's decision to make Mrs Cheveley swear, and not to "dress Goring as Wilde" (202). It also explains the decision to make cuts in Mrs Erlynne's "soliloquies" in *Lady Windermere's Fan*. Prowse suggests that Wilde's initial instinct to refuse to disclose Mrs Erlynne's identity (as Lady Windermere's mother) until Act IV was correct. The change was made because of Alexander's "ghastly middle-class morality" (203). The same explanation is given for Prowse's directions for the end of the play, which—in Kaplan's words—need to be "re-problematized" for a modern audience:

> [Kaplan]: [The end of the play] . . . is usually used to reunite the Windermeres . . . Your Lady Windermere pointed the exchange by striding upstage and striking her husband in the face. Her final line to Lord Augustus . . . completed what was, for her husband, a stinging social rebuke.

> [Prowse]: Well, Windermere is such a prick. After all, he speaks [to Lord Augustus] man to man, in a patronizing, condescending way about this woman who as far as Lady Windermere is concerned has just saved her life. So she thinks "sod that!" and hits him. (204)

Kaplan's piece for the Monaco conference covers more or less the same ground and comes to broadly the same conclusions, that

Prowse's stagings pointed to "Wilde's potential as a playwright of some importance for our own *fin-de-siècle*" (222).

In his short essay, "Wilde's 'Plays of Modern Life' on the Contemporary British Stage" (1994), Robert Gordon is also interested in the stage history of Wilde's plays. Like Kaplan he examines a number of stagings of the Society Comedies, focusing particularly on Philip Prowse's productions for the Glasgow Citizens' Theatre in the mid-1980s and Peter Hall's production of *An Ideal Husband* (1992). Gordon attempts to show how Prowse and Hall "found different methods of releasing in the theatre the complex subtext which in each of the two society dramas [*An Ideal Husband* and *The Importance of Being Earnest*] measures the love of pleasure against the pleasure of love" (166).

In "Wilde Interpretations" (1994) John Stokes also discusses productions of the Society Comedies. He takes his cue from an observation by Jonathan Miller, that "acts of theatrical interpretation must, if they are to be valid, respond to elements already in the work . . . that . . . are still part of the author's intention" (156; Stokes's paraphrase is from Miller's *Subsequent Performances* [1986]). Stokes describes how the "adventurousness" in the staging of modern London productions has tried "to match Wilde's linguistic extravagance" and how those productions have capitalized on the audience's pre-existing knowledge of Wilde's biography (156–57), a point made by a number of other critics. However, Stokes sees the "greatest investment of directorial energy" in bringing out the melodramatic elements in Wilde's plays. Stokes then goes on to test Miller's hypothesis in two ways: first by looking at reviews of three modern productions of the plays "sifted and sorted according to [Stokes's] own memories and impressions"; and second by considering what his survey "might tell us about the theatre of a century ago" (157). He looks at Philip Prowse's 1984 Glasgow production (and 1991 revival) of *A Woman of No Importance*, and Prowse's 1986 Glasgow production of *An Ideal Husband* in relation to Sir Peter Hall's 1992 production of that play at the Globe; and Nicholas Hytner's 1993 production of *Importance of Being Earnest*. He then compares all of these productions to the original stagings of the plays in the West End in the 1890s. Stokes observes that one of the most striking points of continuity between Victorian and modern performances is the dependence upon selling them via the audience's prior knowledge of their author: "the Wildean presence . . . works on stage today because it makes manifest a quality endemic to the plays . . . an interplay between performance, audience, and outside world that was already active in the conditions of late Victorian theatre, though taken to new extremes by Wilde" (171).

The staging of Wilde's plays is also the subject of Richard Allen Cave's "Wilde Designs: Some Thoughts about Recent British Productions of His Plays" (1994). Cave describes the two extant "rudimentary sketches" by Wilde of settings for *Salome* and *Lady Windermere's Fan*, as well as Charles Ricketts's designs for his 1906 production of *Salome*, a topic which is also addressed by Joel Kaplan in his essay for the *Cambridge Companion* (discussed later in this section). The "principle" of design for Ricketts and Wilde, in Cave's view, was "settings that evoked a sense of place or period by suggestion that would activate the audience imaginatively" (177); and Cave argues that Ricketts may have been drawing upon collaboration with Wilde, certainly in the plan to separate the actors into "separate masses of colour" (179). Cave further suggests that it is possible to see, via Ricketts's designs, Wilde's own innovatory ideas about stage design:

> It is clear that Ricketts shared Wilde's preoccupations in the field of stage design and that, when he had the chance after 1906 to put what was till then largely theorising into practice, he began rigorously to investigate how to exploit the dynamics of stage space for psychological and symbolic ends and to explore the potential of colour to achieve a decidedly innovatory kind of visual poetry. (180)

Cave goes to describe the influence of Ricketts (and through him, of Wilde) on stage design in the twentieth century, and in particular how it can be seen in Steven Berkoff's 1988 production of *Salome*, and Philip Prowse's productions of the Society Comedies.

Some of Cave's ideas were rehearsed in an earlier piece—his contribution to the 1993 Monaco conference. In "Power Structuring: The Presentation of Outsider Figures in Wilde's Plays," Cave once again argues for the innovative nature of Wilde's dramaturgy; more precisely, he points to Wilde's use of stage space to define "varying types and degrees of personal power" (39). Cave's evidence is derived once again from a close analysis of a ground-plan for the last act of *Lady Windermere's Fan*, described as "definitely in [Wilde's] own hand," and a stage design for *Salome* drawn up by Charles Ricketts "during a conversation with Wilde" (40). Cave attempts to show how Wilde's "uncluttered" stage in *Salome* permitted him to draw "an audience's attention to the power relations between the characters that structures the whole action" (41); and how the seating of Mrs Erlynne on a sofa in Act IV of *Lady Windermere's Fan* demonstrates "the inner power of the woman" and "enables her rightly to hold the centre of the stage" (45). Cave goes on briefly to examine the handling of "outsider figures" in Wilde's other dramas, describing the way the "visual dynamics" of the staging "focus an audience's attention on the power relations between the central characters" (47). Cave's study can be usefully read alongside David Peter Corbett's 1994 essay "'Collaborative Resistance': Charles Ricketts as Illustrator of Oscar Wilde."

In a manner similar to Richard Allen Cave, Joseph Donohue in "Wilde and the Idea of a Theatre" (1994) also argues for the innovative nature of Wilde's dramaturgy; more precisely, he claims that Wilde conceived "a private, radical notion of the theatre" which was "authentically his own," and which "conjures images of idealized emotional states and crises, an interior theatre of the heart and soul, of suffering and loss" (118–19). Donohue goes on to suggest that attention to the "scintillating wit and engaging characters" (119) of the four Society Comedies can obscure Wilde's interest in these larger and more serious emotional concerns. Opposing the readings of Wilde's dramatic career proposed by Richard Ellmann and Regenia Gagnier, Donohue argues that Wilde's "original and independent intellect . . . led him to resist and partly to subvert the role of the professional dramatist" (124). And it is precisely this recognition of Wilde's "ambivalent" and "complex" reaction to West End theatrical institutions which, Donohue claims, can lead us to a new appreciation of the influence on Wilde of factors traditionally neglected by critics—that is, "French symbolist theatre," "post-Elizabethan poetic drama," and the "Romantic drama of Shelley" (124). Donohue's essay does not explore these dramatic forms in any detail; rather, his aim is simply to point the way to what he terms "a more integral and holistic understanding" of Wilde's drama (125), one which moves beyond the narrow focus on the "capitalistic bourgeois marketplace" proposed by Gagnier, as well as the simplistic recourse to an "autonomous psychological makeup" (121) offered by Ellmann.

An attempt to establish a new paradigm for discussing Wilde's dramatic achievement is to be found in a further essay by Richard Allen

Cave. "Wilde's plays: some lines of influence" (1997) focuses on the competing claims made for Wilde's dramatic talent by Kerry Powell in *Oscar Wilde and the Theatre of the 1890s* (1990) and by Katherine Worth in *Oscar Wilde* (1983). According to Cave, Powell sees Wilde as primarily "Victorian"—that is, as a borrower rather than inventor of dramatic forms. By contrast, Worth's ambition (in Cave's view) is to establish Wilde's "modernity" by emphasizing his role as a "transitional figure" who anticipated "developments in poetic drama" of figures such as W. B. Yeats (219). Cave's argument is that both critical approaches, when pushed to "an extreme," are reductive and distorting, for both "judge Wilde as artistically lazy," He goes on to suggest that an alternative and more productive framework for examining Wilde's plays is one which sees the qualities identified by Powell and Worth as complementary rather than oppositional aspects of his craft. According to Cave, we must acknowledge "the meticulous poise Wilde sustains between the Victorian and the innovatory" (220). This sense of "poise" or "balance" is in its turn interpreted by Cave in the light of what he terms "colonial/postcolonial" and "postmodernist" critical theory: that is to say, it is a position demanded by Wilde's identity as "the despised 'other.'" As an Irishman and homosexual who wanted "to pursue fame in the metropolis," Wilde was required to be "a wearer of masks," to "hold two or more distinct personalities in a tense balance" and "two or more distinct levels of meaning in an equally tense juxtaposition" (221–22).

The proposition that Wilde's use of masks is subversive is hardly a new one. Cave, however, wants to see this strategy (as Declan Kiberd does) as the product of explicitly nationalist concerns—as a reaction to "imperialist rhetoric": Wilde, according to Cave, is "deconstructing Englishness" from "within." Such a view leads Cave to argue (again in terms which are familiar) that the "meaning" of Wilde's plays exists in their "fractures, stylistic shifts, challenging dislocations"—in, that is, their "sub-textual" qualities (224). Cave's analysis focuses on the presentation of character in the plays and on the "tonal insecurity" which he sees as a product of Wilde's deliberate mixing of genres—his simultaneous use of the comic, melodramatic, and farcical. Such a technique, Cave goes on, "provocatively challenges degrees of self-awareness in the engaged spectator" (226). By far the largest part of Cave's essay, however, is devoted to discussing the vexed question of Wilde's "influence." Examining the work of a variety of modern dramatists, including Edward Bond, Tom Stoppard, Joe Orton, Frank McGuinness, and Neil Bartlett, Cave attempts to show how these dramatists learned from Wilde the art of "subverting audience expectation" (229); in these modern works Cave detects "postmodernist techniques of deconstruction and intertextual referencing" similar to features found in Wilde's own plays. Cave's essay should be read in the light of work by cultural critics such as Sinfield and Bristow, and theatre historians such as Donohue, all of whom have questioned the kind of argument which Cave proposes—that is, they question the range of meanings available to Wilde's contemporary audiences and therefore the intentions behind their composition.

Joel Kaplan's 1997 essay "Wilde on the Stage" in some ways complements Cave's work in that his concern is also with the performance aspects of Wilde's drama. His piece opens with the entirely unsurprising observation that the performance history of Wilde's plays is "closely linked to the larger history of their author's social and cultural reception" (249). Kaplan begins his survey of those performances with an examination and a description of the events leading up to the premières of Wilde's four Society Comedies. He shows how acutely both the writing and staging of these plays used the "textures and commodities of Society life" in order to "challenge the world" they "seemed to endorse" (249). Such "contemporaneity" (252), however, had a price: Kaplan argues that the very quality which ensured the plays' success for first-run audiences compromised their appeal for later viewers. According to Kaplan, by the time of his death in 1900 Wilde had become "safely historical" (255), with the result that when the Society Comedies returned to the West End stage in the early years of the twentieth century, it was necessary to update costumes, props, and topical allusions in order that Wilde's "'plays of modern life' . . . reflected not the surfaces of the *fin de siècle* but those of 1904, 1907 and 1914" (257). However, Kaplan argues that such "modernisations" were not entirely successful, largely because the politics articulated in Wilde's plays had moved on: in particular, views about homosexuality and feminism were quite different in 1914 than they had been in 1895. As Kaplan explains, the speech about "separate spheres" when delivered by a Lady Chiltern whose "gowns proclaimed her a contemporary of Asquith was met with open derision" (258).

Kaplan shows how problems in updating the plays continued through productions in the 1920s: he suggests that the only successful staging of this period was Ernst Lubitch's silent cinematic adaptation of *Lady Windermere's Fan* which substituted a contemporary "pictorial language" for Wilde's dated polemic (260). From the 1930s, Kaplan singles out Nigel Playfair's "period" *Earnest*, a production which, he claims, came "to dominate the staging of Wilde's comedies for the next quarter-century" (262). In a similar way, Kaplan sees Lindsay Kemp's 1970 *Salome*, which presented the work "as a homoerotic spectacle," as defining "Wilde as a playwright for our own time" (265). Kaplan also draws attention to what he views as "the most surprising development" in the recent history of the staging of Wilde's plays—the rediscovery, by directors such as Philip Prowse, of Wilde's first three society plays as "complex theatre pieces" (267). Kaplan's informed and entertaining survey ends with a mention of the cross-dressed 1994 production of *Lady Windermere's Fan* by Rough Magic at London's Tricycle Theatre. For Kaplan, it is ironically this most "radically readjusted" staging which brings the modern audience closest to Wilde's original intentions, for it restores to the work "the paradoxes of problem play-making with which Wilde greeted his first audiences over a century ago" (272). Kaplan's essay provides the student with an excellent overview of, and an introduction to the stage history of Wilde's plays. His work should perhaps be read in conjunction with that of Robert Tanitch, whose *Oscar Wilde on Stage and Screen* (1999; discussed in 7. iv.) covers some of the same ground, but with less elegance.

Kaplan's interest in the ways Wilde's dramatic texts are a product of theatrical institutions is also broached in two important essays in *Theatre Notebook* (1992 and 1994), and in what has proved to be an influential book, co-authored with Sheila Stowell, *Theatre and Fashion: Oscar Wilde to the Suffragettes* (1994; discussed below). In "A Puppet's Power: George Alexander, Clement Scott, and the Replotting of *Lady Windermere's Fan*" (1992), Kaplan used recently discovered correspondence between George Alexander and the theatre critic Clement Scott to shed new light on the dispute between Wilde and Alexander over the moment when Mrs Erlynne's identity should be revealed to the audience. Kaplan convincingly demonstrates that Alexander enlisted a hostile review of the first performance from Scott in order to bring Wilde to heel. His larger argument concerns the relative power of late nineteenth-century dramatists and actor-managers; he sees the disagreement between Wilde and Alexander and its resolution through the agency of Scott as a "struggle . . . about who would control the West End stage during a particularly formative period in its history" (70). This theme is picked up in a slightly different way in Kaplan's "Oscar Wilde's Contract for *A Woman of No Importance*" (1994). Again Kaplan draws attention to new archival evidence (on this occasion in the University of Bristol) which forces us to revise our understanding of Wilde's relationship with another actor-manager, Herbert Beerbohm Tree. Kaplan shows that the agreement which Wilde reached with Tree (which first came to light in Hart-Davis's *More Letters*) does not, as critics had tended to assume, represent Wilde setting his own terms. Rather two letters (which Kaplan reprints at the end of his piece) in the Tree archive reveal that Wilde merely "confirms his acceptance of terms dictated by Tree the previous day" (47). Kaplan concludes by noting that Wilde was "given some say in negotiating the position his play would occupy in Tree's 1893 season" but on the whole—and like most contemporary dramatists—he had to "accommodate his producers" rather than "issue 'demands'" (47).

More evidence about Wilde's contracts with theatrical managers is revealed by Russell Jackson in "Oscar Wilde's Contract for a New Play" (1996). Jackson discovered among the papers of Ada Rehan, held at the University of Pennsylvania, a typed carbon-copy of a contract drawn up between her and Wilde in early 1900. Reference to this projected play had appeared in correspondence between Wilde and the London theatrical agent, John Farrington, reproduced in Hart-Davis's *Letters*. The discovery of a copy of the contract reveals for the first time the precise terms which Wilde agreed. They involved percentage royalties on a sliding scale for British, American and Canadian productions, together with an advance of £100 on Wilde's signing the contract and a further £200 on delivery and acceptance of the manuscript. In the event Wilde failed to honour the agreement; moreover he appears never to have returned Rehan's advance. Jackson comments that the decision to commission a play from Wilde in 1900 was certainly highly speculative, and may have been an act of charity. He also draws attention to a clause in the contract which stipulates that Rehan had the right to produce the play anonymously, a requirement which Jackson links to Leonard Smithers's book publication in 1899 of *An Ideal Husband* and *The Importance of Being Earnest* without Wilde's name on their title-pages.

In "How Many 'Bags of Red Gold'?: The Extent of Wilde's Success as a Dramatist" (1999), Josephine M. Guy and I challenge the figures habitually used to describe Wilde's earnings from the theatres which staged his plays. In particular we contest the figure of £7,000 which Hesketh Pearson, and then Richard Ellmann and John Russell Stephens, suggest that Wilde earned from the first production of *Lady Windermere's Fan*. We report on various statement of returns, now held in the Clark Library, which give details of the sums which Wilde received from the various managements for which he worked. The documents held at the Clark allow the terms of some of Wilde's contracts to be reconstructed. The first figures which Guy and I report relate to the first production of *Lady Windermere's Fan* at the St James's Theatre, and some of the returns for that play's North American tour (particularly in New York, Chicago, Montreal and St Louis). Also described are the returns for *A Woman of No Importance* at the Haymarket and some figures relating to the extensive British provincial tour, undertaken by three separate touring companies. In addition we report on returns for *An Ideal Husband*, and for *The Importance of Being Earnest*. We conclude that Wilde's earnings, although considerable, were far less than have been commonly imagined. Moreover those earnings also appear to have fluctuated between 1892 and mid-1895. We also reveal that *A Woman of No Importance* was the play which earned Wilde the most money—a detail corroborated by him in a letter to Frank Harris written a few weeks before his death in 1900.

An interest in the way dramatic works were shaped by non-authorial factors is the subject of Kaplan and Stowell's *Theatre and Fashion*, which examines how the "vexed relationship" between fashion, the stage and society in the last quarter of the nineteenth century affected "phenomena as seemingly disparate as the emergence of the society playhouse, the coming of Ibsen, the rise of the modern fashion show . . . the adoption of 'dress code' by militant suffragettes . . . [and] the production and reception of dramatic texts" (1). In five carefully researched and usefully illustrated chapters Kaplan and Stowell explore these phenomena during the period from 1892 to 1914. A discussion of Wilde's three first three Society Comedies takes a large proportion of Chapter 1 (*Earnest* is not included in this category nor in the book). Kaplan and Stowell argue for a formative but sometimes tense relationship between the costuming, conception, and the writing of the plays. For example, in *Lady Windermere's Fan* they suggest that "costumes would be seen as commodities in their own right" (15), an effect intrinsic to the play's discussion of the debasement of morality into fashion. By contrast, they claim that in *A Woman of No Importance* "the play's status as fashion plate was undermined by its moral organisation and affective power" (23). Their discussion of *An Ideal Husband* focuses on the revisions which Wilde made to the published version of the play; they argue that his aim in the addition of detailed stage-directions concerning the dress of various characters and the stage sets, was "to create for a reading public a sense of visual immediacy" (27). Kaplan and Stowell's account adds useful details to our knowledge of the performance histories of the plays they discuss; in addition, their general attention to the interaction between the worlds of commerce and theatrical culture means that their empirically-based research can be profitably read alongside more abstract and theoretical accounts of Wilde's relationship to commodity culture. (See Talia Schaffer's "Fashioning Aestheticism by Aestheticizing Fashion: Wilde, Beerbohm and the Male Aesthetes' Sartorial Codes" and her *The Forgotten Female Aesthetes: Literary Culture in Late Victorian England* [2000], both of which are discussed in 4. vii.)

In "Oscar Wilde: the resurgence of lying" (1997), Declan Kiberd uses ideas first rehearsed in *Inventing Ireland* (1995; see 3. i.) to explore Wilde's plays. Kiberd argues that a "disenchantment with language" (and particularly and inevitably with the English language) is "strong" in Irish writing (277); he gives examples from the work of other Irish playwrights—Joyce, Beckett, and nearer contemporaries of Wilde such as J. M. Synge and Dion Boucicault. Such disenchantment, according to Kiberd, is manifest in the Irishman's "reputation for deceit, guile and word-play," qualities which in turn are the "result of the distrust by the natives of the coloniser" and also "more directly, the inevitable outcome of a life under martial law" (278). (A similar topic is explored by Kiberd in "Wilde and the English Question" [1994] where his concern is to set the idea of a double life and Bunburying within a Irish context.) Kiberd goes on to assimilate Wilde's interest in lying (in his critical essays and plays) to this tradition. So, for example, he compares Algy's deceits in *Earnest* to Christy Mahon's fantasies in *The Playboy of the Western World*. Kiberd also compares Wilde's and Synge's treatment of issues such as religion, education, and innocence, as well as their protests against what is called "literalism." In the work of both authors, Kiberd argues, "fiction takes on the contours of truth," and in an assertion that seems to embody its own negation, suggests that "if lies are a higher truth, then what passes as truth may be a form of lower lies" (288). Kiberd then examines how Synge furthers and "revises" Wilde's insights: he detects a "sophistication" in the work of Synge which "seems to suspect that the mask of the elegant anti-self purveyed by Wilde is perhaps a subtle latter-day version of the ancient blarney." According to Kiberd, Synge "is less interested in the power of a lie than in that portion of reality which proves resistant to it" (288). Kiberd's essay ends with a brief consideration of the ways in which Wilde's "drama of lying" (289) is renewed in the work of more modern Irish dramatists, particularly Brendan Behan and Tom Murphy.

At this point it is perhaps worth outlining some differences between Kiberd's account of Wilde's dramatic legacy for the Irish theatre and Joel Kaplan's research into the staging of Wilde's plays in England. Kaplan, as I have noted, drew attention to the difficulties experienced by directors in realizing Wilde's radicalism for twentieth-century English audiences. By contrast, Kiberd's account of a dramatic tradition tends to assume that the political agenda which animated Irish playwrights in the 1890s is continuous with that articulated in works written nearly a century later. "Wilde," he argues, "correctly sensed that ownership and understanding of the means of expression would be the question of real consequence in the century to come. Subsequent history has proven just how right he was" (292). Also worth noting is Alan Stanford's argument (see 3. ii.) that it is *Irish* (rather than English) audiences who fail to understand Wilde, to appreciate the "savage satire of his plays."

Connected, but tangentially so, to Kiberd's concerns is J. L. Wisenthal's essay "Wilde, Shaw, and the Play of Conversation" (1994), which points to some similarities between Wilde's view of the relationship between history and talk (in "The Critic As Artist") and Shaw's 1889 lecture on "Acting, by One Who Does Not Believe in It" and his later play, *Caesar and Cleopatra*. Wisenthal acknowledges that the relationship between Shaw and Wilde has been well-documented in recent years; he sees both men being influenced by

Matthew Arnold's attack on English parochialism in "The Function of Criticism," so much so that Wilde's mediation of Arnold's celebration of criticism "anticipates the nature of much of [Shaw's] drama" (209). Wisenthal goes on to suggest that Shaw's reaction to Wilde's Society Comedies, particularly to *An Ideal Husband*, "brings out their connections to [Wilde's] critical essays" (210). Wilde, for Wisenthal, continued Arnold's work in criticism after the latter's death in 1888. In turn, after Wilde's death in 1900 "Shaw continued Wilde's work, with the dialogue of Don Juan in Hell" (211). Wisenthal traces the contours of this succession, acknowledging some clear differences, and quoting the caveat of Shaw himself: "he [Wilde] wrote for the stage as an artist. I am simply a propagandist" (217). Wisenthal's argument is that each of his three subjects revealed a concern for the form of their work, and this is what connects them. Unfortunately he is rather less clear about how precisely we can make a proper political connection between the three figures he discusses, and how can we equate the political thinking of Arnold's non party-political conservatism of the 1860s and Shaw's Fabian socialism of the early twentieth century with Wilde's pseudo-anarchism of the 1890s.

More secure is Peter Raby's argument in "The Origins of *The Importance of Being Earnest*" (1994), where he charts the "complex and obscure" (139) genesis of that play. He describes the first scenario in a letter to George Alexander (written in July or August 1895, the full text of which Raby himself discovered in the Clark Library), and sets it in the context of Wilde's difficulties with John Hare over the production of *An Ideal Husband*, and also in the context of Wilde's dealings in the United States over the same play with the American theatrical impresario Charles Frohman and Elisabeth Marbury (Wilde's agent in the United States). Raby notes that Frohman proposed a complicated arrangement whereby he offered an option on Wilde's "next modern comedy" (that is, the next comedy after *An Ideal Husband*), specifying a royalty of £3 per performance until "you shall have received a sum total of £1,000" (141). These details, Raby suggests, must have been uppermost in Wilde's mind when he haggled with Alexander over the American rights of *The Importance of Being Earnest*. Raby suggests that the Gerald Lancing scenario (which later became *Mr and Mrs Daventry*) was written after a lunch meeting with Alexander on 6 September 1894 (not before it, as Hart-Davis suggests), and that the complications (and lack of transparency) in

Wilde's dealing with Alexander form a "parallel narrative to the way [in which] the play itself developed" (142). Raby goes on to describe the history of the composition of *The Importance of Being Earnest*, its use of Sussex place-names and the significance of its characters' names, together with its parallels with some contemporary drama (including Lestocq's and Robson's *The Foundling*). In all, the history which Raby describes is a salutary corrective to the glib accounts of the relationship between Alexander and Wilde, which I mentioned in chapter 1.

In "Bunbury Pure and Simple" (1998), a piece which draws upon Raby's work, Craven W. Mackie speculates on the origins of the name of Bunbury in *The Importance Of Being Earnest*, commenting that its earliest occurrence is in Wilde's marginal note: "Mr Bunbury—always ill." Mackie observes that the origin of the name has been the topic of critical "speculation" for forty years (327), and gives a history of the most widely accepted alternatives: that proposed by William Green (in "Oscar Wilde and the Bunburys," *Modern Drama*, 21 [1978], 76) which suggests that the source was the names of two acquaintances in Wilde's youth, a thesis silently adopted by Ellmann; a character in an unpublished farce, *Godpapa* (proposed by Kerry Powell); a village in Cheshire (the suggestion of Joseph Donohue and Ruth Berggren); and a name to be found in the Army Lists of 1894 (suggested by Peter Raby). Mackie argues that Wilde could have found the name in the obituary columns of the *Morning Post* and the *Times* in July 1894—a "sudden and convenient Bunbury epidemic" (329) which would have made the name familiar. A different emphasis on the significance of the name "Bunbury" is given in Christopher Craft's account of the (alleged) sub-texts of *The Importance of Being Earnest* in *Another Kind of Love* (1994; see 3. i.).

A further study by Peter Raby—"*The Importance of Being Earnest*: 'The Persons of the Play'" (1995)—examines "the fictional/factual tension" in the names Wilde gives to his characters (68). He traces the social reference of names such as "Bracknell," "Fairfax," "Cardew," "Lane," and "Merriman," commenting on Wilde's remarkable ability to "draw from and lightly suggest the social structures around him, even while he is mocking or undermining them" (71). The second half of Raby's essay compares Wilde's use of names with that to be found in Maria Edgeworth's novel *Ennui*. He also finds a number of plot and thematic similarities between *Earnest* and *Ennui*, and suggests a "possible echo of Edgeworth's Celia and Geraldine in Wilde's Cecily and Gwendolen" (75).

Raby's monograph in the Twayne's Masterworks Series, *The Importance of Being Earnest: A Reader's Companion* (1995), although to some extent limited by the format of the series in which it appears, is nonetheless a useful work. Raby describes the play's dramatic and literary context, its genesis, and the seriousness of some of its concerns, claiming that it "functions through the meticulous imitation, and then subversion, of the tribal customs of upper-class late Victorian society" (41). He also prints photographs and images of the original 1895 production, including some rarely reproduced cartoons from the *Illustrated Sporting and Dramatic News*. Like Joseph Donohue's ambitious reconstruction of the text of the first performance, Raby (in a section which has similarities to his essay on the same topic discussed above) also looks at the significance of the play's use of names, what and how they signify. As with Anne Varty's *A Preface to Oscar Wilde* (see 5.), the merit of Raby's work is its even-handedness, a quality in short supply in many studies.

In "Wilde's comedies of Society" (1997), Raby provides a wide-ranging discussion of the first three Society Comedies. Like Donohue's account of *Salome*, much of the information is familiar. Issues such as Wilde's fraught relationship with George Alexander, his "juxtaposition of the comic and the serious" (147), his "unprecedented attention to dress and accessories" (149), and the "great precision" with which he "places his social world" (151), have all been well documented by earlier literary historians and critics. Moreover few critics would find any quibble with Raby's overall judgement that Wilde "created a particular form of comedy in which to display his mocking imitation of England, a form which satisfied his audience, and which seemed, by its adroit resolutions, to suggest that all was well with Society" (159).

Russell Jackson's essay on *The Importance Of Being Earnest* (1997) complements Raby's account of the other three Society Comedies. It seems intended for the same sort of reader in that it draws together some well-known elements in accounts of the play, providing a short description of its genesis, of the complex process of alterations made during rehearsal, and of its thematic relationship with the rest of Wilde's *oeuvre*. While acknowledging that *Earnest* "remains hospitable to all kinds of significance commentators may identify in it" (173), Jackson is very cautious about interpreting the work in terms of Wilde's biography, and particularly of seeing it as "a specifically gay play" (173). In this respect he shares the reservations of Alan Sinfield (in both *The Wilde Century* and his essay in the *Modern Drama* collection) about the work of gay critics such as Gary Schmidgall (discussed in 2. i.), and their "determined enlisting of Wilde and his works in a gay canon" (176n.).

In "Narcissistic Reflections in a Wilde Mirror," Karl Beckson discusses a theme which has been picked out by other recent critics, notably Alan Sinfield (see 3. i.), what Beckson calls "narcissistic doubling." Beckson sees self-sufficiency in Wilde's dandies, epitomized by Lord Goring's comment that "To love oneself is the beginning of a life-long romance," merging with what he calls "narcissistic self-love" (148). For Beckson, Wilde's dandies see in a mirror an idealized version of themselves, corresponding to the "idealized mirror of [the] mind" (150). Beckson describes the importance of the motif in all the Society Comedies: Lady Windermere's photograph of herself and her son, Mrs Erlynne's gazing into mirrors, the "doubling" relationship between the Duchess of Berwick and Lady Agatha in *Lady Windermere's Fan*; "Herod's belief that mirrors 'do but show us masks'" in *Salome*; the truths or otherwise of looking-glasses in Act I of *A Woman of No Importance*, and so on. Beckson also points out that Wilde kept a bronze statuette of Narcissus in his house in Tite Street. Importantly, however, Beckson reminds us that in his "use of the [Narcissus] myth for the stage" Wilde removes the "homoerotic propensities" associated with it (149). (Beckson's piece can be profitably read alongside Lawrence Goodman's 1995 essay, "Narcissism and Oscar Wilde.")

Beckson's essay finds an echo in Joseph Bristow's contribution to the *Modern Drama* special issue, "Dowdies and Dandies: Oscar Wilde's Refashioning of Society Comedy" (1994), an essay which re-examines the idea of role-reversal in Wilde's comedies, and the inconsistencies that they appear to generate. Of particular concern to Bristow is the slippage between what would appear to be polar opposites, the "dowdy" and the "dandy." As Bristow observes, "dowdies and dandies are . . . hardly discrete. But, there again, they are not quite the same thing either" (56). Bristow's interest is in whether this contradictoriness is (as many other critics have argued) "necessarily progressive or avant-garde" (56). He goes on to study in detail some key scenes in *Lady Windermere's Fan, A Woman of No Importance* and *An Ideal Husband* where this category slippage, or what he calls these "characterological transformations" (66), are particularly puzzling. Bristow speculates that the "inconsistency and contradiction" which appear "as the main structural features of these works" may be "little more than formal devices" (66), which have a self-cancelling effect. He concludes that "it needs to be borne in mind that the reversible structures that shape and define Wilde's writing may well negate their wilful impulse to overturn commonplace assumptions" (69).

Bristow's essay represents an interesting development in understanding the politics of Wilde's plays, and should be read in the context of his other essays which question the ways in which Wilde understood his own sexuality. Bristow's final comment, that Wilde's "verbal pyrotechnics are hardly likely to ignite the fires of any coming revolution" (69), suggests that critics should re-engage with the entertainment values and functions of Wilde's drama, and not be so preoccupied with detecting a politics below its surface. In this sense, Bristow's ideas are congruent with research by Joel Kaplan, Sheila Stowell and Joseph Donohue (discussed above) into the performance histories of Wilde's plays, which also draws attention to their commercial success and their relation to contemporary fashion. It is worth noting that the tenor of this kind of work runs against the tide of much earlier criticism, particularly that of Jonathan Dollimore (see *Oscar Wilde Revalued*, 163), as well as Sos Eltis's more recent study of the composition of Wilde's plays (*Revising Wilde* [1996]; see 5.) which, like Dollimore's pieces, sees them as articulating a subversive politics.

There have been a number of short and less substantial studies of Wilde's plays by Christopher S. Nassaar. In a note entitled "Wilde's *The Picture of Dorian Gray* and *Lady Windermere's Fan*" (1996) he attempts to establish an intertextual connection between Wilde's novel and his first society play. Rather than looking at verbal resonances or self-plagiarism, Nassaar argues for a fundamental similarity in the conception of evil in both works. There are, he suggests, "four states" or stages of evil in *Dorian Gray*, and these find equivalents in different characters in *Lady Windermere's Fan*. In a further essay—"Wilde's *Lady Windermere's Fan* and Shaw's *Mrs Warren's*

Profession" (1998)—Nassaar sees Shaw's play as "a Shavian rework-ing of Wilde's, an attempt to squarely face the issues that Wilde side-stepped. In a nutshell, it is *Lady Windermere's Fan* intellectualized" (137). Nassaar traces thematic similarities in the plays and concludes that the real difference exists in the fact that Wilde defined morality in sexual terms, but Shaw suggests that "sexual corruption is part of ... economic corruption" (138). In the only discussion of *La Sainte Courtisane* ("Wilde's *La Sainte Courtisane*" [1997]), Nassaar dis-cusses the way "the tale—cast in the form of a brief play . . . consti-tutes a thematic bridge" between *Salome* and *The Importance of Being Earnest.*

I noted earlier that the 1990s witnessed a flowering of interest in *Salome.* There have been more pieces devoted to this play than any other dramatic work by Wilde. That said, the quality of these pieces is rather uneven, and some of the observations they make are rather tired. For example, in a short essay entitled "Oscar Wilde and Dra-matic Strategies" (1994), Irène Eynat-Confino examines what she terms "two rhetorical and dramatic strategies . . . encoding and dis-placement" by which Wilde in *Salome* displayed "his views on ho-mosexuality" and gave "voice to his feelings and misgivings about Lord Alfred Douglas" (127). Her overall conclusion is that the centre of *Salome's* "thematics" is not "homosexual lust" but "love between two men, love, that deep feeling that attached Wilde to Alfred Doug-las" (134)—a conclusion which historians and theorists of sexuality will perhaps find naive. In an equally slight essay, "Oscar Wilde's *Salome*: Symbolist Princess" (1994), Patricia Kellogg-Dennis exam-ines feminist interpretations of *Salome,* concluding—perhaps rather predictably—that "Oscar Wilde's Salome wasn't a New Woman: she is a paradigm of the symbolist *femme fatale*" (230). In a more substan-tial piece entitled "Losing One's Head: Wilde's Confession in *Salome,*" Melissa Knox suggests the play reveals "Wilde's early expe-riences and his sexual development" (233). More particularly Knox argues that the "highly dangerous sexuality of the girl-child Salome" (236) relates to Wilde's own attraction to adolescent bodies and, fur-ther back in his past, to his "infantile sexual play" with his sister Isola (240). These controversial ideas are developed more fully in Knox's *Oscar Wilde: A Long and Lovely Suicide* (1994; see 2. i.).

In "Realism and Symbolism in Oscar Wilde's *Salomé*" (1994), Aus-tin E. Quigley discusses the effectiveness of that play. He notes that there have always been problems with staging it, and suggests that these might derive from its "odd combination of historical and avant-garde features" (104). It was precisely this "interaction between invention and convention that was, for Wilde, central to the significance of the story itself" (105). For Quigley—following and acknowledging here Alan Bird's insights in *The Plays of Oscar Wilde* (1977; see *Oscar Wilde Revalued*, 177–78)—the strength of *Salome* existed in the way Wilde combined elements of the "many versions" of the story which were already familiar in literary culture with the "original creations" of the characters of Salome and Herodias. The play thus explores what Quigley sees as extremes of super-human and sub-human behaviour. It does so by partially critiquing the conventions of symbolist writing which Wilde inherited from European models found in the work of Wagner, Mallarmé, Baudelaire and Maeterlinck. It is this which is the source of the play's uniqueness: "somewhere between the physically confirmed truths that sustained naturalism and the psychologically attested truths that were to generate expressionism lies, for Wilde, a symbolist perspective that differs from and is related to both" (108).

Jason P. Mitchell's essay "A Source Victorian or Biblical?: The Integration of Biblical Diction and Symbolism in Oscar Wilde's *Salomé*" (1996) also takes as its point of departure the Symbolist elements of Wilde's play. He notes the popularity of "the Salome theme" up to the time of the Renaissance and how it was "revived" in the hands of nineteenth-century European writers such as Heinrich Heine, Gustave Flaubert, Stéphane Mallarmé, and Joris-Karl Huysmans. Mitchell then comments on Wilde's debts to Maurice Maeterlinck, quoting—via Ellmann—Maeterlinck's (as well as Mallarmé's and Pierre Loti's) reactions to the play. However, the main point of Mitchell's essay (which contains a disproportionate number of errors and misprints) is to argue for and to document closely the "influence of Old Testament verse on *Salomé*" (15). Mitchell concludes by observing that *Salome* is a "work in which diction and symbolism are inextricably linked" (18).

In "Wilde's *Salome*" (1999), Christopher S. Nassaar notes that the play was written immediately after *Lady Windermere's Fan*, and that it contains eight references to a fan. For Nassaar, "the references constitute Wilde's signature," but they also serve "a functional and symbolic purpose" (89) as a weapon and a sexual symbol. Nassaar observes that the last reference to fans in the play is Salome's refusal of four fans made of parrot feathers: "earlier, Salome had used a fan to hide her nature, but now she rejects the fans partly because she no longer wishes to hide her true self in any way" (90).

More substantial and a lot more rewarding is Robert Schweik's argument in "Congruous Incongruities: The Wilde-Beardsley 'Collaboration'" (1994), that both Wilde's text and Beardsley's drawings "undermine efforts to find in them some thesis, subvert undertakings to locate social arguments in them, and thwart attempts to read into them some sexual agenda" (10). Schweik pursues his case by drawing attention to certain "incongruities" in the text and in the illustrations. He shows some "odd conjunctions" in the play's language (between, for example, the solipsistic speeches of Salome and the cynicism of Herodias), in Wilde's "handling of his characters," and in biblical allusions and comic elements. Schweik concludes that "inconsistency, disconnectedness, lack of match between its elements—these are among some of the most distinctive features of Wilde's play" (15). He finds similar incongruity and disconnection in Beardsley's illustrations—in, for example, the use of androgyny, of anachronistic details (such as the furniture depicted in the toilet of Salome) and in contrasting portrayals of Salome herself, who appears at times "hawk-like" and at other times "girlish" (23). Schweik concludes that the "lack of match" between texts and illustrations ironically gives a sense of overall coherence, even though that "coherence" was unintended, the result of a "happy historical accident" rather than any "effective effort and collaboration" (24). (For a different account of Beardsley's illustrations to *Salome*, see Linda Gertner Zatlin, "Aubrey Beardsley's 'Japanese' Grotesques" (1997), and Zatlin, *Beardsley, Japonisme and the Perversion of the Victorian Ideal* (1997).

Brad Bucknell's essay "On 'Seeing' Salome" (1993) also looks at the relationship between Wilde's English text and Beardsley's drawings, but in a context much wider than that of Schweik. He is interested in Wilde only insofar as his play is part of a particular nineteenth-century tradition of representing Salome, one which relies upon an "interplay of verbal and visual signifying practices" (503). He focuses on the representations of Salome to be found in the biblical narrative, in Joris-Karl Huysmans's *A Rebours*, Gustave Moreau's "Salomé Dancing before Herod" and "The Apparition," and in Wilde's drama.

Bucknell notes that the biblical texts "are strikingly short on description" (506), but it precisely the "visual aspects" of the story which are exploited in the nineteenth-century "Salome iconography" (508). Bucknell argues that in Wilde's *Salome*, "the volatile realm of the drama exploits the problem of boundaries between viewer and viewed" (514), and as a result "there is a sense that nothing will stand still . . . seeing, then, may be treacherous" (516). In his concluding remarks, Bucknell concedes that the answer to his opening question, "Is it possible to talk about *seeing* Salome?" (503), may seem "striking in its banality," because "to 'see' Salome is to see the eye of the male beholder looking back at itself" (523). Edward Burns in "*Salome*: Wilde's Radical Tragedy" (1994) also examines the motif of the gaze, but in a far less satisfying manner. His general argument is that the play's radicalism lies in "its reworking of . . . the relation between spectacle[,] word and meaning" (30).

William Tydeman's and Steven Price's *Wilde: Salome* (1996) in Cambridge University Press's Plays in Performance series is a study-aid with a strong bibliographical emphasis. It gives a brief but useful account of the play's genesis, acknowledging the problems of identifying the numbers of "other hands" who assisted Wilde in producing the French version, as well as the complexities involved in tracing Wilde's many influences and sources. The book then documents and describes selected early European productions of *Salomé*; here the material assembled by Tydeman and Price is much more reliable than that collected by Tanitch (see 7. iv.), giving the reader a smaller selection of productions, but a much fuller sense of what each performance entailed. A further chapter concentrates on what the writers call "the English stage" from 1911 to 1990, and connects changes in the way in which *Salome* was produced with larger cultural preoccupations. For example, the writers describe a "recent American production which placed the play's imagery of disease in the context of the contemporary AIDS crisis" (112). Similarly, the marginalization of the play in the years following the Second World War is explained in terms of "the conservatism of the [post-war] theatre" (95). A final chapter entitled "Transformations" concentrates on appropriations of the text for other media: Beardsley's illustrations for the 1894 Bodley Head English-language edition, Richard Strauss's opera, performances of the dance of the seven veils as a separate routine, and screen versions of *Salome*. In all the book is one of most useful accounts of the textual and stage history of the play, and is a salutary reminder that it is a performance as much as a reading text, a circumstance which many literary historians have tended to overlook. (For example, Nicholas Frankel's account of *Salome* in *Oscar Wilde's Decorated Books* [2000],discussed in 3. iii., is concerned with it solely as a reading text.)

Joseph Donohue's "Distance, death and desire in *Salome*" (1997) covers some of the same ground as Tydeman's and Price's study, although Donohue's emphasis is on explaining how recent approaches to the play have brought it "decisively into a new sphere of understanding." He claims that a "far-reaching revaluation of *Salome* [is] now under way" (120). Donohue begins with an account of the play's genesis and a summary of research into Wilde's sources for it, but comments that "the real extent of Wilde's originality" has yet to be assessed (124–25). He also examines that line of criticism, inaugurated by Kate Millett, which has read *Salome* as a "covert homosexual work" (127). In Donohue's view, there is "no clear line between heterosexual and homosexual concerns" in the play (129). Finally, Donohue examines the play's symbolism, particularly as it relates to desire, and what Donohue sees as its most problematic elements, its "visionary pronouncements" (136). Donohue's final judgement is that *Salome* should be seen not as an exception in Wilde's dramatic *oeuvre*, but rather as central to understanding "the generative forces of his dramaturgy" (137). Although his essay presents few genuinely original insights into the work, it does give a very useful and cogent overview of the state of research into *Salome*. Of course a proper appreciation of this play has been hampered by the absence of an authoritative scholarly edition, one which will settle many of the problems surrounding its composition and the provenance of the English-language version. Although he is too modest to mention it, Donohue himself is working on such an edition; if it comes close to matching the meticulousness of his edition of *The Importance of Being Earnest* (see 6. ii.), it will be more than welcome.

4. v.   The Writer of Fiction

I noted in *Oscar Wilde Revalued* that the short fiction was perhaps the most consistently neglected area of Wilde's *oeuvre*. This state of affairs has persisted during the 1990s; there have been some useful studies identifying sources and influences (see 4. vi.) and a couple of pieces offering new ways of reading Wilde's stories; but there has been nothing which approaches a full-scale assessment.

The themes of some of Wilde's fairy stories—principally those in *The Happy Prince and Other Tales*—are the subject of Clifton Snider's "Eros and Logos in Some Fairy Stories by Oscar Wilde: A Jungian Interpretation" (1993). Snider's premise is that fairy tales (in Wilde's case "literary" fairy tales, or those whose authors can be identified) "appeal to our collective unconscious" and that Wilde's stories appeal to "something in the collective psyche of the English-speaking peoples" (1). For Snider, the Victorian period tended to be "unbalanced on the side of what Jung would call the Logos principle as opposed to Eros," when Logos means the principle of knowledge, traditionally associated with masculinity, and Eros means the "principle of connection," traditionally identified with women and femininity (2). For Snider, the ease and spontaneity with which Wilde told tales suggest that "they arose at least in part from unconscious sources that even he was not aware of" (3). In the tales the "Eros principle is honored and shown to be needed. Wilde, as a homosexual man, was able unconsciously to portray the need for psychic wholeness in non-patriarchal ways" and in his later work "both males and female figures discover the need for connection" (7). In the end, Snider's view of the fairy stories is perhaps not quite as radical as he leads the reader to believe: its persuasiveness will depend upon his readers' views of the coherence and validity of the Jungian paradigm he uses to explain them.

In "Wilde's Gracious Enclosures: A Brief Tour" (1997), Gareth Noon surveys Wilde's fiction (and some of his poetry and *Salome*). Taking his cue from an observation from Gary Schmidgall (see 2. i.) that Wilde was "always testing the securities of the boundaries presented to him," Noon identifies "zones of privilege" in Wilde's work—what he calls "'gracious enclosures': walled gardens, intimate temples, sequestered palaces from whose precincts the undistinguished, the ugly, and the poor are firmly excluded" (17). According to Noon the function of these boundaries is to protect "an indifferent beauty" (17). On some occasions, particularly in "The Happy Prince," "Charmides" and "The Selfish Giant," boundaries protect the privileges of a social elite. On others, particularly in *The Picture of Dorian Gray*, "The Birthday of the Infanta," *Salome*, "The Star-Child," and *The Sphinx*, the activity of enclosure is more metaphorical or figurative, and involves protecting beauty from what Noon calls the "devouring energies of life and the relentless metamorphosis of the flesh" (19). Noon claims that Wilde "repeatedly stresses the corrosive effect of involvement in the reality beyond the boundaries of the gracious enclosure" (19); this in turn results in a paradox in which beauty "being perfect . . . is aloof from change" but isolated "into a chill and barren stasis" (20). Noon concludes that "it is in the face of this spotless sterility, and against the resistance of its vulnerable barrier, that convulsions of empathy, lust, rebellion, proliferating growth and the hunger for sensation force themselves" (20). Noon cites as a possible source for Wilde's interest in boundaries Davis Coakley's observation that the Wilde family had privileged access to a walled garden in Merrion Square, Dublin (Coakley's book is discussed in 3. ii.). An interested reader could also profitably look at Leonore Davidoff's account (in *The Best Circles* [1973]) of the various walled gardens and privileged spaces to be found in late nineteenth-century London. Finally reference to Wilde's short fiction can be found in general surveys of Victorian fairy-tales. (See, for example, Carole G. Silver, *Strange and Secret Peoples: Fairies and the Victorian Consciousness* [1999].)

In contrast to the short fiction, *The Picture of Dorian Gray* continues to generate considerable interest among critics, although—and as I noted in my introduction—not all of the pieces discussed below are as original as their authors seem to believe. C. George Sandulescu's collection of essays, *Rediscovering Oscar Wilde* (1994), which reproduces the proceeding of the 1993 Monaco Conference, has a number of short pieces on *The Picture of Dorian Gray*. In "The Mirror of Narcissus in *The Picture of Dorian Gray*," Antonio Ballesteros González discusses a familiar theme: Wilde's exploration in that novel of the issues of identity and duality via the Narcissus myth. In "Dorian Gray's Rooms and Cyberspace," Pia Brînzeu examines the relationship between various "story events" in the novel and the "descriptions of rooms" in which they are located (22), observing that all the chapters begin and end with characters entering or leaving a room—a device which "gives rhythm and movement to an otherwise completely static novel" (25). Brînzeu goes on to suggest that such a "spatially centred narrative" permits "a cybernetic reader" to "construct different types of topological frames for the same story." Such a reader, for example, could move characters from "one spatial frame ... to different other rooms and analyse differences" or "re-live the novel from a different angle" (27–28). In a slightly more interesting piece, "Intellectual Wordplay in Wilde's Characterization of Henry Wotton," Jean M. Ellis D'Alessandro attempts to show how the characterization of Wotton, particularly in his conversation, is informed by the work of "Herbert Francis" Bradley, a philosopher who might be better known to most readers as F. H. (Francis Herbert) Bradley. D'Alessandro focuses in particular on Wotton's views on the "question of appearance and reality" (61), on his talk of "subjective sensation" (63)—both of which are seen to be evidence of a *trait d'union* between Wotton and Bradley" (63). D'Alessandro's thesis, however, is somewhat weakened by the fact that Bradley's famous *Appearance and Reality* was published in 1893, some years after *Dorian Gray*, and by the fact that there is no evidence that Wilde ever read Bradley. Much of D'Alessandro's essay concentrates on analysing Wotton's general rhetorical skills—his sophistry—which is seen as deriving from Wilde's classical scholarship. D'Alessandro concludes with the observation that "Wilde's characterisation of Wotton required the traits of a metaphysician and a dialectician to complete it" (72). (D'Alessandro's piece could be usefully contrasted with Michael Patrick Gillespie's "'What's in a Name?': Representing *The Picture of Dorian Gray*" [1994].)

Lawrence Danson's contribution to Sandulescu's Monaco collection is more ambitious than many of the other pieces on Wilde's novel. In "'Each Man Kills the Thing he Loves': The Impermanence of Personality in Oscar Wilde" Danson attempts to unpick the meaning of the term "personality," which he sees as "a Wildean keyword from the time of his earliest reviews and lectures through his writing of *De Profundis*" (82). Danson compares Wilde's use of the term with that by contemporaries such as Walter Pater and the psychologist Henry Maudsley; and he goes on to identify and examine a number of different senses of the term at work in *Dorian Gray*, including "the scientific, the commodified, and the aesthetic" as well as the idea of a personality as "sexually *sympathique*" (88). Danson's overall argument is that Wilde "never produced a unified field theory of personality to reconcile the contradictions which animate the word" (91)—a conclusion which is broadly in keeping with Danson's discussion of the contradictions underlying other aspects of Wilde's terminology in *Wilde's Intentions: The Artist in his Criticism* (1997; see 5.).

In her contribution to the 1993 Monaco conference, "John Melmoth and Dorian Gray: The Two-Faced Mirror," Marie-Noëlle Zeender argues for the influence of Maturin's "romantic satanic hero" on Wilde's *Dorian Gray* (432)—a topic which is perhaps not quite as original as Zeender believes. After what she herself admits to be "a short survey" of the two novels, Zeender offers a conclusion which seems to undermine her project: "Wilde's indebtedness to Maturin is real, but on the whole it remains superficial because the message is different. *Melmoth* is a profoundly religious work, *Dorian Gray* is not" (439). In "Eros and Thanatos in *The Picture of Dorian Gray*" Sylvia Ostermann also pursues an over-familiar theme; her concern is to explain what she terms "the integrated structure of the novel" by reference to the Freudian conflict between Eros and Thanatos (297). So, for example, she sees Dorian as "the victim of the constraints between Eros and Thanatos which can only be reconciled by love itself" (303).

In "Wilde's *The Picture of Dorian Gray*" (1995) Deborah McCollister notes that the word "charming" is used over sixty times in the novel. She sees the term possessing two meanings—"pleasing" and, less obviously, "the ability to control the thoughts and deeds of others" (17), one associated in the nineteenth century with mesmerism. She acknowledges the work of Kerry Powell in locating Wilde's tale among other mesmeric stories, and suggests that "most of the characters possess at least some power to charm, as well as some vulnerability to mesmeric spells" (20).

In "The Physiological Determinism Debate in Oscar Wilde's *The Picture of Dorian Gray*" (1993), Terri Hasseler examines the "separation of soul and body" in *The Picture of Dorian Gray* in terms of what is identified as "the Victorian controversy over physiological determinism." The argument of the essay is that Wilde offers a materialistic understanding of destiny, one which replaces the supernatural idea of fate: "in *Dorian Gray* the control over a personal destiny seems to be seated in the soul: once that soul is lost, the body, like an animal without a soul, determines action" (31). For Hasseler, Dorian is "the essence of the Huxleyan predetermined automaton" (31). Hasseler's essay can be read alongside John Wilson Foster's "Against Nature? Science and Oscar Wilde" (1998; see 3. ii.)

John Gall's concern in his essay "The Pregnant Death of Dorian Gray" (1992, but not included in *Oscar Wilde Revalued*) is to trace the presence in the novel of the grotesque (as it is defined by Mikhail Bakhtin in *Problems of Doestevsky's Poetics* [1984]) and the carnivalesque (as it is defined by Terry Castle in *Masquerade and Carnival* [1986]). Gall argues that Wilde's novel proves a "rich source" for these tropes and themes, and they in turn allow for a "complex investigation of the themes of metamorphosis and initiation . . . renewal and failure" (57). Gall's account of the novel adds to our sense of its multiple generic identities: the presence of Symbolist, Decadent and Gothic themes, detective and magic-picture sub-genres—they have all been isolated by recent critics. With these studies of influences and sources, however, an important issue has generally been overlooked: how such different generic and thematic identities can easily co-exist.

The thesis explored by Curtis Marez in "The Other Addict: Reflections on Colonialism and Oscar Wilde's Opium Smoke Screen" (1997) is that the juxtaposition in *Dorian Gray* "of non-Western art and opium allows Wilde to restage . . . questions of racial representation." For Marez, that is, Wilde's novel "narrates . . . one of the constitutive contradictions of *fin-de-siècle* British colonization": the dissemination of "imperial ideologies" allows them to be appropriated by "colonial subjects" at the same time that the Empire, by relying on the "absolute racial difference of colonizer and colonized . . . bans the ideological traffic between the two" (259). Marez's account begins with a subtle discussion of the contradictions in Wilde's "colonial" identity. Marez argues that Wilde developed a "notion of Aesthetic Empire," derived from a "British heritage encapsulated in a canon of beauty" (262–63) in order to resolve these tensions. Wilde could argue that art or culture could be an alternative to colonial conflict, but only when his idea of art had been derived from the terms of an English debate about English literature and an English national identity. As Marez pertinently comments, "even though he sometimes criticized the British Empire and identified with Irish nationalism and the Celtic 'race,' Wilde more usually idealized English culture" (264). In the second section of his essay Marez describes the way in which Wilde tried to resist being figured as Irish by "displacing his own differences onto non-Western ornaments and the people who produced them" (264); "Wilde can only appear British and European in contrast to people he regards as even less British and European than himself" (266). Examining a number of caricatures and cartoons of Wilde (held in the Clark Library) Marez notes that the strategy met with only "limited success since many of his critics continued to link him with the very types of 'wildness' he was trying to transcend" (266)—Wilde was represented as "Black, Native American and Chinese" (272). The final section of Marez's essay focuses on *The Picture of Dorian Gray*, arguing that Dorian's opium addiction "becomes a foil for Wilde's redemptive appropriation of non-Western culture: Dorian's dependency orientalizes him, threatening to dissolve his British identity" (274). Marez's essay is subtly argued and represents an interesting engagement with many of the questions raised in *Wilde the Irishman* (see 3. iii.) about art and nationalism.

One of Christopher S. Nassaar's many brief essays on Wilde in the *Explicator* is devoted to the weight of Dorian Gray's portrait. In "Wilde's *The Picture of Dorian Gray*" (1999) Nassaar describes how the portrait becomes heavier, as it changes from simple canvas to framed picture; by the time it is stored it is "a load to carry," and only leant against the wall. Nassaar notes that when his servants discover Dorian's body, the picture is once more hanging on the wall—"the weight of the supernatural portrait is lightened dramatically, enabling it at last to rise up and hang itself on the wall in an assertion of its renewed innocence" (217).

In "Wilde's *The Picture of Dorian Gray* and *Salome*" (1998) Nassaar alludes to some of the novel's many intertextual elements, describing a reference to the Marquis de Sade which "has gone unnoticed" (33). Nassaar notes that Wilde knew de Sade's work well, and suggests that "he would have been attracted to [him] as a fellow-criminal-artist" (34). However, Lord Henry's comment that "crime belongs to the lower orders" is a conscious paradoxical "jab" at de Sade. For Nassaar, however, *Salome* is explicitly de Sadeian: whereas "in *Dorian Gray* Wilde criticized Sade, in *Salome*—written at the height of his homosexual affair with Lord Alfred Douglas—he seems to adopt most of Sade's idea and his technique, wrapping it in a biblical veil" (35). (See also an earlier piece by Martin Meisel, "The World, The Flesh, and Oscar Wilde: Bodily Politics in *Salome* and *Dorian Gray*" [1992, but overlooked in *Oscar Wilde Revalued*].)

I suggested that the critical attention which *The Picture of Dorian Gray* has attracted greatly exceeds that given to the three other volumes of fiction. However book-length studies of the novel have been rare. Michael Patrick Gillespie's *The Picture of Dorian Gray: "What the World Thinks Me"* (1995) is one of those few to buck the trend. Part of the Twayne Masterworks Series, its intended readership is principally the advanced undergraduate or first-year postgraduate. As with Anne Varty's study, *A Preface to Oscar Wilde* (see 5.), the anticipated audience and the series dictate the format and to some extent the tone of Gillespie's book. So there is an extended chronology which acts as a chronicle of the life; then a section entitled "The Extratextual Milieu," which includes a chapter on the novel's "historical context." Few Wilde scholars will be unaware of the pitfalls of such ambitions: new historicist critics have been insisting for twenty years or more that a simple distinction between text and context is theoretically naive, and that any "context" is a construction which present-day critics place upon the past. Nevertheless in practice few teachers would disagree fundamentally with Gillespie's main points; they might, though, wish to add to them. The next chapter, "The Importance of the Work in Defining the Context of Ambiguity," outlines both the similarities between *Dorian Gray* and more conventional Victorian fictions, and the complex "interpretative challenges" (15) which Wilde's novel poses for the reader. Gillespie's indebtedness to reader-response theories is most evident at this point. The final chapter in Gillespie's first section is an account of the novel's critical reception.

The second section is devoted to exegesis: in his "Prefatory Note" to this section, Gillespie argues that his ambition is to demonstrate "the idea that Wilde's narrative actively encourages the reader to view the work from a range of perspectives, in turn fostering multiple interpretations" (31). These plural perspectives, however, turn out to be fewer than we might have expected, and in practice are reduced to three. The first "questions the assumption that one reads to find the meaning hidden beneath the surface" and examines instead how a "reader's background and expectations" shape literary responses. The next two chapters attend to the importance of "social, cultural, and historical conditions" and the "operation of the narrative " (32) in the novel. Gillespie's concluding chapter is a examination of the connections between the novel's preface and the novel itself. He suggests that the work demands an "imaginative pluralism" (106) in the reader; however, it is not easy to see how practically a reader squares this notion of polyvocality with the Gillespie's other declared ambition, that of providing contextualizing information.

Many of the ideas in Gillespie's book were deployed in slightly different ways (and for a significantly different readership) in a number of essays published a few years earlier. For example, in "Picturing Dorian Gray: Resistant Readings in Wilde's Novel" (1992), Gillespie broached his idea about the "indeterminacy" of Wilde's novel, and what he called its resistance to "closure" (23). He argued that "the individual reader must depend upon a range of Modern and post-Modern approaches to exploit the hypostatic multiplicity inherent in the text" (23). He located his argument in relation to what was, in the early 1990s, recent work—by critics such Regenia Gagnier (1986) and Ed Cohen (1987). However, his underlying thesis is more reminiscent of the arguments of structuralist critics of the late 1970s than it is of the concern with sexual politics and consumerism which has dominated interpretations of the novel in the 1990s.

In "Ethics and Aesthetics in *The Picture of Dorian Gray*" (1994), Gillespie again dwells on the issue of the novel's interpretative plurality. He focuses on what he terms "an aesthetic/ethical" reading of the novel (140), arguing that Wilde's work "does not and should not bring us to a new ethical position or reinforce our old one" (153). Rather Gillespie suggests that *Dorian Gray* gives us "the opportunity to enhance the mix of our aesthetic and ethical views by extending our sense of the possibilities for interpretation beyond those delineated by our immediate hermeneutic system" (154). More generally Gillespie argues for what he terms "the both/and approach to interpretation," one which unfortunately he does not describe with any clarity.

In an essay entitled "Art as Symptom: A Portrait of Child Abuse in *The Picture of Dorian Gray*" (1997), Esther Rashkin, like Gillespie, acknowledges the variety of interpretations which Wilde's novel has elicited. She claims, however, to add a new reading which until the present "has been entirely overlooked" (69). Rashkin's thesis is that

Dorian Gray is concerned "with the effects of psychological child abuse" (69). Drawing on the work of the Hungarian psychoanalyst Sandor Ferenczi, Rashkin attempts to show "how Wilde's text presents a case of emotional abuse and dramatizes the ramifications of the abuse for the 'life' of the main character" and how this in turn "exposes the heretofore unseen connection between abuse and aesthetic creation" in Wilde's novel (69). Rashkin's argument focuses on Dorian's relationship with his grandfather and suggests that Dorian's "plunge into decadence and criminality represents his acting out of an imago or portrait, created and violently imposed upon him by his oppressive grandfather" (74). Such an interpretation, according to Rashkin, requires the reader to rethink the role of Lord Henry as the corrupter of innocence. Rashkin goes on to describe Dorian's murder of Basil as "a reaction to his abused childhood" (76), and Dorian's stabbing of his picture in his old schoolroom as a symbolic attempt to destroy "the figure of his grandfather" (77). Rashkin's reading is ingenious, but relies on an overdetermined interpretation of the very few references to Lord Kelso in the novel. For critics who have little sympathy for psychoanalysis, there will be some disquiet in interpreting a novel from the early 1890s in the flickering light of a 1933 essay which is concerned with sexual abuse.

4. vi. *Sources & Intertexts*

There has been a considerable amount of literary detective work on Wilde's *oeuvre* over the past decade. Most of this has involved the identification of sources or possible sources in individual works, increasing our sense of Wilde's openness to (and recall of) the ideas of others. Few essays, however, have addressed the relationship between particular borrowings and Wilde's creativity as a whole. An exception is "Self-Plagiarism, Creativity and Craftsmanship in Oscar Wilde" (1998), where Josephine M. Guy confronts the issues involved in Wilde's use of multiple "sources." She suggests that several recent studies of Wilde's writing practices (some of which are described in 5.) have shown apparently contradictory creative strategies at work. The first is that of the "journeyman" Wilde, carefully transforming (and in the process partly subverting) the material and conventions with which he engages. The second, for Guy, is more disturbing, for it involves Wilde's "willingness to 'borrow' silently the work of others and himself" (7). This self-plagiarism proves to be the "hard case" for understanding Wilde's creativity, and Guy identifies two ways of explaining it. She suggests that some critics have related it to Wilde the professional writer: "when Wilde identified a winning formula[,] he 'understandably' milked it for all it was worth" (8). Other critics have employed the idea of Wilde the iconoclast—self-plagiarism or self-referentiality in this view becomes an example of Wilde locating "aesthetic value in linguistic *jouissance*" (9). Guy proceeds to ask whether these two recent explanations of Wilde's creativity can be satisfactorily brought together. As a test case she examines some of Wilde's aphorisms and jokes, the material most often transposed from one work to another. She argues that when material is re-used it is often subtly changed and that a decision to re-use a joke is based on a sense of its appropriateness—on Wilde's judgement whether or not it will continue to work in a new context. She concludes that Wilde's plagiarism may be strategic and executed with a journalist's sensitivity to public opinion and audiences: "if Wilde's self-plagiarism *is* a game, then it is one which is perfected by the professional writer's careful attention to the occasion" (20). (For a different account of Wilde's humour, see Mariano Baselga's "Oscar Wilde and the Semantic Mechanisms of Humour: The Satire of Social Habits" [1994]; see 4. vii.)

In "Plagiarist, or Pioneer?" (1994), Merlin Holland also addresses the vexed question of Wilde's plagiarism by trying to assess the scope of his reading through identifying some of the books which he may have read. In particular, he describes how he obtained a photocopy of the Tite St sale catalogue of Wilde's possessions (following his bankruptcy) which specified lots referring to Wilde's books. Holland also examined account sheets from publishers (including David Nutt) from whom Wilde purchased books. From this material he tries to assess the nature of Wilde's borrowings, concluding that Wilde's reading gives evidence of "profound learning and scholarship" even if defining the precise nature of his literary debts remains an "elusive" task (211).

In "Shavian Comedy and the Shadow of Wilde" (1998), David J. Gordon explores the similarities between the careers of those writers, noting that initially the two men had much in common (their families, for example, were acquainted in Dublin). Gordon goes on to comment on the professional respect each had for the other, although he judges their personal relationship to be no more than "courteous"

(125). Gordon then identifies what he sees as essential similarities in their artistic ambitions. They both "from the start attacked similar targets: duty, respectability, the sentimental view of poverty, the danger of self-denial and of ideal-driven goodness" (126). Finally, however, it is the differences between Shaw and Wilde which most interest Gordon, and importantly, these concern "the place of art itself in relation to life" (127):

> If Wilde's creative imagination was stirred by the socially transgressive act or word made charming by high style, Shaw's was stirred by the idea of a Life Force. . . . If Wilde's aestheticism morally polarized the beautiful and the ugly, Shaw's vitalism morally polarized energy and conventionality. . . . [Shaw] certainly believed that art itself refined and improved us. . . . For Wilde, in contrast, art leads and should lead, nowhere." (127–28)

Gordon goes on to analyse this opposition by contrasting Wilde's *An Ideal Husband* and *The Importance of Being Earnest* with Shaw's "comedies of the nineties"—*Arms and the Man* (1894), *You Never Can Tell* (1896) and *The Devil's Disciple* (1897). Gordon concludes by noticing the way in which the reputations of the two Irish playwrights were mirror-images of each other in the twentieth century, suggesting that Wilde's present popularity has to do with the ways he taps into "our postmodern skepticism regarding objectivity, truth, and art" (139). (Also interested in the relationship between Shaw and Wilde is Terry Eagleton in "Oscar and George" [1994].)

In "The Aesthetics of Exile" (1993), Jay Losey follows the example of a number of critics by examining Wilde's intertextuality in a much more local way, by looking at the influence of just one writer, tracing the importance of Dante in Wilde's writing, from his earliest appearances in *Ravenna* and "At Verona." Losey suggests that in the poems "Wilde assumes a Dantean mask to create a fictionalized exile." The "reference to being exiled" (Dante actually from Florence, Wilde only imaginatively from Ireland and then from England) indicates a poetic identification: speaker and poet have felt "exile's galling chain." Losey then traces the frequent uses of the Florentine poet in *Intentions* (in "The Decay of Lying," but more especially in "The Critic as Artist"), suggesting that the use of the *Commedia* has by this time become more complex: "it may be possible to discern a dialogue not between Gilbert and Ernest but between Wilde and Dante." Rather unsurprisingly, perhaps, "Wilde occasionally subverts Dante's meanng to convey his own aesthetics" (433). *De Profundis* represents the most profound engagement with Dante, the condition of both writers finding an echo in Ovid's description of Marsyas—"like Wilde and Dante, Ovid died in exile" (445). Losey's account is an interesting addition to Wilde's propensity to what we might call "creative misreading"; it is also an addition to our knowledge of the importance of Dante's work for early modernists and modernist literary culture. However, like the work of commentators such as Kiberd (see 3. ii.), it does beg some questions about the nature of exile.

In a brief and much less convincing essay, "Wilde's *The Ballad of Reading Gaol*" (1995), Christopher S. Nassaar also detects the influence of Dante on Wilde: this time in what he sees as the "pervasive" influence of the *Inferno* on *The Ballad of Reading Gaol*. He comments on the similarities between Dante's circles of Hell and the rather more literal "two circles or rings in Reading Gaol, one inhabited by the guardsman . . . and one inhabited by himself and the other prisoners" (159). He also notes that in both Wilde's and Dante's poems "there is a dramatic movement toward intensity of horror," and in both hells "there are monsters and demons and grotesques of various sorts" (160). For Nassaar, then, the basic stylistic principle of *The Ballad of Reading Gaol* is "the exploration of hell" and Dante's *Inferno* provides him with a "basic model of this exploration" (160).

In "The Reading Gaol of Henry James's *In the Cage*" (1999), Nicola Nixon argues that James's novella, written six months after the appearance of *The Ballad Of Reading Gaol*, was "seemingly inspired by Wilde's text" (180). Understanding the relationship between these two works, according to Nixon, allows us to appreciate better the historical specificity of James's story. More precisely, Nixon suggests that James was responding polemically to what she terms the idea of the "romantic prison" (180) articulated by Wilde. She describes *The Ballad Of Reading Gaol* as "an almost paradigmatic romantic prison poem, symptomatically infused with only traces of representative hardships and vast amounts of maudlin Christian consolation" (183). According to Nixon, *In the Cage* recasts the romantic prisoner as female; this in turn allows James to "interrogate the gender codifications of the romantic prison and question whether its assumptions about the rightness of docile compliance to social authorities are appropriate" (185–86). Nixon explores this thesis through a detailed discussion of James's novella, concluding that his "critique of Wilde's . . .

romantic prison ends up exposing a deep conservatism within a genre that celebrates the acceptance of one's lot." She continues: "Wilde's 'Ballad' reveals only the melioristic romance of educative hardship; James's telegraphist displays the results of such a romance when gender and birth determine that such meliorism is, finally, inconsequential" (197). Nixon's interest is mainly in James and her account certainly casts more light on *In the Cage* than on Wilde's poem. It is perhaps also worth pointing out that Nixon's comparison between the two works ignores the very different material circumstances in which they were written. Wilde's copious correspondence with Leonard Smithers suggests that *The Ballad of Reading Gaol* was written in part with the specific intention of achieving popularity and to make money (rather than to be expressive of Wilde's experiences, which are in any case more fully described in *De Profundis*). If this is so, what Nixon calls the poem's "gestures back to . . . sentimental favourites" (183) are entirely to be expected.

In "Matthew Arnold and Oscar Wilde's Commonplace Book" (1994) Horst Schroeder notes how a number of Wilde's entries in his undergraduate commonplace book derive, often verbatim, from Matthew Arnold's essay "The French Play in London," published in the *Nineteenth Century* in August 1879. In particular he traces Wilde's entries on "Metre," "Thought," "Tragedy," "Culture," and "Progress" to Arnold's work. Further essays by Schroeder reveal his abiding interest in the contexts of Wilde's works. In "Bimetallism: A Topical Reference in Oscar Wilde" (1993), he observes that Mabel Chiltern's joke about bimetallism is one that occurs elsewhere in the *oeuvre*. He notes that there is a reference to it in "The English Renaissance of Art," and that by the time the term is repeated in *A Woman of No Importance* ("Bimetallism! Is that quite a nice subject?") it formed "part of Wilde's comic stock-in-trade" (57). Schroeder further comments that the joke is repeated again in the four-act version of *The Importance of Being Earnest*, and finally in an interview in the *St James's Gazette* in 1895. Schroeder attributes the repetition of the joke to the fact that "the phenomenon must have been a hotly discussed topic in the 1880s and 1890s" (57), and goes on to outline the main elements of that discussion: J. W. Cross's essay on bimetallism in 1895 in the *Nineteenth Century*, a Parliamentary Committee and a Royal Commission in Britain, and three monetary conferences in Paris and Brussels, as well as the "vast number of books on the subject' (58). As is the case with a number of other recent studies, the logic of Schroeder's point (although he does not generalize from his information) is that a great many of Wilde's jokes were re-used precisely because they were still topical (see Guy [1998], discussed above).

A further short study by Horst Schroeder is "Wilde's Commonplace Book and Symonds's *Studies of the Greek Poets*" (1993). He observes that Philip E. Smith and Michael S. Helfand laboured to identify Wilde's sources in his Oxford Commonplace Book, commenting also that they invite readers to "help fill the remaining *lacunae*" (53). Consequently Schroeder proceeds to do precisely that by citing "ten passages from J. A. Symonds's *Studies of the Greek Poets* (1873) and *Studies of the Greek Poets: Second Series* (1876) as the points of reference for . . . unidentified and, respectively, misunderstood entries in Wilde's Commonplace Book [which give] ... renewed emphasis to the great impact Symonds made on Wilde" (53). The Wilde which Schroeder describes is a writer of almost encyclopedic reading and phenomenal powers of memory, a point which he also makes in his note (with Timothy D'Arch Smith) on the origins of the phrase "feasting with panthers" (discussed below). In "ΕΡΩΣ ΤΩΝ ΑΔΥΝΑΤΩΝ —*L'Amour de l'Impossible*: A Graeco-French Collocation in 'The Critic As Artist'" (1993), Schroeder continues his detective work by tracing the source of the collocation of those Greek and French phrases. He notes that the sentiment—the love of the impossible—is to be found in *The Picture of Dorian Gray* and in a letter of 1885 from Wilde to H. C. Marillier. The origins of the collocation, Schroeder suggests, derive from John Addington Symonds's *Studies of the Greek Poets* (1873) (and ultimately Diogenes Laertius, *Lives of the Eminent Philosophers*). Schroeder also notes that the Greek phrase is to be found in Wilde's Oxford Commonplace Book.

In another piece, "Pausanias and 'The Critic As Artist'" (1993), Schroeder turns his attention to the sources for some of the references to works of Greek art made by Ernest in "The Critic as Artist." He traces Ernest's descriptions to accounts by Pausanias of the battle of Marathon, of "Polygnotus' celebrated paintings in the Cnidian Lesche at Delphi" (55), and of Polyxeni of Polycleitus. Schroeder also detects "some visual details taken from Herodotus" (55). In his concluding remarks, Schroeder points out "a subtle irony" in a line occurring later in the dialogue when "it is suggested that the two interlocutors should not talk of 'Lucian and Longinus, of Quinctilian and Dionysius, of Pliny and Fronto and Pausanias, of all those who in the antique world lectured and wrote on art matters'" (56). As Schroeder's findings have made clear, it was Pausanias who had "already played a considerable role in the preceding discussion" (56).

Classical sources are also the concern of Emmanuel Vernadakis in "Wilde's Reading of Clemens Alexandrinus" (1994). In his essay, Vernadakis takes on the ambitious task of attempting to show how "Greek philosophy" and "Christian religion" are "exploited" in Wilde's work (421). His short essay focuses on the alleged influence of Clemens of Alexandria. Vernadakis admits that Wilde "never mentions" Clemens's name, and that "proof that [Wilde] had read Clemens's work can only be established indirectly" (422). Nevertheless Vernadakis goes on to claim that passages from "The Happy Prince" as well as "the very conception of *Salome*" are "inspired" by Clemens's writings, particularly his *Exhortation of the Gentiles* (424–25). He also detects Clemens's influence on "The Soul of Man Under Socialism" and *De Profundis*. Vernadakis concludes, perhaps a little defensively: "Wilde does not share the same views as Clemens. But the work of the latter certainly stimulated positively the imagination of the former. If he never mentions Clemens, it is because the influence of the Alexandrine is profound and genuine, and in Wilde the profound and genuine are neither flaunted nor taught, but are to be detected and discerned" (430).

In another investigation into Wilde's use of sources, "A Source for 'Pen, Pencil, and Poison'" (1994), Schroeder continues his detective work for sources and contexts by tracing the origins of four passages in Wilde's essay "Pen, Pencil, and Poison" to Alexander Gilchrist's *Life of William Blake*, a new edition of which had been published in 1880. In "An Unacknowledged Quotation in 'Pen, Pencil, and Poison'" (1996) Schroeder went on note yet another of Wilde's borrowings. In this instance Wilde's description of Wainewright's attitude towards Barry Cornwall, Allan Cunningham, Hazlitt, Elton and Leigh Hunt—existing "without anything of the malice of a friend"—is traced back to Edward Young's *Love of Fame, the Universal Passion* via Hazlitt's work, and particularly *A View of the English Stage*. For Schroeder, the phrase "malice of a friend" assumes "that subversive character which makes it indistinguishable from his other caustic remarks" (52). In "Wilde, Wainewright, and Fuseli" (1996),

Schroeder noted another, more complex borrowing at work in the same essay. Wilde's description of Thomas Wainewright's art criticism derives from Wainewright himself in a review of an exhibition at the British Institution in 1821 which was reprinted in 1880 in *Essays and Criticisms by Thomas Griffiths Wainewright* (ed. W. Carew Hazlitt), a piece which, as Schroeder notes, was itself taken from Henry Fuseli's *Lectures on Painting Delivered at the Royal Academy.*

In "A Homeric Epithet in 'The Critic as Artist'" (1994) Schroeder elaborates on the significance of Wilde's phrase "hyacinth-like curls" in "The Critic as Artist," pointing out that it is not, as Regenia Gagnier holds, simply "purple prose," but a phrase repeated elsewhere in Wilde (in, for example, the essay "English Poetesses" and the story "The Star-Child"). Schroeder explains that the "image of the flower-like hair, so dear to Wilde, is derived from Book VI of the *Odyssey,*" and that it reflects a "sentiment recurrent in English literature," occurring in Sidney, Milton, Byron, and Poe (362).

In "Feasting with Panthers" Timothy D'Arch Smith and Horst Schroeder make the brief observation that that phrase in *De Profundis,* which Rupert Croft-Cooke took as the title of his influential 1967 monograph, derives from a passage in Balzac's *Illusions perdues* ("me semble-t-il que je soupe avec des lions et des panthèrs"). D'Arch Smith and Schroeder see the phrase as "another instance of Wilde's well-known habit of creative borrowing and of his truly astonishing memory; they further suggest that it "corroborates Wilde's claim . . . of his life-long admiration for the great French novelist" (202). French influences are also the concern of Christa Satzinger's *The French Influences on Oscar Wilde's "The Picture of Dorian Gray" and "Salome"* (1994), a work which usefully supplements earlier studies on the importance of French culture in Wilde's work, such as Patricia Clements's *Baudelaire And The French Tradition* (1985) and Christophe Campos's *The View of France From Arnold To Bloomsbury* (1965; both are discussed in *Oscar Wilde Revalued,* 158–60).

Schroeder continues his indefatigable quest for Wilde's sources in "The Reference to Mantegna in 'The Critic as Artist'" (1997). The comments on that painter in Wilde's essay are traced to John Addington Symonds's *Renaissance in Italy: The Fine Arts* (1877), and especially to remarks on Mantegna's *Triumphs of Caesar* at Hampton

Court (which, according to Schroeder, occur on 273f). Schroeder also notes that Wilde explicitly mentions Mantegna's work in "The Truth of Masks" and alludes to it in his review of Pater's *Imaginary Portraits*.

Theoharis Constantine Theoharis's concern is Wilde's relationship with the philosophy of Aristotle and of Friedrich Nietzsche. The familiar starting-point of his piece, "Will to Power, Poetic Justice, and Mimesis in *The Picture of Dorian Gray*" (1994), is the idea that the novel is "Wilde's supreme and most sustained venture into paradox" (397). The particular paradox which engages Theoharis's interest is Wilde's simultaneous concern with "traditional as well as contemporary authority" (397). In Theoharis's essay these authorities become Aristotle and Nietzsche. In an often dense argument, Theoharis attempts to trace various "points of contact" between Wilde's novel and the ideas of these two philosophers, focusing in particular on the relevance of Aristotelian and Nietzschean conceptions of tragedy to the fate which befalls Dorian. Theoharis concludes: "Dorian succumbs to the rage of nineteenth century [*sic*] realism, Aristotle's progeny, and the rage of nineteenth century [*sic*] Romanticism, Nietzsche's forebear. He dies of seeing and not seeing his face in art's stylized glass" (404). Another account of the indirect influence of the German philosopher on Wilde is "Entre Dionysos et Apollon: Pour une lecture Nietzschéenne de Wilde" (1996), in which Pascal Aquien suggests, in the words of the abstract of his paper, that "the meeting points" of the two are numerous, including "the denunciation of abstraction and reason or the coexistence of Apollo and Dionysos as dynamic fundamentals" (168).

In "Oscar Wilde's Celebrated Remark on Bernard Shaw" (1994), Karl Beckson gives the history of Wilde's description of Shaw (according to W. B. Yeats) as a man "who has no enemies but who is intensely disliked by his friends," and traces its source to chapter 15 of the book version of *Dorian Gray*. In "Oscar Wilde in his Literary Element: Yet Another Source for *Dorian Gray*?" (1994) Isobel Murray pursues a topic which occupied many of her earlier essays, the number and nature of the influences upon Wilde when he wrote *The Picture of Dorian Gray*. On this occasion the source she identifies is Louisa May Alcott's sensational novel, *A Modern Mephistopheles*, published pseudonymously in 1877 and posthumously under the author's own name in 1899. Much of Murray's essay is devoted to summarizing the plot and describing the characters of this little-known work. She concludes that Wilde's "temporary engagement" with the novel centres on the development of the main character, Jasper Helwyze, who may have been "inspirational" for Wilde's Lord Henry Wotton (294).

A further presence in *The Picture of Dorian Gray* and *Salome*, according to Christopher S. Nassaar (in "Wilde's *The Picture of Dorian Gray* and *Salome*" [1995]) is none other than Jack the Ripper. Nassaar argues that Dorian's method of killing Basil Hallward is "reminiscent of the Jack the Ripper murders" (218), and that the source "serves to deepen and intensify the horror of Dorian's act" (219). He sees a similar influence at work in Wilde's presentation of the killing of John the Baptist. "Salome," Nassaar argues, "both reflects the Ripper and goes beyond him. Not only does she commit a savage sex murder, but she feasts lustfully on her victim's blood-soaked severed head" (219).

In "Andersen's 'The Shadow' and Wilde's 'The Fisherman and His Soul': A Case of Influence" (1995), Nassaar details the influence of Hans Christian Andersen's tale upon Wilde. Nassaar notes how Wilde's source is usually identified as "The Little Mermaid," but suggests that "'The Shadow' is by far the deeper influence" (218). He goes on to demonstrate when Wilde borrows and when he reworks Andersen's themes, concluding that while "The Fisherman and His Soul" is "rooted" in the earlier tale, it asserts "Christian values as opposed to Andersen's nihilistic ones" (224). A further account of the influence of the Danish author on the Irish writer is to be found in Nassaar's later piece, "Andersen's 'The Ugly Duckling' and Wilde's 'The Birthday of the Infanta'" (1997). Nassaar sees the influence of Velasquez and Tennyson, as well as that of "Beauty and the Beast," but in a Blakean manner (because of its thematic reversals), "An Ugly Duckling" is an "idyllic 'song of innocence,'" while Wilde's story is a "powerful 'song of experience'" (85).

In "An Allusion in Wilde's 'The Canterville Ghost'" (1998), Josephine M. Guy discusses Wilde's addition of a subtitle to "The Canterville Ghost"—"A Hylo-Idealistic Romance"—and how a satisfactory account of its origin (in the work of Constance Naden) has not been forthcoming from critics and editors alike. Guy points out that the subtitle was not present on the story's first publication in *The Court and Society Review* in 1887. She suggests that the later and posthumous re-publication of Naden's work might have ensured "sufficient publicity" for the joke to "work" (226).

In "Prunes and Prism: Wilde and Dickens" (1997) S. J. Harrison suggests that the name of Miss Prism in *The Importance of Being Earnest* may derive from the figure of the governess, Mrs General, in Dickens's *Little Dorrit*, and particularly from Mrs General's repeated phrase "prunes and prism": the "repeated 'Prism' associated with a proper governess-figure suggests that Wilde's name came from . . . passages in Dickens; in both cases the word is no doubt also chosen for its closeness to 'prim,' a quality which both characters show" (351).

In "Wilde, Browning and the 'New Obscurity'" (1999) Leslie White takes on a much larger theme, examining the significance of Wilde's reading of Browning in "The Critic as Artist." White briefly traces the troubled history of Browning's own reputation, including the "persistent charges of unintelligibility" levelled at his work (5). White also locates Wilde's account of Browning in relation to discussions of his work by Rossetti, Swinburne and Alfred Austin (but, oddly, not the equally important critiques by Walter Pater and Arthur Symons). All of this provides a context for a lengthy discussion of Wilde's interest in what White calls "the 'obscurity question'" (9)—an issue addressed in works such as "Pen, Pencil, and Poison," "The Decay of Lying," "The Portrait of Mr W. H." as well as "The Critic As Artist." It is in this last work, however, that White sees Wilde articulating his ideas most cogently. Wilde's justification of Browning's obscurity, according to White, "focuses elements of [Wilde's] own idealist aesthetic, itself selectively derived from Hegelian dialectical thought" (11). In that defence, Wilde presented Browning "as a philosophical ironist, a poet whose work reveals thematically and technically a resistance to harmonious closure," an argument which "establishes ways of approaching [Browning's poetry] that mark Wilde a perspicacious and prescient early critic of him" (16). It is worth noting that there has been more commentary on the Wilde-Browning connection than White seems aware of. The general issue of obscurity in late nineteenth-century literary culture, for example, was addressed in detail by Allon White in *The Uses of Obscurity* as long ago as 1981. Moreover Wilde's engagement with the debate about obscurity (made via the work of Browning) was the subject of part of Josephine M. Guy's *The British Avant-Garde* (1991).

In "Wilde's Shadow in Conrad's 'The Return'" (1993), Paul Kirschner identifies a series of similarities between Conrad's story "The Return" (begun in May 1897, the month of Wilde' release from prison) and *Lady Windermere's Fan*. These involve thematic parallels, such as a concern with "the artificiality of fashionable society and the broadening of moral vision in one of its members"; the use of similar props (of a fan and a letter); and "verbal echoes" (495). However, Kirschner claims that "the strongest hint of Wilde's presence" is to be found in the description of Mrs Hervey's lover, who is described as "the verse-writing editor of a 'society paper,' who has big front teeth, a 'thick-lipped smile,' an air of effeminacy, elegance and bulkiness" (496). Kirschner concludes that what he terms the "reminders of Wilde and his play" in "The Return" do not "seem polemical so much as a covert salute to a brilliant contemporary achievement" (496).

In "The Gothic Wilde" (1994), Donald Lawler explores Wilde's appropriation of "Gothic resources of expression, effects [and] genre-framing" (249) in *The Picture of Dorian Gray*, *Salome* and *The Sphinx*. He argues that the "foundations" of these three works "as decadent masterpieces seem dependent upon Wilde's decision to use the gothic as the most effective means for resolving artistically competing claims of the aesthetic, sexual, tragic, and supernatural aspects of works representing portions of his own inner life" (261–62). Lawler also sees Wilde's use of the gothic as "a brief, brilliant episode in an experimental phase of his career" (262).

Wilde's influence on the work of later writers has also been the subject of a number of studies. In "Re-Discovering Wilde in Travesties by Joyce and Stoppard" (1994) Gerd Rohmann traces what he terms the "intertextual relationships" between *The Importance of Being Earnest*, the "Circe" chapter in *Ulysses*, and Tom Stoppard's play *Travesties*. The link between the three works is Henry Carr. An amateur actor and employee of the British Consulate, Carr played the part of Algernon in a performance of *Earnest* in 1918 which was directed by Joyce. Rohmann describes how Joyce and Carr fell out and sued each other in the Zurich district court; Joyce lost, and took revenge through his characterization of "Private Carr" in *Ulysses*. These incidents in turn are the subject of Stoppard's *Travesties* where Carr appears as a senile madman. Rohmann's argument is that through Wilde both Joyce and Stoppard "take their literary revenge on Carr and philistinism" (345). His larger (if less secure) claim is that "Wilde's work and the legend of his life make modern and post-modern literature break boundaries between historical and fictional worlds" (346). In "Wilde's *The Importance of Being Earnest* and Stoppard's *Rosencrantz and Guildenstern are Dead*" (2000), Christopher S. Nassaar reminds us that Stoppard's line "The bad ended unhappily, the good unluckily. That is what tragedy means" derives from Miss Prism's observations on the fates of fictional characters. He also argues that the plays have a similar concern with the issues of free will and determinism. The audience's knowledge of the fate of Rosencrantz and Guildenstern (because of its familiarity with *Hamlet*) is mirrored by an audience's knowledge of Wilde's fate. A further reason for Stoppard to "echo" *The Importance of Being Earnest* is to be found in the fact that Wilde's play "blindly parodied determinism" (92). The relationship between Wilde and another group of twentieth-century writers is the subject of Neil Bartlett's "The Uses of Monotony: Repetition In The Language Of Oscar Wilde, Jean Genet, Edmund White and Juan Goytisolo" (1997).

The influence of Wilde on a very different sort of writer is the subject of Peter Musolf in "Bunburying and the Art of Kabuki: or, Wilde, Mishima and the Importance of Being a Sardine Seller" (1996). Musolf identifies what he sees as central themes in Wilde's work, especially that of the "deceitful artistic moulding of our world" (333), which determines how it is apprehended, and Wilde's sense of the fluidity of the individual ("what we would call a personal fiction, a creation both by a person and of a persona" [333]). Musolf sees similarities to these ideas in the work of the enigmatic twentieth-century Japanese writer Mishima. Indeed, noting Wilde's talk in 1882 of visiting Japan, he suggests that Japan catalysed Wilde's thought; in particular the "imagination's sovereignty over nature" (334). Musolf suggests that Mishima's 1954 kabuki play, *Iwashiuri no Hikiami* (*The Sardine Seller*) shares many concerns and themes of *The Importance of Being Earnest*—it is "a cross-cultural cousin" (335).

The intertextual relationship between Wilde and Mishima Yukio is the subject of James Raeside's "The Spirit is Willing but the Flesh is Strong: Mishima Yukio's *Kinjiki* and Oscar Wilde" (1999). He draws particular attention to the parallels between *Kinjiki* and *The Picture of Dorian Gray*, and to what he calls the "many implicit references" to Wilde in the novel (20). The piece will be of more interest to students of Japanese literature than to those wishing to understand Wilde. For more details of Wilde's transactions with Japanese culture, see Zhou Xiaoyi, "Oscar Wilde's Orientalism and late Nineteenth-Century European Consumer Culture" (1997); see also Jeff Nunokawa, "Oscar Wilde in Japan: Aestheticism, Orientalism, and the De-realization of the Homosexual" (1995).

4. vii. Thematic Studies

Peter Allan Dale's subtle, intelligent and densely argued essay, "Oscar Wilde: Crime and the 'Glorious Shapes of Art'" (1995) in the *Victorian Newsletter*, describes how for Wilde "criminality and artistry somehow complement one another." The thesis which his essay explores is that an understanding of "the congruity between art and crime" has a "bearing on the development of late-Victorian aestheticism" (1). For Wilde, according to Dale, the value of art was its ability to bring about self-realization; but Wilde considered that criminality possessed a "still deeper" ability to express "individuality" and his "need to tell stories about crime" (2) testified to that conviction. Dale contextualizes Wilde's fascination with crime in terms of an Oxford ideology of culture, which derived in part from Hegel, and which had an aesthetic as well as a political "form" (1). Dale then compares Wilde's views of art and crime with other (nineteenth- and twentieth-century) ways of modelling their relationship, including what he terms "the model . . . of *sublimation*," "the *transgressive* model," and Foucauldian theory (which, like Wilde's views, also derives from Hegel). Dale concludes that Wilde's Foucauldian-like understanding of art and crime allowed him to negotiate "a critical paradigm shift in the Victorian reading of Hegel" (4) which in turn implies "a shift in aesthetic theory" (4). That shift centred on embracing a more politicized understanding of the aesthetic as "an experience which energizes and validates the discontent (one may say the criminal discontent) within us" (4).

Talia Schaffer's "Fashioning Aestheticism by Aestheticizing Fashion: Wilde, Beerbohm and the Male Aesthetes' Sartorial Codes" (2000) takes up a topic broached in different ways by Sheila Stowell and Joel Kaplan in *Theatre and Fashion* (1994; discussed in 4. iv.). In an interesting and closely argued article, Schaffer contends that "Aesthetic fashion was the focus of late-Victorian attention because it so clearly displayed the anxieties, stresses, and formulations of the movement. It was a battlefield for competing voices within Aestheticism; it was a stage whereon the various gender notions of the movement could be displayed" (39). Schaffer goes on to suggest that the Aesthetes (especially Wilde) were condemned for effeminacy, principally because in their desire to "beautify everyday life, they moved into areas which historically had been associated with women" (40). Wilde in particular offered the possibility of a connoisseurship which would "frankly acknowledge the Aesthetic debt to women's culture"; as a consequence Wilde, especially as editor of the *Woman's World*, revealed himself to be a "grateful and appreciative inheritor" of that culture (41). Schaffer goes on to suggest that in "the Aesthetes' favorite genres . . . women were strong presences. . . . In both literature and culture, then, the male Aesthetes saw themselves as radical reformist outsiders invading a field which already belonged to women" (42). Schaffer maintains that in matters of dress, the Aesthetes "set out to reconnect dress with art, bypassing fashion altogether" (43), a project which changed, with "Wilde's fashion innovations cunningly [mediating] between women's culture and men's art theory"; Wilde "was implying that men's and women's spheres might be contiguous properties similar enough to contain nearly identical, interchangeable, commodities" (44).

Schaffer then compares Wilde's aestheticism with that of Max Beerbohm and with George Du Maurier's images of the Aesthete, concluding that "only Wilde was able to enjoy fashion wholeheartedly, perhaps because Wilde's alternative sexual activities already positioned him so far outside the traditional masculine role that he was more interested in challenging than in conforming to the rules of Victorian masculine propriety" (51). It is worth noting that Aestheticism, in Schaffer's argument, is a term which involves no problems of definition. So she can talk about "Aesthetic" men or "Aesthetic" fashion as if her frame of reference is obvious. Moreover she resists defining Aestheticism as a serious philosophical movement, derived from the work of, say, Pater, Ruskin and Swinburne, on the grounds that such a view marginalizes the importance of fashion. Whether or not this is true (and biographers of Pater invariably draw attention to his dress in the late 1860s) the fact that Schaffer's account largely ignores these figures limits its usefulness as an account of Aestheticism, rather than of fashion. Schaffer gives fuller account of

Aestheticism in *The Forgotten Female Aesthetes: Literary Culture in Late Victorian England* (2000). The aim of that book is to draw attention to "the female aesthetes whose critical and popular success made them formidable contemporaries" (2) to their more familiar male counterparts, including Wilde. The focus of Schaffer's study is the "world of women," what she terms the "missing half of aestheticism" (2). Nonetheless Wilde figures prominently in her discussion; for example, in chapter 4 she sees *The Picture of Dorian Gray* as an attempt by Wilde to take over and "masculinize" the aestheticism of Ouida (Marie Louise de la Ramée). A fuller knowledge of these female Aesthetes may change how we understand the gendering of late nineteenth-century literary culture and the novelty of male Aesthetes such as Wilde.

A study which has many points of connection with Schaffer's essay, and more particularly with her book, is Mary Warner Blanchard's *Oscar Wilde's America: Counter Culture in the Gilded Age* (1998). Blanchard's interest is in aspects of late nineteenth-century American Aestheticism, which she refers to as "a few modes—interior decoration, artistic dress, aesthetic icons—and a few figures—Wilde, and the four female aesthetic visionaries, [Candice] Wheeler, [Celia] Thaxter, [Mary Louise] McLaughlin, and [Maria Griswold] Van Rensselaer" (xv). Blanchard's principal concern is to recuperate the reputations of her four female Aesthetes. However, she has a long opening chapter on Wilde, whom she sees as defining a form of artistic life which inspired these women. In a manner very similar to Sarah Burns's account of Wilde's American lecture tour in *Inventing the Modern Artist* (1996), Blanchard argues that Wilde's appearance in America "introduced a daring new category of the masculine self, the 'invert,' a definition greeted cautiously by an interested America" (10). Blanchard documents reactions to Wilde in the American press, noting that in some parts of the United States he was seen as effeminate, but in the West he was "applauded as 'manly'" (27). Blanchard gives considerable attention to the ways in which Wilde's dress and his lectures on decoration contributed to new definitions of masculinity. Like Talia Schaffer, Blanchard shows how Wilde allowed masculinity to encompass spheres usually identified with femininity; these included a concern with fashion and house decoration. Like Sarah Burns, Blanchard suggests that at the end of the nineteenth century this new form of masculinity was superseded or replaced by one dependent upon a more traditional association between men and work, particularly the male world defined by a new professional class of business associations. One of the most interesting aspects of Blanchard's research is her re-characterization of Wilde's reception in the United States: he was, she claims, greeted "with tolerant good humour" (17). In contrast to the accounts of critics like Sandra Siegel, Blanchard views the famous homophobic attack on Wilde by Thomas Wentworth Higginson as untypical, in that it derived from Higginson's aberrant personality.

Wilde's humour is the subject of Mariano Baselga's "Oscar Wilde and the Semantic Mechanisms of Humour: The Satire of Social Habits" (1994); the specific question which is addressed is "how does Wilde work the meaning into humour and what has his social attitude to do with it?" (14). Baselga locates Wilde's humour in his "social rebelliousness" and proceeds to describe the variety of "linguistic forms" which Wilde's "social non-conformism" adopts (14–15). The essay's overall premise, derived from the work of linguists such as Dick Leith and Jean Athison, is that there is "a direct—though obviously not simple—relationship between linguistic and social usages" (17). Baselga's short essay concludes with the perhaps over-familiar observation that Wilde "uses semantic mechanisms to *deconstruct . . .* social habits" (20).

Gail Finney's altogether more ambitious essay, "Comparative Perspectives on Gender and Comedy: The Examples of Wilde, Hofmannsthal, and Ebner-Eschenbach" (1994) sets out to contrast British and American comedy with a number of German varieties. The Anglo-American tradition (a tradition which for Finney also includes French comic writing) is that of "male comedy" whose "ideology" is to support the established [male] order" (638–39). British and American women's comedy, by contrast, typically has a "destabilizing tendency" and rebels against the "conventions of male comedy" (639). Finney suggests that German comedy, produced by a regional rather than a national identity, resists closure, and thus "has much in common with women's comedy in British and American traditions" (641). Finney goes on to test her thesis by contrasting three plays "set at the turn of the century, all [treating] the aristocracy, and all [sharing] the classic comic plot" (643): *Earnest,* Hugo von Hofmannsthal's *Der Schwierige* (1921) and Marie von Ebner-Eschenbach's *Ohne Liebe* (1891), suggesting that the last play is concerned more with "sexual parity" than the "gender generalizations of Wilde and Hofmannsthal" (648). (Related to these last two pieces is Rolf Breuer, "Paradox in Oscar Wilde" [1993].)

In her short essay "The Once and Future Dandy" (1994), Jerusha McCormack draws attention to certain parallels between Wilde's dandyism and Mohandas Gandhi's political career. According to McCormack both Wilde and Gandhi "were from the margins of the British Empire. . . . Both took their careers from their sense of exclusion" (271). She further claims that the "strategy of protest" adopted by both figures centred on "a kind of ritual provocation that effectively hands over control to the audience" (271). McCormack's proposition that dandyism should be understood as a form of political dissent is explored more fully in her contribution to *Wilde the Irishman* (see 3. ii.).

The less than original aim of Bart Moore-Gilbert's essay, "From Miss Prism to Misprision: Oscar Wilde and Contemporary Theory" (1994), is to show how Wilde's critical essays—particularly "The Critic as Artist"—"anticipate the arguments" of reader-response theories proposed by modern theorists such as Wolfgang Iser and Stanley Fish (274). Moore-Gilbert's argument is that Wilde's "foundational attempt to turn the critical focus away from the text's relationship with author and world to its relationship with the reader . . . requires critical history to be rewritten" (281). Moore-Gilbert seems unaware that this has indeed been done (and many times).

Finally I conclude this section with a mention of Dariusz Pestka's somewhat idiosyncratic *Oscar Wilde: Between Aestheticism and Anticipation of Modernism*. The book is structured as a survey of Wilde's *oeuvre*; its overall thesis—that of Wilde as a transitional writer—is hardly novel.

| 5 |

Critical &
Introductory Studies

The amount of attention given in critical essays to Wilde's nationality and sexuality might lead one to think that they were the only new ways of conceptualizing his life and work in the 1990s. Although it is true that the past decade has not seen a large number of book-length studies of Wilde, those which have appeared have been surprisingly diverse, and many have been controversial in the claims they make. They range from attempts to redescribe Wilde's aesthetic in religious terms to an ambition to reassess him as a political theorist. There are also studies which provide new contextualizations, attempting to set his work against phenomena as disparate as a transnational European world of ideas or the day-to-day realities of the professional writer's trade in London in the 1890s. Despite these differences, however, all seem to share a common ambition—to describe a new framework within (or by means of) which the whole of the *oeuvre* can be reinterpreted and revalued. Of course, whether individual studies do in fact account for all Wilde's works is a moot point: certainly the utility of these monographs is likely to be measured in terms of their ability to explain satisfactorily the totality of Wilde's writing career.

◆ ◆ ◆

In *Art and Christhood: The Aesthetics of Oscar Wilde*, a work which appeared too late in 1993 to be included in *Oscar Wilde Revalued*, Guy Willoughby draws attention to what he calls the "veritable babel of opinions" which "have always surrounded" Wilde's *oeuvre*, "largely because few can agree on a single critical perspective of his work" (15). Willoughby's thesis is that "a coherent view" does emerge "if we consider a recurrent but neglected figure: that of Jesus Christ" (15). Such a forceful claim may strike the reader as odd, for many recent critics have indeed tried to establish "a coherent view" of Wilde—by highlighting, for example, his sexuality or his nationality as the animating principle behind his creativity. The price of such coherence, though, has inevitably been partiality or selectivity, a problem which Willoughby's book is aware of but not free from. Willoughby proceeds to discuss Wilde's "remodelled Jesus," claiming that Wilde's Christ "embodies a commitment to the community at large, and to an expanded organic view of self and society that derives from aesthetic appreciation, rather than moral instinct" (15–16). In other words, Willoughby claims to detect a serious ethical interest in what he calls the "public engagement" in Wilde's writing. The strengths of Willoughby's book lie in his close exegesis of individual works by Wilde. In the main these works are *The Happy Prince and Other Tales*, *A House of Pomegranates*, *The Soul of Man*, *The Picture of Dorian Gray*, *Salome*, "La Sainte Courtisane," "The Poems in Prose," *De Profundis* and *The Ballad of Reading Gaol*; in addition there is a short appendix which discusses *Poems* (1881). In its turn, however, it is precisely the selectivity of this list which reveals the weakness of Willoughby's argument. For a thesis which claims to produce "a coherent view" which "unifies [Wilde's] diverse literary achievement," the omission of Wilde's most successful and enduring works, the Society Comedies, speaks volumes. There is more than a suspicion here that Willoughby fails to admit any text which could provide counter evidence. So, for example, religion in the Society Comedies—whether it is misguided Puritanism, or enfeebled clergymen, or the spiritual inconsequentiality of baptism—is a constant target for Wilde's satire.

A second and more serious limitation to Willoughby's argument is a methodological one. He claims that his study has been informed by the insights of recent critical theory, but his arguments invariably employ a close engagement with his chosen texts which is reminiscent of the practices of New Criticism. This in turn leads to a failure to attend to the social and institutional aspects involved in literary production. Willoughby's analytical method tends to treat works written at different moments in time and for very different occasions as one continuous piece of text. Such a practice leads to a bibliographical carelessness which tells its own story. For example, Willoughby talks of "the utopian *Soul of Man Under Socialism* (1891) . . . the apologetic *De Profundis* (1897) . . . [and] *La Saint Courtisane* (1892–4)." The errors here are as follows: there is no work called *Soul of Man Under Socialism*; rather there is an essay of 1891, "The Soul of Man Under Socialism," and a book of 1895 entitled *The Soul of Man*. There is no work published in 1897 called *De Profundis*; rather there are Ross's two abridged works of this name (1905 and 1908) and Wilde's full letter to Douglas which was published by Rupert Hart-Davis in 1962 (but not under the title *De Profundis*). Even the manuscript which Hart-Davis published cannot be dated with certainty to 1897. *La Saint Courtisane* is misspelt (it should be *La Sainte Courtisane*). Moreover it is by no means clear that it was begun in 1892; certainly it was not finished in 1894. Willoughby's later confusing description of it as a "near-complete fragment" (87) obscures the complexities of the relationship between the extant manuscript (in the Clark Library) and the provenance of the text printed by Ross which is the base text for the 1966 Collins edition used by Willoughby. None of them can be described as "near-complete."

One of the reasons why critics have found it so difficult to explain Wilde's *oeuvre* in terms of any single and coherent set of ambitions is precisely because his works were produced under a wide variety of quite distinct social and commercial pressures and were addressed to very different sorts of audiences. Of course if this information is ignored—that is, if one overlooks the material reasons why Wilde wrote as he did—and if one is selective in one's choice of textual examples, then coherence and unity are easily contrived. (It is worth noting that a similar limitation can be seen in Julia Prewitt Brown's study, discussed below.) Finally, Willoughby's bibliographical carelessness has led him to compile a list of "the writings that have been of use in the making of the book" which is not to be trusted. It is easy to see how a typographical error can change the date of the publication of Mason's bibliography, turn the *Dalhousie Review* into an improbable *Dolhousie Review*, or almost convert J. E. Chamberlin into one of Wilde's favourite red Burgundies ("Chambertin"); but some errors are of scholarship, not typography.

Julia Prewitt Brown's interest in *Cosmopolitan Criticism* (1997) is similar to that of Willoughby in that she too is concerned to re-describe Wilde's aesthetics, and she once again concentrates on the relationship of art to life in his works. Unlike Willoughby, however, Brown contextualizes Wilde's ideas in terms of a nineteenth-century continental (European) philosophical tradition, rather than in rela-tion to Christ or religion. Much more alert to recent trends in Wilde scholarship, she aims to correct what she sees as an over-materialist bias in modern accounts of Wilde, particularly those associated with the studies of Gagnier (1986) and Dollimore (1991). The intellectual tradition Brown describes includes Schiller, Carlyle, Ruskin, and Baudelaire; moreover she sees important analogues for Wilde's sense of the interrelatedness of the ethical and the aesthetic in the work of European contemporaries such as Kierkegaard (in *Either/Or*) and Ni-etzsche. (It is worth stressing that *Either/Or* can only be an analogue, not an influence, because although it was published in 1843, years be-fore Wilde began his career, it was not translated until forty years af-ter his death (1944). Similarly there is no evidence for Wilde engaging with Nietzsche's work.) In Brown's reading, the goal of Wilde's intel-lectual journey is a new accommodation of the aesthetic and the ethi-cal, the opposition of which she sees as a fundamental characteristic of nineteenth-century British intellectual life. This revaluation of Wilde has important consequences for understanding the shape of the *oeuvre*. For example, it gives a central role to material not published in Wilde's lifetime, his first and last works, the *Oxford Notebooks* and *De Profundis* (again like Willoughby, at the expense of the Soci-ety Comedies). According to Brown, the *Notebooks* indicate Wilde's early sense of the importance of engaging with "the incapacity of the individual [nineteenth-century] systems themselves to integrate both ethical and aesthetic experience" (36); while *De Profundis* be-comes a philosophical, rather than an autobiographical piece (or in-deed a letter to a lover).

Brown's study is indebted both to the scholarship and ambitions of Philip E. Smith's and Michael S. Helfand's edition of the *Oxford Notebooks* (1989). Smith and Helfand also described Wilde as an in-tellectual, engaging with an eclectic tradition of philosophical thought and contemporary scientific writing, including the work of Hegel, Spencer, Thomas Huxley, John Tyndall, Henry Buckle, and W. E. H. Lecky. They see in Wilde's undergraduate notes on these writers a set of intellectual concerns which animate the rest of the *oeuvre*. Brown also seeks to make connections between Wilde's earlier writing and the rest of the *oeuvre*, although she describes a different set of interests from those seen by Smith and Helfand, and she also takes issue with their claim that Wilde achieved an intellectual "synthesis" of his diverse reading. Brown argues that "throughout his career Wilde maintained a paradoxical interrelatedness of opposites" (xv). In some ways the overall concept of Brown's study is reminiscent of an older tradition of Wilde scholarship, which located his work in relation to Ruskin, Arnold, and Pater. In extending the range of Wilde's intellectual interests, she attempts to deepen and strengthen our understanding of Wilde as a serious philosophical thinker. Like Willoughby, however, Brown's refusal to engage more than glancingly with other accounts of Wilde will lessen the appeal of her book for some readers: so it would be interesting to see how Wilde the "cosmopolitan critic" is compatible with the newly emerged "Irish Wilde."

Brown also shares with Willoughby (and indeed with Smith and Helfand) a methodology which erases crucial distinctions between works and between different kinds of works. For example, the textual condition of the undergraduate notebooks, presumably never intended to be read by anyone other than Wilde, is wholly distinct from that of "The Decay of Lying" (written to commission for the *Nineteenth Century*), and both of these are different again from *De Profundis* (written in part as a semi-private letter). Yet Brown can see all three pieces in terms of a continuing engagement with her idea of an intellectual cosmopolitanism. Perhaps the fundamental disappointment of her book is Brown's failure to *engage* with her opening premise, that material accounts of Wilde diminish our sense of him as a serious intellectual. If Brown is correct, then the Wilde she describes is deeply incompatible with the consumerist Wilde who emerges from recent accounts of the materiality of his texts. It would be refreshing if some future study attempted to reconcile these opposed views, to show how and whether Brown's "idealist" Wilde can be made to confirm what we know about how he wrote his works, and who he wrote them for.

Jody Price's *"A Map of Utopia": Oscar Wilde's Theory for Social Transformation* (1996) argues for Wilde's importance as a political theorist. She suggests that some of his views, particularly the idea of self-realization, anticipate late twentieth-century theories of social change. Price concentrates on Wilde's concept of individualism which, she argues, is distinguished from other earlier concepts by positing a form of self-realization which also involves a connectedness with other individuals. Price examines Wilde's attitudes towards consumerism, suggesting that his aestheticism—the separation of art and utility—provides an alternative realm of cultural value. In the course of her study, Wilde's works are read rather programmatically; there are also some difficulties with her overdependence upon "The Soul of Man Under Socialism," and her apparent lack of sensitivity to its irony. Perhaps the major limitation of Price's book, however, is her failure to connect properly Wilde's thesis about the individual with the whole range of contemporary political thought, particularly late nineteenth-century individualist pressure groups, whose far-right politics have many similarities with Wilde's position, but which are today considered to be an historical embarrassment. In its turn, this limitation leads Price, like George Woodcock before her in his study *Anarchism* (1962), to overstate Wilde's influence on twentieth-century political thought. (See also George Woodcock, *Oscar Wilde: The Double Image* [1989].)

Another but very different attempt to characterize Wilde as a political writer also appeared in 1996—Sos Eltis's *Revising Wilde: Society and Subversion in the Plays of Oscar Wilde*. Unlike Price, Eltis concentrates on Wilde's dramatic works; by examining various drafts of selected plays, she attempts to show that "Wilde's revisions carefully drew his texts away from his conventional origins, transforming them from derivative imitations of the plays on which they were modelled into far more subtle and subversive works" (4). Her opening chapter attempts to establish Wilde's political beliefs as "anarchist, socialist, and feminist" (6): she draws mainly upon his work for the *Woman's World* and (like Price) upon "The Soul of Man Under Socialism." Subsequent chapters go on to describe how these politics are progressively worked into *Vera*, *Lady Windermere's Fan*, *A Woman of No Importance*, *An Ideal Husband* and *The Importance of Being Earnest*. So, for example, Eltis can claim that in the last of these works "Wilde created the perfect dramatic form for his philosophy. Within a deceptively familiar farcical structure, he not only smuggled in smart satirical criticism of his society and its mores, he also gave imaginative life to his perfect anarchist state" (199).

Eltis's study was the first attempt to synthesize the local and individual work of textual editors of Wilde's dramas into an overall thesis about his creativity. Although her ambition is to be lauded, the actual results of her work have a number of difficulties and drawbacks. First, and as many reviewers pointed out, her account of a subversive politics fits ill with what theatre historians have uncovered about the commercial nature of late nineteenth-century theatrical institutions and the power-relationships between Wilde and his managers (see for example, Kaplan on Wilde and Beerbohm Tree and on Wilde and Alexander [1994 and 1992; discussed in 4. iv.]). In addition her general analysis of the late nineteenth-century political milieu is brief and as a result often naive. Second, Eltis's interpretation of Wilde's process of revision through the various drafts of his plays tends to obscure (at times perhaps misrepresent) the complexities of the textual evidence—that, for example, it is extremely difficult to determine the order of various drafts (to establish a stemma), and therefore it is unwise to take for granted a teleological process of textual development. It is certainly not a development to be found anywhere else in the *oeuvre*—there is no evidence, for example, that the book version of *Dorian Gray*, or the essays in *Intentions*, were revised to make them more radical. The most disappointing aspect of the book, however, is its selectivity. A consideration of *The Duchess of Padua* and *Salome*, not to mention Wilde's unfinished drafts and scenarios, would give us a very different understanding of his ambitions as a dramatist. So, for example, would it be possible to describe Wilde's revisions of *The Duchess of Padua* for Lawrence Barrett's American production as being politically driven? Or, perhaps more pertinently, what would Eltis make of the fact that in the winter of 1891, when he was supposed to be finishing *Lady Windermere's Fan*, Wilde was actually still trying to sell *Padua* to uninterested English managers. There is a suspicion that Eltis's reluctance to consider these two works may be because they do not yet exist in scholarly editions, and such knowledge of their textual conditions that we do possess tends to undermine her argument about Wilde's political use of the theatre.

Like his essays discussed in 4. iii., Lawrence Danson's *Wilde's Intentions: The Artist in his Criticism* (1997) is written with elegance and wit, and is uncluttered with the jargon of so much contemporary (and theoretically-driven) criticism. It is as if Danson wishes his style to emulate the urbanity of his subject. While this makes for a very readable book, the eschewing of theory has demanded a price. Often Danson is naive about the premises of his arguments: his notion of a simple distinction between text and context is hard to sustain, especially when his subject-matter, the essays which form *Intentions*, had their origins in the periodical press, exactly that genre which so persistently dissolves the distinction. Equally difficult is the apparently arbitrary manner in which the notion of context is limited. Much of the contextual material which Danson does refer to is far from new, and some of it (particularly Wilde's use of Arnold and Pater) is rather tired. Furthermore, if Arnold and Pater are Wilde's "context," then why not more of Spencer (who is mentioned by Danson only twice), of Darwin (who appears just once), or of Hegel, Kant, Mill, Schiller (none of whom are given any mention). Other critics have devoted book-length studies to the influence of these writers on Wilde's social and art-criticism, but without making any claims to being definitive. Another surprising *lacuna* in Danson's book (and his essays) is the omission of any detailed account of the journalistic context of Wilde's work, despite the fact that critics such as Stokes (1997) have insisted that Wilde's periodical publications drew heavily on other contemporary journalism. Danson's book and essays are an entertaining introduction to Wilde's critical thought, but provide few new insights for the scholar or researcher.

In *Oscar Wilde: The Critic as Humanist* (1999), Bruce Bashford attempts to reassess Wilde's role as a critical thinker and in the process develops ideas he first explored in a number of essays written in the late 1970s and 1980s (for an account of which, see *Oscar Wilde Revalued*, 182, 184, 191, and 200). His declared aim is "to place Wilde in a tradition of interpretive theory represented by a thinker like Dilthey" (21). The scope of Bashford's study is therefore wider than that of Danson in that he does not restrict himself solely to the critical essays. Rather the figure of Wilde as a critical theorist is detected in works as early as "The Rise of Historical Criticism," an undergraduate essay, and as late as *De Profundis*. In addition to these two works, Bashford's book contains chapters on "The Portrait of Mr W. H." and the critical dialogues. He also devotes chapters not to humanism in general but to Wilde's particular brand of it, a decision that some readers might regret. A much greater disappointment is Bashford's decision not to engage with the most recent accounts of Wilde as a critic. In a note to the introduction, Bashford declares that "in order to declare my project done at last, I had at a certain point to simply ignore further scholarship on Wilde" (161). It is for this reason, Bashford claims, that Danson's and Brown's monographs are not discussed. In a study which sets out to rework ideas which have been in gestation for twenty years, such a decision will be regretted as a missed opportunity.

A book which examines Wilde's writing practices is Josephine M. Guy and my *Oscar Wilde's Profession: Writing and the Culture Industry in the Late Nineteenth Century* (2000). Drawing on new evidence about Wilde's earnings, contracts, and negotiations with publishers and theatre managers, we document the material aspects of Wilde's creativity and argue that he was much more complicit with than critical of the emergent consumerism of the time, and that his career was shaped in significant ways by the various professionals with whom he worked. We then use this information to examine Wilde's methods of composition; in particular, we give a new interpretation of Wilde's habit of plagiarism and self-plagiarism and also question critical assumptions about how and why he revised. *Oscar Wilde's Profession* takes evidence from across Wilde's *oeuvre* in an attempt to generate a coherent and comprehensive thesis about his creativity, one which can encompass the various and often contradictory aspects of his writing.

Michael Patrick Gillespie's study, *Oscar Wilde and the Poetics of Ambiguity* (1996), takes up some of the issues broached in his booklength account of *The Picture of Dorian Gray* in the Twayne Masterworks series and some periodical articles (see 4. v.). There Gillespie proposed that Wilde's novel was one capable of "fostering multiple interpretations." In his later book this polyvocality is a quality seen in all of Wilde's *oeuvre*. In keeping with Wilde's own critical prescriptions, it produces the "greatest amount of pleasure" in the work. In his study of *Dorian Gray*, Gillespie also attended to what he called "the extratextual milieu," the literary and cultural forces which shaped the novel. In his later book, this idea too is extended to cover the *oeuvre*. Gillespie gives considerable importance to *Salome*. Like Brad Bucknell (1993; discussed in 4. iv.) he sees the indeterminacy of that play arising from an interplay between text and illustrations (on this topic, see also Robert Schweik [1994] and Richard Allen Cave [1994]; both these pieces are also discussed in 4. iv.).

In keeping with a number of other recent studies, Gillespie's Wilde is a writer remarkably responsive to public taste, especially in his first three West End plays. Such an observation is not particularly novel (Gillespie, for example, notes the pioneering work of Kerry Powell who identified the importance of Wilde's audiences for understanding his theatrical output.) It is also worth observing that there is some tension between the Wilde who writes polyvocal texts and the Wilde who writes in order to please the tastes of particular audiences. It is not obvious how works with plural meanings could be marketed.

Karl Beckson's survey of 1890s British metropolitan culture, *London in the 1890s* (1992, but too late to be included in *Oscar Wilde Revalued*), contains, as one might expect, a significant number of references to Wilde; in the index there are as many references to him as there are to W. B. Yeats, Arthur Symons and George Bernard Shaw; indeed Wilde has almost as many as London itself does. The subtitle of Beckson's work is "A Cultural History," and he includes chapters on socialist and anarchist politics, prostitution, "empire builders and destroyers," and the New Woman. Nonetheless "culture" itself is mainly understood as referring to what some might wish to call "high" culture—the Rhymers' Club, the New Drama, Whistler, Wagner, and so on. Beckson's account is, as one would expect, supported by an immensely detailed knowledge of the period, and he also carefully traces the origins of those "high" cultural practices of the 1890s back to the 1880s and 1870s and to their European equivalents and antecedents. Wilde figures most prominently in Beckson's chapters entitled "The New Drama," "Love in Earnest: The Importance of Being Uranian," "Trials and Tribulations" and "Whistler, the Fantastic Butterfly." More importantly, however, Wilde is seen as the key transitional figure between the literary culture of the nineteenth and twentieth centuries:

> As public symbol and secret cipher by which the age can be read, he converted to Roman Catholicism on his death bed while in a semi-comatose state, an admirer of the beauty and pageantry of its rituals. Modernist in his aesthetic criticism and attitudes, though essentially traditional in his use of literary forms . . . Wilde sought to transform Victorian culture. A serious dandy who performed before a trivial audience, he remains the decade's tragic figure who sensed the underlying rot of civilization. (379)

This view of Wilde is a familiar one, and the most useful function of Beckson's history for students will be his contextualization of Wilde in relation to the "high" literary culture of some of his contemporaries. On the other hand, researchers into Wilde will want to supplement the information in Beckson's book with those accounts (described in 3. iii.) which emphasize Wilde's transactions with popular culture and an emergent consumerism. A cultural history which focuses on late nineteenth-century Paris rather than London is David Sweetman's *Explosive Acts: Toulouse-Lautrec, Oscar Wilde, Félix Fénéon, and the Art and Anarchy of the Fin de Siècle* (2000). Toulouse-Lautrec is the main focus of the study, but Wilde also figures as one of the extravagant personalities which Sweetman sees characterizing the period.

Anne Varty's *A Preface to Oscar Wilde* (1998) is a thoroughly impressive piece of work. Its target audience is similar to that of Peter Raby's *Cambridge Companion* (1997; discussed in 7. iii.), and in many ways it fulfils better the remit of that collection—that is, Varty's single voice ironically gives a more liberating sense of the diversity and challenges in Wilde's *oeuvre* than the many voices in Raby's volume do. It also represents an improvement on all other introductory accounts of Wilde, including Donald H. Ericksen's 1977 study *Oscar Wilde* (for Twayne), John Stokes's *Oscar Wilde* (1978) in the British Council's Writers and their Works series, and Peter Raby's introductory account for Cambridge University Press, *Oscar Wilde* (1988). Varty's volume is organized in four parts. The first, entitled "The Writer and his Setting," begins with a chronology of the main details of Wilde's life tied to a brief chronicle of other social, cultural, and political events which broadly relate to Wilde's work. Wisely, Varty does not attempt to give the reader a "potted" biography or a cultural survey; instead she focuses on four issues which she sees affecting the ways in which we read Wilde's work: his family life, Ireland, homosexuality, and what she terms "the myth of Wilde." The second and third sections give short critical introductions to each of the works. In her arrangement of this material, however, there are some surprises. By including in her section on "Critical Writings" Wilde's lectures, journalism, as well as the "The Soul of Man Under Socialism" and *Intentions*, Varty gives the reader a sense of the range of Wilde's critical output as well as the populist origins of the more famous pieces. A short section on "Theatre Practice and Innovation" provides a useful connection between the journalist and the dramatist, as it reminds readers that Wilde was an informed theatre-goer and reviewer well before he was a successful playwright. There are also sections on "Poetry" and "Short Fiction" (in which Varty usefully distinguishes between the more literary ambitions of what she calls Wilde's "aesthetic prose"—such as "The Fisherman and his Soul"—and the more explicitly commercial "Newspaper Fiction," such as *Lord Arthur Savile's Crime and Other Stories*). These are followed by discussions of *Dorian Gray*, *Salome* (which is examined both in relation to Symbolist theatre and Wilde's earlier interest in Decadent themes and exotic subjects), what Varty calls the "Social Comedies," and a section entitled "Letters" (which includes *De Profundis*). The fourth part of the book is a reference section which includes short accounts of Wilde's circle, a gazetteer, a very brief (and unfortunately incomplete) account of the whereabouts of the manuscripts, a glossary of literary terms, and a highly selective but annotated list of suggestions for further reading.

Introductory accounts invariably suffer from two limitations— those of space and of tone. Varty's volume is inevitably constrained by the remit of the series to which she contributes. As a consequence some of her sections are extremely brief, and some of the reference material is too compressed to be of much practical use. (For example, the student interested in locating Wilde's manuscripts will not be given much help in this book; likewise a student unfamiliar with literary-critical terminology will need a much fuller guide than the definitions which Varty provides.) On the other hand, she writes with poise and intelligence and her book, though scholarly, has both elegance and clarity. Moreover, her lucid and entertaining reading of individual works is designed to open them up, to invite the student to think about them further. In this respect *A Preface to Oscar Wilde*, though of limited use to the research student, is nonetheless probably the best introduction available for an undergraduate and general readership.

Finally it is worth mentioning a reprint of Jonathan Goodman's *The Oscar Wilde File* (1996; see *Oscar Wilde Revalued*, 17). Advertised to appear in 2000, but too late to be inspected, is Neil Sammells's *Wilde Style: The Plays and Prose of Oscar Wilde*, in Longman's Studies in Eighteen- and Nineteenth-Century Literature series.

| 6 |

Editions

6. i. Collections

In *Oscar Wilde Revalued* I noted that there was still not a satisfactory complete edition of Wilde and although a full edition had been commissioned it was "at least three years in the future" (201). That edition was the Oxford English Texts Complete Works. Three years proved to be an optimistic prediction. Nevertheless the first volume, *Poems and Poems in Prose* (discussed in 6. ii.), appeared in 2000, and successive volumes will follow at regular intervals.

In the meantime, the Collins edition of the *Complete Works*, which first appeared as long ago as 1948, is the nearest we have to a collected edition. That first volume was edited by G. F. Maine; a second edition was produced in 1966 with an introduction by Vyvyan Holland. Its rationale seems to have been to provide the general reader with a fuller account of the *oeuvre*. Thus the 1966 edition included several poems (such as "Chorus of Cloud Maidens" and "Lotus Leaves") which were not to be found in Maine's edition, as well as the four-act version of *The Importance of Earnest*. In 1994 Merlin Holland produced a revised edition, with various sections edited by Holland, Owen Dudley Edwards, Terence Brown and Declan Kiberd. This revised edition is the fullest to date, and was reprinted as a centennial edition in 1999. It prints further new material: fifteen "new" poems are included, together with a much expanded section on Wilde's journalism. Holland argues in his introduction to this last section that publishers and editors have tended to sell Wilde short by persisting in reproducing only the most popular works: "Wilde at his most thought-provoking," Holland claims, "has not been in demand" (907). By "thought-provoking" Holland is referring to the serious journalism and letters where he claims the reader can find the "unadorned Wilde" (907). What is immediately striking about all the Collins editions is their growing ambition to get closer to a complete Wilde, when the notion of completeness is defined by current trends in criticism. As Holland makes clear, the latest additions to the Collins Wilde reflect an academic emphasis on his role as a professional writer rather than simply an entertainer. In addition, the 1994 Collins also contains lively and intelligent introductions; so, for example, attention is given not only to the professional journalist, but also to Wilde's Irishness. Nonetheless, the Collins edition has two short-comings: the absence of explanatory notes and also a total silence about the rationale for its choices of copy-text. In some cases we can make informed guesses about the last set of choices—as with the decision by Terence Brown to print the four-act version of *The Importance of Being Earnest*. Generally, though, it remains true that the editorial problems presented by the fact that some of Wilde's works exist in competing versions are simply ignored.

By contrast, Anthony Fothergill's *Plays, Prose Writings and Poems* (1996) does provide explanatory annotation, most of which is helpful and some of which is excellent; however it is achieved at the expense of the comprehensiveness of the Collins edition. More importantly, the problems of copy-text are once again not satisfactorily explained. In *The Oscar Wilde Anthology* (2000), Merlin Holland makes a selection of what he judges to be the most enduring of his grandfather's literary achievements. Isobel Murray's anthology, *Oscar Wilde—The Major Works* (2000, but not available for examination at the time of writing) promises to be a similar sort of volume.

Collections of Wilde's writing organized by genre have generally given the reader more information than those which aim at completeness. Peter Raby's volume of Wilde's best-known plays (*Lady Windermere's Fan, Salome, A Woman of No Importance, An Ideal Husband* and *The Importance of Being Earnest*) was published in Oxford University Press's Drama In World's Classics series in 1995. Raby prints the first published edition of each play and the English text of *Salome*. There is no systematic account of textual variants; however Raby draws upon the work of the editors of the New Mermaid editions in order to give alternative readings "where these are judged to clarify textual or performance aspects" (xxvi). The volume contains a useful introduction and bibliography; moreover the explanatory notes are economical but informative. In addition Raby prints in full the first scenario for *The Importance of Being Earnest*, a document which he himself discovered in the archives of the Clark Library. At £4.99 (or $6.95) the anthology is very reasonably priced, and is a candidate to be considered as one of the best volumes of plays for the student market.

In 2000 Richard Allen Cave edited a collection, *The Importance of Being Earnest and Other Plays*, which will be a strong competitor for that same market. In addition to printing, like Raby, *Lady Windermere's Fan, Salome, A Woman of No Importance, An Ideal Husband* and *The Importance of Being Earnest*, Cave also includes *A Florentine Tragedy*, his copy-text for this last work being Ross's 1908 edition. The copy-text for *Salome* is the 1894 Bodley Head edition. The textual situation with the other plays is a little less clear. Cave claims to have used as his "base-text" those printed in the old (1954) Penguin edition which were set from Ross. Cave, though, corrects these texts "by collating them against the texts published in the New Mermaid Series" (xxvii). Unfortunately in his notes, Cave does not indicate when he has preferred the New Mermaid reading. Likewise, when he discusses variants from the manuscript and theatre drafts, he does not indicate their precise source, nor indeed who was responsible for those changes. Cave does give a short history of the composition of each play; however these are inaccurate in some details. For example, he claims (apropos of *Earnest*) that Wilde "had contracted himself to George Alexander . . . for an advance of £150 in Summer 1894, after submitting a detailed outline of the plot in four acts" (419). As the *Letters* reveal, this detail is incorrect; as importantly, it glosses over the complexities of Wilde's relationship with Alexander, all of which are available in the Donohue edition of *Earnest* which Cave cites in his bibliography. Similarly, with *A Woman of No Importance*, he claims that "six manuscript or typescript draft versions of the play are extant, including the licensing copy" (388). Cave seems to have arrived at this figure by consulting the grid of versions printed in the first New Mermaid edition of the play (in *Two Society Comedies* [1983]). Yet the explanation of that grid identifies a further version which the editors were unable to consult, as well as multiple copies of some drafts of Act II (held at the Harry Ransom Humanities Research Center in Texas). In addition in 1987 the New Mermaid editors drew attention to many further drafts of the play in the Herbert Tree Collection in the University of Bristol; in turn these were noted in the account of the stemma in the 1993 revised New Mermaid edition of *A Woman of No Importance*. It is not surprising that a popular edition is not based on primary research, but it is a little disappointing that Cave has not made the best use of the editorial work he has drawn upon.

Cave's introduction focuses on Wilde's stage-craft, a topic which he discusses in a number of recent critical essays (see 4. iv.). This interest is also to be seen in the explanatory notes. As well as identifying nuances of social etiquette, Cave frequently comments on the significance of stage directions to Wilde's plotting and characterization. However, as with Cave's handling of the textual genesis of the plays, his discussion of stage directions tends to blur the distinction between those to be found in the reading texts (published by the Bodley Head and Leonard Smithers), and those from performance texts, which were often the result of collaboration or an actor-manager's intervention. As a result, the reader is given a slightly misleading view of the circumstances of Wilde's composing habits. These caveats aside, Cave's edition will be useful to the student reader.

In *Oscar Wilde: Complete Short Fiction* (1994), I print and annotate the first book-versions of Wilde's three volumes of short stories (*The Happy Prince and Other Tales* (1888), *A House of Pomegranates* (1891), and *Lord Arthur Savile's Crime and Other Stories* (1891). Also printed are the Blackwood's version of "The Portrait of Mr W. H." (1889), and the six published "Poems in Prose" from *The Fortnightly Review* in 1894. Apart from an ambition for comprehensiveness, the argument for including these last works rests on their generically anomalous status—that they can all be read as prose fictions. Also printed as appendices are the fragment of an unfinished prose poem ("Elder-tree") and Robert Ross's text of "For Love of the King." Although the provenance of this last piece is uncertain, it shares some interesting stylistic similarities with the Wilde canon. Since the publication of this edition, the reasons for Wilde's use of the subtitle of "The Canterville Ghost" have been explained (see Guy, 1998; discussed in 4. vi.). Also since its publication, private correspondence from Mrs M. Adams to the editor has provided information about the biography of the dedicatee of "The Birthday of the Infanta" in *A House of Pomegranates*, "Mrs William H. Grenfell, of Taplow

Court." Taplow Court, in Buckinghamshire, was the residence of Mrs Grenfell and her husband (that is, Lord and Lady Desborough), who in turn were members of a group calling itself "The Souls." Wilde (and Rudyard Kipling) were frequent visitors to Taplow Court. (See Jane Abdy and Charlotte Gere, *The Souls* [London: Sidgwick and Jackson, 1984]; and Angela Lambert, *Unquiet Souls* [London: Macmillan, 1984].)

To coincide with the release of the Brian Gilbert film *Wilde* in 1997, Penguin Books published a short anthology of Wilde's "wit and wisdom" under the title *Nothing . . . Except My Genius* (the introductory essay by Stephen Fry, which reflects on his portrayal of Wilde in the film, as well as on his own homosexuality, is usefully read alongside Robert Tanitch's *Oscar Wilde on Stage and Screen*; see 7. iv.). A similar volume is Karl Beckson's anthology *I Can Resist Everything Except Temptation and Other Quotations from Oscar Wilde* (1996), which arranges quotations alphabetically by subject.

6. ii. *Individual Works*

The titles of the New Mermaid editions of the society comedies were bought from their original publishers, Ernest Benn, by A. and C. Black some years ago and the new publishers have been revising some titles in the series. *A Woman of No Importance* and *An Ideal Husband*, originally published together as *Two Society Comedies*, were issued separately with new and updated introductory material in 1993. A new edition of *Lady Windermere's Fan* was published in 1999. In all three cases, however, the economics of academic publishing has dictated that the texts themselves remain substantially the same. The main consequence of this state of affairs is that the stemmata of the plays described in the textual apparatus—particularly of *A Woman of No Importance*—is not as full as it could or should be. The same is true of the New Mermaid edition of *The Importance of Being Earnest*, which (because of the play's popularity) has gone through a number of new impressions over the past twenty years. With the exception of *Earnest*, the New Mermaid editions of Wilde are probably still the best available, but they are inevitably beginning to show their age: the scholarly apparatus and explanatory annotation of Joseph Donohue's (with Ruth Berggren) 1995 edition of *The*

Importance of Being Earnest in most ways supersedes that contained in Jackson's edition.

It should be noted, however, that Donohue's ambition was different from that of the New Mermaids' editor, in that he aimed to reconstruct the text of the first performance, and not to reproduce Leonard Smithers's 1899 reading text. This endeavour in its turn has highlighted some particular problems of editing and annotation. The problem of copy-text is discussed at length by Donohue in the introduction and apparatus, and in the process he gives the fullest account available of the commissioning, composition and staging of the play. He is admirably transparent in the way he tries to "deal evenhandedly with [the] varying claims to authority" of the texts he has used, and lists very clearly the "set of principles" which inform his choices (93). Donohue also attempts to describe and justify the principles which inform the extensive annotation in his edition. Indeed it is the amount and detail of the annotated material which is the most striking feature of his volume: on occasions there can be as much as seven columns of notes to explain ten short lines of text. For example, Algernon's speech in Act I about Jack's name and address generates around 2,500 words of commentary. Such profusion of information inevitably raises questions. First, there is the issue of editorial display: practically this has been resolved by setting explanatory notes in a column beside a (thinner) column of text and textual notes. The result, though, is to give a much greater prominence to the annotation than to the text, to the extent that the reading experience is similar to that produced by a medieval manuscript in which the marginal gloss has more significance than the text being explained. Second, there are questions about Donohue's criteria of relevance. He is of course aware of the issues involved, but there are some contradictions in the rationale he gives in the preface. Donohue talks of "context" as something "not fixed" and not "easily determined"—that it is produced by the annotator's sense of the function of his edition, that it is "purpose-shaped" (12). On the other hand, however, Donohue insists that there is a body of "fundamental knowledge" which the annotator has to convey. Donohue seems to be labouring a distinction between annotation which is necessary for some basic ("fundamental") understanding of a text, and annotation which opens it up. He tries to use this distinction to defend the superabundance of his notes:

Most annotations that impart basic information about a subject contain additional material of a more sophisticated, recondite, or anecdotal nature that may shield them from the charge of pedantry and perhaps shed on the relevant text an uncommon light. Other notes adduce fresh perspectives on the familiar or even enter on a new and unknown territory. (12)

Not all editors and annotators will be persuaded by this argument, particularly when it is applied to the understanding of a performance text. Setting aside the difficulties posed by the diversity of the audiences for Wilde's play and therefore their different cultural knowledge and expectations, there is a further difficulty in recovering both the nature of that audience's contemporary knowledge, as well as which elements of it contributed to their experience of the play. Not surprisingly, then, there is room for considerable debate about the relevance of much of Donohue's commentary. The annotation to the opening stage direction—"*Discovered: LANE arranging afternoon tea on table . . .*" (103)—provides a good example. Donohue glosses the direction by an extensive quotation from an 1877 manual entry on tea services, which begins as follows:

The tea services of modern times are very different to those in use some years ago. In the days when tea was regarded as an expensive luxury the cups were very small and narrow in shape, and were made without handles. Now that the exorbitant duty on tea has been abolished, and it may be obtained at a reasonable rate, the cups are made of comparatively large size and are conveniently shaped. . . . (103)

The appropriateness of an 1877 manual to an 1895 theatrical performance is not immediately obvious. The gloss goes on to refer the reader to two illustrations of contemporary advertisements for tea sets and to a recipe for Queen's tea cakes, all of which are reproduced much later in Donohue's volume (275, 276, 279). Once again it is difficult to see how any of this information contributes to our understanding of the way in which a contemporary audience would have experienced Lane's arrangement of a tea-table on the stage: would that first-night audience have noticed (or indeed have been able to see) whether the tea service was French porcelain from Harrods or Prince's Plate from Mappin and Webb (as in Donohue's reproduced advertisements)? And who in the audience would have known (or cared about) the recipes for Queen's tea cakes? Ironically, the elaborate note misses one of the more important signifiers of Lane's actions. It allows us to locate immediately the time of the action—tea-time (as we are told some lines later), an elaborate afternoon ritual, well known to contemporary audiences but now lost to some younger British and most American readers.

These caveats do not detract from the fascination of many of the details of Donohue's annotation. Taken together they constitute an intriguing account of upper middle-class domestic British culture of the 1890s. Whether such detail is necessary for a "fundamental" understanding of the play, though, and whether it does produce "fresh perspectives" are moot points. In Donohue's defence, however, it needs to be acknowledged that the subjective nature of explanatory annotation means that its range will always be open to dispute. On the other hand, the sheer volume of Donohue's material does lend support to his fear, expressed in the Preface, that his edition is "breaking a butterfly upon a wheel" (12).

Creation Books published in 1996 what they labelled (with rather casual arithmetic) a "joint centennial edition" (7) of *Salome* and Beardsley's *Under the Hill*. While the edition reproduces Beardsley's illustrations, and is nicely printed, it has no editorial or textual apparatus and a foreword of just three pages, most of which is devoted to plot summary and some of which is inaccurate—the title page, for example, unequivocally asserts that *Salome* is "translated from the French by Lord Alfred Douglas," a claim which the introductory matter nowhere substantiates. *Salomé* is also edited by Pascal Aquien (*Salomé. With English version by Lord Alfred Douglas* [1993]).

The rather cavalier attitude to textual matters noted in the discussion of collections of Wilde is also a feature of recent new editions of single works, including Peter Faulkner's edition of *The Picture of Dorian Gray* (1996), and James Havoc's edition of *Salome* (1996). For example, Faulkner says his text is "based" on Robert Ross's edition without explaining what "based" actually entails, nor, equally importantly, why he goes to Ross in the first place. More problematically, Havoc's edition of *Salome* gives us no textual history or provenance at all. Norman Page's edition of *The Picture of Dorian Gray* (1998) for the Broadview Literary Texts series is less disappointing, but it is still unsatisfactory in matters of explanatory annotation. Page's introduction gives a clear description of the homoerotic subtexts of the novel, and usefully details some of its the social and literary contexts, going so far as to print as appendices passages from Pater and Huysmans, from other works by Wilde, exchanges in the first trial, and reviews of the novel. Yet *as an edition* it has many short-comings. The introduction demonstrates an awareness of the problems posed by the two texts of the novel. Page reprints the book version, but without giving a convincing reason for his choice. Moreover he does not give a textual apparatus, nor an account of the stemma of the work. Page discusses the importance of intertextuality to the effect of *Dorian Gray*, even noting the importance of self-quotation: "an epigram already used in one of his essays can turn up in his novel, one in his novel in due course reappear in one of his stage comedies" (7). Yet the explanatory annotation does not really provide the evidence for this claim.

For example, at a local level we are told that Curzon Street is a "fashionable" address (57), but we are not told that it is re-used for the parvenue Mrs Erlynne in *Lady Windermere's Fan*. Similarly, the phrase "taedium vitae" (177) is translated for the reader, but we are not told that it forms the title of one of Wilde's poems. More importantly the jokes or the situations which were to be re-used in later works are not identified. So, for example, the exchange between Dorian and the Duchess of Monmouth (225–27), reminiscent of the structure and many of the details of the exchange between Lord Illingworth and Mrs Allonby in the first act of *A Woman of No Importance*, has no annotation, despite the fact that Wilde raided the novel for many lines for the play. Perhaps this doesn't particularly matter, but Page's practice is not consistent. He does note, for example, that the "delicate grace of that Tanagra figurine" (113) has an exact analogue in a passage in "The Critic as Artist." (It is worth noting that the Lippincott text has been published by Creation Books [2000]; in 1999 Oxford University Press's World's Classics series published a hardcover version of the novel, edited by Edmund White.)

A number of other unimpressive editions of works by Wilde appeared in the 1990s. Malcolm Hicks's selection of Wilde's poems, which was published in 1992 and just too late to be discussed in *Oscar Wilde Revalued*, is perhaps the strangest. Hicks has a brief note on the text, telling us (apropos of the 1881 edition) that "a modest number of poems, with revisions . . . had been previously published in periodicals" (17), but does not tell us which these poems were. The same note mentions the 1892 edition issued by the Bodley Head, calling it the "Author's Edition." It is identified in this way in Stuart Mason's *Bibliography*, but Hicks fails to mention that the edition itself was made up from the remaindered sheets of the two identical 1882 Bogue editions, and he further omits to identify the publisher (a glance at Mason, ironically listed as a suggestion for further reading, would have given all of this information). Strangely, Hicks takes as his copy-text for those poems collected in the 1881 edition the text published by Ross in his 1908 edition, stating that this collection "restores two stanzas of 'Charmides' which were cancelled in the 1892 *editions*" (17; my italics). There was of course only one 1892 edition, and that inevitably was identical to 1882 editions, and therefore the deletions from "Charmides" represent Wilde's (rather than Ross's) last thoughts on the poem. Of course, the modern editor is quite free to follow Ross's tastes in matters of editorial judgement, but the poor reader should at least be told the reasons for that choice. More perplexing is Hicks's decision to give us just one page of explanatory notes. His reasoning is that "to document the wealth of reference and allusion" in Wilde "would result in a pedantic clutter at odds with the spirit of the reading experience" (127). The high ground would have been to argue that any annotation inevitably mediates a text, a position which in turn would require a facsimile of a particular edition. However, Hicks concedes this high ground by giving sixteen notes, seven of which are translations or explanations of Greek or Latin phrases. Yet if the reader turns to him for help to gloss Wilde's reference to "red leaves of rose from Sapphic Mitylene" in *Ravenna*, she will be disappointed. (By contrast, Isobel Murray's edition of the poems, described below, does explain the reference.) The point is that any reader who knows that Mitylene was the chief city of Lesbos, will surely be able to translate the simple Latin of Wilde's title "Quia Multum Amavi." Rather perversely, perhaps, Hicks does translate the line, but doesn't tell us that it is borrowed from Swinburne. Even more oddly, he doesn't translate the title of the next poem in his selection, "Silentium Amoris." Many modern critics have been at pains to argue that Wilde's complex attitude to intertextual matters (that "clutter" which Hicks so cavalierly deprecates) is precisely what the "spirit of the reading experience" of his works amounts to.

More laudable and much more valuable is Isobel Murray's edition of the *Complete Poetry* (1997). Murray follows the chronology of Wilde's poems established by Bobby Fong in his unpublished PhD thesis (University of California at Los Angeles, 1978). Her edition gives the ordering of the poems in the 1882 Bogue edition, and over thirty pages of notes. It prints *The Sphinx, The Ballad of Reading Gaol* and some of the uncollected poems. Also included is a chronology of the writer's life and a useful introduction. Priced as it is (at the time of writing £3.99 in the UK and $9.95 in the USA) it is certainly the edition of the poems representing the best value for any student.

I noted that Murray drew upon the pioneering work of Bobby Fong. So too does Fong himself re-use elements of his own work, for his thesis, which for a long time has been known to scholars fortunate enough to be able to visit UCLA and the Clark Library, forms the basis of the textual work for his and Karl Beckson's edition of the *Poems and Poems in Prose* (2000) for Oxford University Press. The volume is the first in the Oxford English Texts edition, and prints all the poems known to have been written by Wilde, including 21 never published in his lifetime. Establishing the texts of the poems, the textual introduction, and the textual apparatus was the work of Fong: he provides locations of manuscripts, details of each poem's publishing history, emendations and variant readings in all known or extant manuscript and printed editions. Karl Beckson provides the explanatory annotation, which gives the biographical and literary contexts to each poem, and identifies Wilde's borrowings; the introduction is by one of the general editors. An important textual discovery in Fong's and Beckson's edition is the publication of a fragment of a manuscript draft of one of the four poems in prose, "The Poet," reprinted by Vyvyan Holland in *Son of Oscar Wilde* (1954; 1999). The manuscript is substantially different from Holland's source, which was a privately printed twelve-page pamphlet entitled *Echoes* assembled by Mrs Gabrielle Enthoven (1868–1950), the theatre historian and collector who had been a friend of Wilde. Fong and Beckson argue that the draft fragment may support the claim that the poems in prose in *Echoes* were derived from stories told by Wilde, but that the discovery of the fragment does not justify the assumption that the texts in *Echoes* therefore have Wilde's authority. (Fong and Beckson contribute an essay on Wilde's poems to Peter Raby's *Cambridge Companion to Oscar Wilde* claiming that Wilde's poetry has been wrongly undervalued; see 4. i.) Fong and Beckson noted their discovery of a new "lyric by Oscar Wilde" in the *Times Literary Supplement* in 1995. They announced that a manuscript of a lyric entitled "The Faithful Shepherd" had been discovered in the Milton S. Eisenhower Library at the

Johns Hopkins University. With it was a letter to John Mais Capel, a London actor, composer and musical director, in which Wilde proposed that the lyric be set to music (for the spinet). A further new discovery (described in an addendum to *Poems and Poems in Prose*) is an undergraduate notebook belonging to Wilde in which he comments on, corrects and annotates, some of his early poems published in periodicals. A fuller description of this document is given in 7. i.

Facsimile reproductions of the first (1898) Leonard Smithers's edition of *The Ballad of Reading Gaol* and the 1892 Bodley Head edition of *Poems* are included in the Decadent, Symbolists, Anti-Decadents: Poetry of the 1890s series edited by R. K. R. Thornton and me for Woodstock Books. Unfortunately not noted in *Oscar Wilde Revalued* was the facsimile reproduction of the autograph fair copy and early manuscript version of Wilde's poem "The Grave of Shelley" in Jeremy Mason's privately printed edition of *Oscar Wilde and the Grave of Shelley* (Edinburgh: Tragara Press, 1992).

In "'Amiel and Lord Beaconsfield': An Unpublished Review by Oscar Wilde" (1996), Anya Clayworth and I print with explanatory annotation the text of the manuscript (held at the Clark Library) of an unfinished review by Wilde of Mary Humphry Ward's translation of Henri-Frédéric Amiel's *Journal intime* and two volumes of Benjamin Disraeli's (Lord Beaconsfield) *Letters*. We speculate that the review was unfinished because Wilde was unable to place it. We also draw attention to its similarities to Wilde's "Chatterton lecture" also held at the Clark: both pieces comprise copious quotation.

A difficult book to categorize, but one whose appearance should be noted, is Thomas Wright's *The Table Talk of Oscar Wilde*, a reworking of Guillot de Saix's Le *Chant du sygne: contes parlés d'Oscar Wilde* (1942).

| 7 |

Research Resources

7. i. *Documents*

With two significant exceptions, during the past eight years very little new manuscript material has come to light. The first exception is the newly discovered correspondence collected and edited by Merlin Holland (see 7. ii.). The second is the reappearance of a scrap-book (held in a private collection) which Wilde put together as an undergraduate and which was presumably a casualty of the Tite St bankruptcy sale. The scrap-book contains clippings from periodicals of some of Wilde's earliest publications, principally his poems for Irish journals. Sometimes these are annotated simply with the date of publication. On other occasions Wilde includes a note on where they were composed. There are also some poems which contain manuscript corrections to the periodical texts; these represent variants different from those in any previously known manuscript or printed version. In addition there are several lists in which Wilde orders his poems, apparently in a chronological sequence of composition. A number of titles appear to relate to poems which have not survived. Taken as a whole the document demonstrates how, from his undergraduate days onwards, Wilde took himself seriously as a poet. Fuller details of this document are given in Fong and Beckson (2000).

The Gale Group's Primary Source Media Division announced in 2000 its microfilmed "Oscar Wilde Collection." The actual resource was not available for me to inspect, but its advertising material claims that the project will reproduce in approximately forty microfilm reels the William Andrews Clark Library's "holdings of Wilde's manuscripts and rare print editions." Elsewhere it suggests that it will reproduce "literary manuscripts and typescripts of poems and plays including unpublished poems and lecture notes and drafts of works," "first and rare editions" of the works, and "autograph correspondence of Wilde and the Wilde family including his wife Constance, his mother Jane, his sister-in-law Lily." The materials "previously unpublished" are to include: "*Amiel and Lord Beaconsfield*[,] . . . 'La Belle Gabrielle': an unpublished poem from the French[,] . . . 'Choir-Boy' and other fragments of unpublished poems[,] . . . [the] Commonplace book: A collection of unpublished personal notes[,] . . . unpublished extracts of *De Profundis*[,] . . . 'Helena': an unpublished poem[,] . . . 'Love song': an unpublished poem[,] . . . typescripts of two prose essays: 'Hellenism' and 'Greek Women.'"

The claims made by this advertising material are not correct. "Amiel and Lord Beaconsfield" was published by *English Literature in Transition* in 1996; the unpublished poems were published separately by Bobby Fong and by Fong and Beckson, and have been collected in their edition of the *Poems and Poems in Prose*. Oxford University Press published the Commonplace book and Notebooks in Michael S. Helfand and Philip E. Smith's thorough and scholarly edition in 1989; "Hellenism" was published in a limited edition by the Tragara Press (Edinburgh) in 1979, one which collated the Clark typescript and manuscripts with the manuscript in the Hyde collection. Finally the "unpublished" extracts of *De Profundis* actually refers to the labels (made by the cataloguers at the Clark) of typescripts of *De Profundis* made before Hart-Davis published the manuscript in 1962. They do contain variants from the manuscript in the British Library, but all date from after Wilde's death, and on occasions their provenance is unfounded. While the reproduction of the resources at the Clark will be highly appreciated by scholars who cannot easily commute to Los Angeles, the misrepresentations in its advertising material do not fill one with confidence.

In terms of the taxonomy of this survey, it is difficult to know quite where to place Karl Beckson's *The Oscar Wilde Encyclopedia* (1998). It is not bibliography, nor biography, nor textual scholarship, but it contains hugely useful quantities of these sorts of information, and is one of the most important resources to have been made available to the scholarly community over the past decade. Along with Mason's bibliography, the *Letters* (both in Rupert Hart-Davis's original editions and Merlin Holland's revised and enlarged edition, discussed in 7. ii.) and Ellmann's biography, Beckson's superbly marshalled volume will become a key tool for writers and researchers. Beckson's scholarship is generally impeccable; moreover the *Encyclopedia* is clearly set out, easy to use, with helpful references for further reading, and it has an excellent index. Although few facts are "new" (in the sense that many can be found in other sources, such as Mason's *Bibliography of Oscar Wilde*, the *Letters*, or library and sale catalogues), their compilation in one volume provides the student (or, more likely, the professional scholar) with the most useful and accessible reference book currently available. Particularly impressive is the bibliographical information on the poems, much of which has been difficult to access. Scholars will also find useful entries on "minor" late nineteenth-century figures of Wilde's acquaintance, such as Julia Ward Howe, Stewart Headlam, and Clyde Fitch. *The Oscar Wilde Encyclopedia* is informed by a strong sense of the kind of writer Wilde was, and this in turn is structured by Beckson's understanding of the 1890s. So we find substantial entries on writers such as Arthur Symons and Richard Le Gallienne who have been seen to epitomize the "quintessence" of the 1890s. In addition there are entries on George Alexander (the manager of the St James's Theatre), Herbert Beerbohm Tree (the manager of the Haymarket) and the Bodley Head, but regrettably there is no separate entry on John Hare or Lewis Waller or H. H. Morell, all of whom were involved in negotiations with Wilde over the staging of his plays. The one shortcoming of the book is the absence of any attempt to describe the work of several recent critics who have set Wilde in the context of the emergence of late nineteenth-century consumerism, and this is perhaps an inevitable consequence of the author's understanding of what it means to "do" literary or cultural history.

One of the most interesting volumes of documentary evidence to have been printed in the last decade is Merlin Holland's *Wilde Album* (1997). It is tempting to think that the idea (although not the details of the text) nor many of the images, may have had its origins in the private publication of Gallimard's *Album Oscar Wilde* (Paris, 1996) which, as Holland says in his acknowledgements, marked Gallimard's publication of their edition of the *Oeuvres* of Wilde. In his introduction to *The Wilde Album*, Holland recalls that Wilde's three family albums, together with "three volumes of press cuttings, caricatures of him and parodies of his work" were seized and sold just before his first trial. Nonetheless the volume does print some striking family images: of Speranza and William Wilde, and of Thomas Wilde, Oscar's grandfather; of Oscar as a toddler and as a young boy; of the envelope which he decorated in memory of his sister Isola and in which he kept a lock of her hair; and his extraordinary sketch of the "view from Moytura House, the Wildes' property on Lough Corrib" (between 16 and 17).

Another important scholarly resource, Karl Beckson's *Critical Heritage* (Routledge and Kegan Paul, 1970) was reprinted in 1997.

7. ii. *Letters*

For almost forty years Rupert Hart-Davis's editions of Wilde's letters have remained an invaluable resource for scholars. In 2000 a new single-volume edition of Hart-Davis's two collections, re-edited by Merlin Holland, appeared under the title of *The Complete Letters of Oscar Wilde*. Holland includes over three hundred letters which Hart-Davis ignored or was unaware of. He also corrects numerous errors of dating made by Hart-Davis (allowing, for example, Wilde's first meeting with Richard Le Gallienne to be dated precisely), and gives the reader a considerable amount of further contextual information. These revisions will have major implications for any new biography of Wilde.

In "Notes on Oscar Wilde" (1998), Anya Clayworth prints a letter from Wilde to R. C. H. Morison, an organizer of amateur theatricals in Edinburgh, in which Wilde refuses permission for Morison to stage *A Woman of No Importance* and points Morison instead to the recently published *Lady Windermere's Fan*, a detail which Clayworth uses to date the letter. She goes on to speculate that Wilde's decision might have been motivated by a reluctance to compromise the prospects of a touring production of *A Woman of No Importance*. (She does not, however, describe the copyright implications of Morison's request.) In the same article, Clayworth also prints a letter of October 1883 from Richard Lees, a Galashiels solicitor, to J. S. Blackie, professor of Greek at Edinburgh University, about Wilde's lecture on 16 October on "Personal Impressions of America," in which Lees suggested that Wilde may have been "repeating" Blackie's views on education.

In "Some Unpublished Wilde Letters" (1998), I print four hitherto unknown letters by Wilde held in the Department of Special Collections at Syracuse University Library. (All four are included in Holland's new edition of the correspondence.) The first and longest is a letter to the painter Lawrence Alma-Tadema in response to Tadema's request for archeological details, perhaps for his picture *Sappho and Alceus*; Wilde's reply lists details of Greek orthography. The second is to James Knowles and concerns the omission of part of Wilde's essay "The Critic as Artist" in its first periodical publication in the *Nineteenth Century*. The third is to an unknown correspondent written when Wilde was at Goring-on-Thames, and the fourth is a letter of thanks to Frank Harris, hitherto only known through its publication in the Maggs catalogue.

Horst Schroeder (1998) reports on the sale by J. A. Stargardt of Marburg in 1979 of an ALS by Wilde. In it Wilde returns a letter "in which somebody had obviously taken exception to an article in the March 1888 number of his journal" (224). Schroeder connects Wilde's ALS with correspondence from the painter William P. Frith published earlier in the *Pall Mall Gazette* referring to an article by Ouida published by Wilde in *The Woman's World*.

7. iii. *Essay Collections & Reprinted Material*

There have been a number of major collections of essays published in the last seven years, including Peter Raby's *Cambridge Companion to Oscar Wilde* (1997), the 1994 special issue of *Modern Drama* edited by Joel H. Kaplan and devoted to Wilde, Jerusha McCormack's collection of essays, *Wilde the Irishman*, and Jonathan Freedman's *Oscar Wilde: A Collection of Critical Essays*. Unfortunately this last volume has eluded all my efforts to track it down in Britain. Even the British Library does not possess a copy. Regrettably, then, I am forced to do as Wittgenstein advised and pass it by in silence. 1994 saw the publication of the proceedings of the 1993 Monaco conference on Wilde, held under the aegis of The Princess Grace Irish Library. Entitled *Rediscovering Oscar Wilde*, and edited by C. George Sandulescu, it represents the largest range of essays, with 37 individual contributions in a volume a little over 400 pages long. This inclusiveness, however, has exacted a price. The majority of the pieces are very short indeed with the result that their arguments are undeveloped and generally lack sustained supporting evidence. It is also the case that a disappointingly large number of contributors tackle topics which are already over-familiar. It is perhaps revealing too that the most original pieces appear to be only a "first take" on arguments developed in more detail elsewhere. The individual essays are discussed in the appropriate sections of this volume and where an overlap with a contributor's other work occurs, this is noted.

By contrast, Peter Raby's collection brings together much more substantial pieces of work. It also gives the reader a useful snapshot of the state of Wilde research in the late 1990s, as well as covering an impressive range of the *oeuvre* (there are essays on the poetry, the journalism, as well as more familiar topics such as the plays and the biography). The contributors are nearly all well-established in their fields, and their pieces cover the range of disciplines in Wilde studies, from bibliography to biography, theatre history, culture and gender criticism to textual scholarship. As editor of *The Cambridge Companion*, Raby was perhaps best placed to interpret its remit and gauge its potential readership. The survey quality of his and Joseph Donohue's pieces (discussed in 4. iv.) suggests that they had in mind the educated general reader and student, rather than the specialist—that is, they had the ambition of providing what the book's cover terms "an essential introduction . . . a general overview and some of the latest thinking on Wilde." However, not all of the essays in the *Companion* are of this sort. Some, such as Gagnier's and Danson's (see 3. iii. and 4. iii. respectively), work more as an introduction to particular critics' views; others, such as Stokes's (4. ii.), are highly specialized. It was precisely this variety of approaches which prompted some reviewers to ask for which readers the *Companion* was intended to be a companion. These quibbles notwithstanding, the book's bibliography is helpful and full, and will be a useful resource for junior researchers and postgraduates. The individual essays are discussed in the appropriate sections of this volume.

Joel H. Kaplan's collection of fifteen essays on the drama (once again specially commissioned) has, as one would expect, a more precise focus. Once again its contributors are well established in their particular fields, and their subjects range from modern productions, to the editorial assumptions of many editions of the plays, to the sexual politics of Wilde's comedies and his relationship with other dramatists of his time. Unlike Raby's collection, there is no bibliography, but like his volume the *Modern Drama* issue does provide a useful resource for researchers. Individual essays are once again discussed in the appropriate sections of this volume.

Jerusha McCormack's collection also has, as its title suggests, a focused theme, that of Wilde's nationality. The essays are more uneven than those contained in Kaplan's and Raby's collections, and in some the reader has to strain to understand their relevance to the book's overall subject; nonetheless the volume represents a new and significant, if contentious, direction in Wilde studies. Its contents are described in detail in 3. iii.

To commemorate the centenary of Wilde's trials in 1995, the Fales Library and the English Department in New York University held an exhibition, *Reading Wilde: Querying Spaces*. A collection of nine essays, "written by graduate students in the Victorian Studies Group" at New York University, also bearing the title *Reading Wilde: Querying Spaces*, was published (1995). The essays are of variable quality, and they are mostly interpretative. Sarah Blake (in "The Tired Chameleon: A Study in Hues") connects part of Mr Justice Wills summing-up (as reported by Ellmann) with some of Wilde's works. Francesca Coppa ("I Seem to Recognize a Device that Has Done Duty in Bygone Plays: Oscar Wilde and the Theatre of Epigram") discusses the importance of the epigram in the plays, suggesting that the identities of the characters are "also epigrammatic"—the plays are about "negotiations for a personal space" (18). Frederick S. Roden ("The Scarlet Woman") discusses the tensions between Hellenism and Roman Catholicism which he suggests Wilde experienced at Oxford, and writes about the importance of religious themes in the early poetry. Peter Chapin ("Wilde at Oxford / Oxford Gone Wilde") describes Wilde's intellectual development as an undergraduate. Chatham Ewing's essay ("American Wildes") takes as its subject Wilde's project of explaining "aesthetics to a popular [American] audience unfamiliar with the details of its Oxford origin" (35), arguing that "Wilde connects the individuality within aestheticism with American poets, American myths, and American industry" (40). Lisa A. Golmitz ("The Artist's Studio") sets Wilde in the context of the visual culture of his time. In "Oscar Wilde Plays on Two Stages: The Club and The Home," Allison Pease examines how Wilde, having "successfully created his home-as-stage" began to play the "role of society gentleman" (62). In "Restyling the Secret of the Opium Den," Timothy L. Carens contrasts Wilde's description of the opium den—a "doubly exotic site" (65)—with other Victorian "opium den narratives." Finally Anjali Gallup-Diaz discusses (in "The Author, his Friends, and *The Ballad of Reading Gaol*: Epistolary Acts") the significance of six unpublished letters from Robert Ross to Leonard Smithers (held in the Fales Library) for understanding Wilde's post-prison writing career and how the "'after-Reading' market for Wilde was negotiated" (77).

Lyn Pykett's anthology in the Longman Critical Readers series, *Reading Fin de Siècle Fictions* (1996) reprints three important essays on Wilde from the preceding decade: Ed Cohen's "Writing Gone Wilde: Homoerotic Desire in the Closet of Representation" (1987), Jonathan Dollimore's "Different Desires: Subjectivity and Transgression in Wilde and Gide" (1987), and Richard Dellamora's "Homosexual Scandal and Compulsory Heterosexuality in the 1890s" (taken from *Masculine Desire* [1990]). In a collection which takes "issues of gender, class, race and ethnicity" as its main subject, it is not surprising that Wilde figures so prominently. In addition, Harold Bloom's Chelsea House anthology of essays on Wilde was reissued in June 2000.

7. iv. Resources

In 1993 Thomas A. Mikolyzk published a bibliography which crossed, as it were, in the press with *Oscar Wilde Revalued*. In a modest but disarmingly accurate preface, Mikolyzk claims that "as with the case of all bibliographies, this one is incomplete" (viii). It devotes sections to book publications by Wilde, listed and discussed chronologically and by title. Then follows a section on periodical publications by Wilde; the remainder of Mikolyzk's volume lists and annotates books wholly on Wilde, books partly on Wilde, articles on Wilde, and dissertations on Wilde. Used in conjunction with other bibliographical material, the collection is a useful additional resource for students and scholars who want to "survey" the field.

Mikolyzk's work, however, does contain errors, omissions, and some misjudgements. Some errors are typographical and trivial; for example, on page 2 David Bogue quietly but amusingly metamorphoses into David Brogue. But there are too many such mistakes (at times one wonders whether the book was proof-read). Some are more serious: Mikolyzk does not seem to have carefully compared the 1881 Bogue editions of *Poems* with the revised 1882 editions—the changes are more thoroughgoing than the "few textual variations" which he mentions. More curiously, there is no account of the 1892 Bodley Head edition of *Poems*. Nor are modern editions of Wilde's works listed, and sometimes those published in Wilde's lifetime are wrongly described. So the first (1893) Bodley Head edition of *Lady Windermere's Fan* is specified as "the original production copy of Wilde's play." As Joel H. Kaplan has shown, the whole concept of the "original production" text of a play is a vexed one, particularly in the case of *Lady Windermere's Fan*, which was significantly changed after the first night performance. More importantly, the first book edition differs quite markedly from what records there are of the play's first run. Occasionally, too, there are entries describing recent works which seem to reveal lapses of judgement. So the entry on the 1988 American edition of Ellmann's biography reads as follows:

> The definitive, Pulitzer Prize winning biography by perhaps the finest Anglo-Irish scholar of the twentieth century. Ellmann used virtually every primary source available throughout the world in crafting this meticulously documented and highly readable biography. . . . Not enough can be said of this work. (57)

It hardly needs to be noted that there is an element of hyperbole here, understandable perhaps in 1987 and 1988, but less so in the early 1990s. Ellmann certainly did not use "every primary source available throughout the world"—and anyway, what exactly could such a claim mean? From 1987 onwards, research has questioned many of Ellmann's presuppositions and corrected the (not negligible) inaccuracies of his work. Oddly, Horst Schroeder's book of corrections is listed in Mikolyzk's bibliography, but Schroeder's careful work does not seem to have informed Mikolyzk's judgement of Ellmann. This circumstance illustrates both the strengths and weakness of the bibliography. In attempting to describe research objectively (a laudable enough ambition) Mikolyzk fails to note how individual projects relate to each other and he does not therefore identify patterns in that scholarship. A number of major works, such R. K. R. Thornton's *Decadent Dilemma* (1983), Stokes's *In The Nineties* (1989), Kevin O'Brien's *Oscar Wilde in Canada* (1982), find no mention at all. These qualifications notwithstanding, Mikolyzk's work lists and describes an enormous amount of material, some of it difficult to trace.

Still one of the main bibiographical resources, Stuart Mason's *Bibliography of Oscar Wilde* (1914), was reprinted in 1999 by Martino Publishers.

Robert Tanitch in *Oscar Wilde on Stage and Screen* (1999) has attempted to give a systematic catalogue of all the theatrical, film and television productions of Wilde's works as well as dramatizations (once again on stage, screen and television) of his life. He claims that his book thereby represents a "record" of Wilde's "fame" and "notoriety" (foreword). The first section is entitled "Life" and is a series of annotated chronological lists of key events in Wilde's biography, and in contemporary affairs (which include the trials and what Tanitch calls "Scandal"). This information is sparse and seems rather arbitrarily chosen. For example, the Dilke divorce case of 1884 is listed as one of the scandals, but the circumstances surrounding the death of Douglas's half-brother, Viscount Drumlanrig, are not. There is also an odd section entitled "Presentiments" in which Tanitch singles out a number of quotations from a limited selection of Wilde's works which in his view "vividly anticipate Wilde's downfall" (10). The "second-sight" thesis underlying this section is both tired and of dubious value. More importantly, it is hard to see what relationship it has with the book's larger project. Tanitch then lists nineteenth-century dramatic productions which were taken to allude to Wilde and the Aesthetic Movement (such as Gilbert and Sullivan's opera *Patience* and Robert Buchanan's play *The Charlatan*). The section on "Life" finishes with a long account of twentieth-century dramatizations of Wilde's life. They range from Leslie and Sewell Stokes's 1936 production at the Gate Theatre Studio of *Oscar Wilde* to the 1999 revival at the Gielgud Theatre of Moisés Kaufman's *Gross Indecency—The Three Trials of Oscar Wilde*. Tanitch gives cast-lists, a selection of contemporary reviews and his own description of the productions concerned. The resulting entries combine descriptive bibliography, contemporary reviews and the judgement of the modern critic. It is not clear that these roles are compatible with each other, nor—more importantly—that they can address the same audience. So the reader who wishes to know that in 1997 the Savoy Theatre revived Micheál Mac Liammóir's *The Importance of Being Oscar* is also given brief snippets of reviews by John Gross, Paul Taylor, and Sheridan Morley (why these three is a question Tanitch leaves unanswered), together with a page of Tanitch's own views, which tell us, for example, that Simon Callow's performance "was unexpectedly subdued" (65).

The remainder of the book provides similar information, together with plot summaries, and the occasional detail of a work's genesis for Wilde's plays, his "novels [sic] and tales." A final section documents performances of "other works" ("The Critic as Artist," *De Profundis* and *The Ballad of Reading Gaol*). In these sections Tanitch's knowledge of twentieth-century productions appears much more secure than his knowledge of nineteenth-century ones. For example, there are no details of the touring productions of the Society Comedies in the 1890s, either in Britain or in the USA, nor of productions in Australia. There are also some worrying errors of fact. For example, the claims that "*Salomé* was written in French in the autumn of 1890" and that the play was "translated by Lord Alfred Douglas" (136 and 138) are both misleading. The assertion that "at Alexander's request Wilde cut the play [*Earnest*] from four acts to three" (256) is simply wrong. There are also some worrying sins of omission in which the partiality of the material presented is distorting. So, for example, the account of the structural changes to *Lady Windermere's Fan* makes no mention of the role played by Clement Scott in bringing about those changes (97; for details, see Kaplan, 1992; see 4. iv.). My feeling is that, as in the section on Wilde's life, there is an arbitrary quality to Tanitch's principles of selection, and this threatens to undermine the utility of the volume as a whole: there is not enough factual accuracy or comprehensiveness to satisfy the bibliographer, not enough contemporary detail for the cultural historian, but too much of both for the reader interested only in reviews.

Finally a different but equally valuable kind of resource is represented by the various exhibitions timed to commemorate the centenary of Wilde's death. These include *The House Beautiful: Oscar Wilde and the Aesthetic Interior* at the Geffrye Museum, London from July 2000 to January 2001 (Charlotte Gere's and Lesley Hoskins's book to accompany it is discussed in 3. iii.); *The Wilde Years: Oscar Wilde and his Times* at the Barbican Arts Centre, London from October 2000 to January 2001; and *Oscar Wilde: "Spendthrift of Genius"* at the British Library, London from November 2000 to February 2001.

| 8 |

Bibliography

8. i.   Alphabetical by Author

Abdy, Jane and Charlotte Gere. *The Souls*. London: Sidgwick and Jackson, 1984.

Alkalay-Gut, Karen. "The Thing He Loves: Murder as Aesthetic Experience in *The Ballad of Reading Gaol*," *Victorian Poetry*, 35 (1997), 349–66.

Aquien, Pascal, ed. *Oscar Wilde. Salomé. With an English version by Lord Alfred Douglas*. Paris: Flammarion, 1993.

Aquien, Pascal. "Entre Dionysos et Apollon: Pour une lecture Nietzschéenne de Wilde," *Etudes Anglaises*, 49 (1996), 168–79.

Bartlett, Neil. "The Uses of Monotony: Repetition in the Language of Oscar Wilde, Jean Genet, Edmund White and Juan Goytisolo," in *Flowers and Revolution: A Collection of Writings on Jean Genet*, Barbara Read and Ian Birchall, eds. London: Middlesex University Press, 1997. 113–27.

Baselga, Mariano. "Oscar Wilde and the Semantic Mechanisms of Humour: The Satire of Social Habits," in *Rediscovering Oscar Wilde*, C. George Sandulescu, ed. Gerrards Cross: Colin Smythe, 1994. 13–20.

Bashford, Bruce. *The Critic as Humanist*. London: Fairleigh Dickinson University Press, 1999.

Baylen Joseph, and Robert L. McBath. "A Note on Oscar Wilde, Alfred Douglas and Lord Rosebery, 1897," *English Language Notes*, 23 (1985), 42–48.

Beckson, Karl. *London in the 1890s: A Cultural History.* New York: W. W. Norton, 1992.

_____. "Narcissistic Reflections in a Wilde Mirror," *Modern Drama,* 37 (1994), 148–55.

_____. "Oscar Wilde's Celebrated Remark on Bernard Shaw," *Notes and Queries,* ns 41 (1994), 360–61.

_____. ed. *I Can Resist Everything Except Temptation and Other Quotations from Oscar Wilde.* New York: Columbia University Press, 1996.

_____. ed. *Oscar Wilde: The Critical Heritage.* 1970; London: Routledge, 1997.

_____. *The Oscar Wilde Encyclopedia.* New York: AMS Press, 1998.

Beckson, Karl and Bobby Fong. "A Newly Discovered Lyric by Oscar Wilde," *Times Literary Supplement* (17 February 1995), 9.

Belford, Barbara. *Oscar Wilde: A Certain Genius.* New York: Random House, 2000.

Blake, Sarah. "The Tired Chameleon: A Study in Hues," *Reading Wilde, Querying Spaces: An Exhibition Commemorating the 100th Anniversary of the Trials of Oscar Wilde.* New York: Fales Library, 1995. 1–10.

Blanchard, Mary Warner. *Counter Culture in the Gilded Age.* London: Yale University Press, 1998.

Bloom, Harold, ed. *Oscar Wilde: Modern Critical Views.* New York: Chelsea House, 2000.

Boroughs, Rod. "Oscar Wilde's Translation of Petronius: The Story of a Literary Hoax," *English Literature in Transition,* 38 (1995), 9–49.

Bourke, Angela. "Hunting Out the Fairies: E. F. Benson, Oscar Wilde and the Burning of Bridget Cleary," in *Wilde the Irishman,* Jerusha McCormack, ed. New Haven: Yale University Press, 1998. 36–46.

Bowlby, Rachel. *Shopping with Freud.* London: Routledge, 1993.

Brake, Laurel. *Subjugated Knowledges: Journalism, Gender and Literature in the Nineteenth Century*. London: Macmillan, 1994.

Brantlinger, Patrick. *Fictions of State: Culture and Credit in Britain 1694–1994*. New York: Cornell University Press, 1996.

Breuer Rolf. "Paradox in Oscar Wilde," *Irish Universities Review*, 23 (1993), 224–35.

Brînzeu, Pia. "Dorian Gray's Rooms and Cyberspace," in *Rediscovering Oscar Wilde*, C. George Sandulescu, ed. Gerrards Cross: Colin Smythe, 1994. 21–29.

Bristow, Joseph. "Dowdies and Dandies: Oscar Wilde's Refashioning of Society Comedy," *Modern Drama*, 37 (1994), 53–70.

_____. *Effeminate England: Homoerotic Writing After 1885*. New York: Columbia University Press, 1995.

_____. "'A complex multiform creature': Wilde's sexual identities," in *The Cambridge Companion to Oscar Wilde*, Peter Raby, ed. Cambridge: Cambridge University Press, 1997. 195–218.

_____ *Sexuality*. London: Routledge, 1997.

Brown, Julia Prewitt. *Cosmopolitan Criticism: Oscar Wilde's Philosophy of Art*. Charlottesville: University of Virginia Press, 1997.

Bucknell, Brad. "On 'Seeing' Salome," *English Literary History*, 60 (1993), 503–26.

Burns, Edward. "*Salome*: Wilde's Radical Tragedy," in *Rediscovering Oscar Wilde*, C. George Sandulescu, ed. Gerrards Cross: Colin Smythe, 1994. 30–36.

Burns, Sarah, *Inventing the Modern Artist*. New Haven: Yale University Press, 1996.

Calloway, Stephen, "Wilde and the Dandyism of the Senses," in *The Cambridge Companion to Oscar Wilde*, Peter Raby, ed. Cambridge: Cambridge University Press, 1997. 34–54.

Calloway, Stephen and David Colvin. *The Exquisite Life of Oscar Wilde*. London: Orion Media, 1997.

Campos, Christophe. *The View of France From Arnold To Bloomsbury*. London: Oxford University Press, 1965.

Carens, Timothy L. "Restyling the Secret of the Opium Den," *Reading Wilde, Querying Spaces: An Exhibition Commemorating the 100th Anniversary of the Trials of Oscar Wilde*. New York: Fales Library, 1995. 65–75.

Cave, Richard Allen. "Power Structuring: The Presentation of Outsider Figures in Wilde's Plays," in *Rediscovering Oscar Wilde*, C. George Sandulescu, ed. Gerrards Cross: Colin Smythe, 1994. 37–50.

_____ "Wilde Designs: Some Thoughts about Recent British Productions of His Plays," *Modern Drama*, 37 (1994), 175–81.

_____. "Wilde's plays: some lines of influence," in *The Cambridge Companion to Oscar Wilde*, Peter Raby, ed. Cambridge: Cambridge University Press, 1997. 219–48.

_____. ed. *The Importance of Being Earnest and Other Plays*. Harmondsworth: Penguin, 2000.

Chapin, Peter. "Wilde at Oxford / Oxford Gone Wilde," *Reading Wilde, Querying Spaces: An Exhibition Commemorating the 100th Anniversary of the Trials of Oscar Wilde*. New York: Fales Library, 1995. 27–34.

Clayworth, Anya. "*The Woman's World*: Oscar Wilde as Editor," *Victorian Periodicals Review*, 30 (1997), 84–101.

_____. "Notes on Oscar Wilde: Two Unpublished Letters from the National Library of Scotland," *Notes and Queries*, ns 45 (1998), 221–24.

Clayworth Anya, and Ian Small, eds. "'Amiel and Lord Beaconsfield': An Unpublished Review by Oscar Wilde," *English Literature in Transition*, 39 (1996), 284–97.

Clements, Patricia. *Baudelaire and The French Tradition*. Princeton: Princeton University Press, 1985.

Coakley, Davis. "The Neglected Years: Wilde in Dublin," in *Rediscovering Oscar Wilde*, C. George Sandulescu, ed. Gerrards Cross: Colin Smythe, 1994. 52–60.

_____. *Oscar Wilde: The Importance of Being Irish*. Dublin: Town House, 1994.

Cohen, Ed. "Writing Gone Wilde: Homoerotic Desire in the Closet of Representation," *Publications Of The Modern Language Association*, 102 (1987), 801–13.

_____. *Talk on the Wilde Side: Toward a Genealogy of Discourse on Male Sexualities*. New York: Routledge, 1993.

Coppa, Francesca. "I Seem to Recognize a Device that Has Done Duty in Bygone Plays: Oscar Wilde and the Theatre of Epigram," *Reading Wilde, Querying Spaces: An Exhibition Commemorating the 100th Anniversary of the Trials of Oscar Wilde*. New York: Fales Library, 1995. 11–19.

Corbett, David Peter. "'Collaborative Resistance': Charles Ricketts as Illustrator of Oscar Wilde," *Word and Image*, 10 (1994), 22–37.

Craft, Christopher. *Another Kind of Love: Male Homosexual Desire in English Discourse, 1850–1920*. London: University of California Press, 1994.

D'Alessandro, Jean M. Ellis. "Intellectual Wordplay in Wilde's Characterization of Henry Wotton," in *Rediscovering Oscar Wilde*, C. George Sandulescu, ed. Gerrards Cross: Colin Smythe, 1994. 61–75.

D'Amico, Masolino. "Oscar Wilde in Naples," in *Rediscovering Oscar Wilde*, C. George Sandulescu, ed. Gerrards Cross: Colin Smythe, 1994. 76–81.

D'Arch Smith, Timothy, and Horst Schroeder. "Feasting with Panthers," *Notes and Queries*, ns 42 (1995), 201–202.

Dale, Peter Allan. "Oscar Wilde: Crime and the 'Glorious Shapes of Art,'" *Victorian Newsletter*, 88 (1995), 1–5.

Danson, Lawrence. "Oscar Wilde, W. H., and the Unspoken Name of Love," *English Literary History*, 58 (1991), 979–1000.

_____. "'Each Man Kills the Thing he Loves': The Impermanence of Personality in Oscar Wilde," in *Rediscovering Oscar Wilde*, C. George Sandulescu, ed. Gerrards Cross: Colin Smythe, 1994. 82–93.

_____. "Wilde in Arden, or the Masks of Truth," *Modern Drama*, 37 (1994), 12–33.

_____. "Wilde as critic and theorist," in *The Cambridge Companion to Oscar Wilde*, Peter Raby, ed. Cambridge: Cambridge University Press, 1997. 80–95.

_____. *Wilde's Intentions: The Artist in His Criticism*. Oxford: Clarendon Press, 1997.

Dellamora, Richard. *Masculine Desire: The Sexual Politics of Victorian Aestheticism*. Chapel Hill: University of North Carolina Press, 1990.

_____. "Oscar Wilde, Social Purity, and *An Ideal Husband*," *Modern Drama*, 37 (1994), 120–38.

_____. *Apocalyptic Overtures: Sexual Politics and the Sense of An Ending*. New Brunswick, NJ: Rutgers University Press, 1994.

_____. ed. *Victorian Sexual Dissidence* (Chicago: University of Chicago Press, 1999.

Dollimore, Jonathan. "Different Desires: Subjectivity and Transgression in Wilde and Gide," *Textual Practice*, 1 (1987), 48–67.

_____. *Sexual Dissidence: Augustine to Wilde, Freud to Foucault*. Oxford: Clarendon Press, 1991.

Donoghue, Denis. "The Oxford of Pater, Hopkins, and Wilde," in *Rediscovering Oscar Wilde*, C. George Sandulescu, ed. Gerrards Cross: Colin Smythe, 1994. 94–117.

Donohue, Joseph. "Recent Studies of Oscar Wilde," *Nineteenth Century Theatre*, 16 (1988), 126–36.

_____. "*Salome* and the Wildean Art of Symbolist Theatre," *Modern Drama*, 37 (1994), 84–103.

_____. "Wilde and the Idea of a Theatre," in *Rediscovering Oscar Wilde*, C. George Sandulescu, ed. Gerrards Cross: Colin Smythe, 1994. 118–26.

Donohue, Joseph (with Ruth Berggren), ed. *Oscar Wilde's The Importance of Being Earnest: A Reconstructive Critical Edition of the Text of the First Production, St James's Theatre, London, 1895.* The Princess Grace Irish Library, 10. Gerrards Cross, Bucks: Colin Smythe, 1995.

Donohue, Joseph. "Distance, death and desire in *Salome*," in *The Cambridge Companion to Oscar Wilde*, Peter Raby, ed. Cambridge: Cambridge University Press, 1997. 118–42.

Douglas, Aileen, and Ian Campbell Ross. "Singularity and the Syllabus," in *Locating Swift*, Aileen Douglas, Patrick Kelly and Ian Campbell Ross, eds. Dublin: Four Courts Press, 1998. 167–79.

Dowling, Linda. *Hellenism and Homosexuality in Victorian Oxford*. Ithaca: Cornell University Press, 1994.

Doylen, Michael R. "Oscar Wilde's *De Profundis*: Homosexual Self-Fashioning on the Other Side of Scandal," *Victorian Literature and Culture*, 27 (1999), 547–66.

Eagleton, Terry. "Oscar and George," *Nineteenth Century Contexts*, 18 (1994), 205–23.

_____. *Saint Oscar and Other Plays*. Oxford: Blackwell, 1997.

Edwards, Owen Dudley. "Impressions of an Irish Sphinx," in *Wilde the Irishman*, Jerusha McCormack, ed. New Haven: Yale University Press, 1998. 47–70.

Elfman, Clare [Blossom]. *The Case of the Pederast's Wife: A Novel*. Forthcoming, 2000.

Eltis, Sos. *Revising Wilde: Society and Subversion in the Plays of Oscar Wilde*. Oxford: Clarendon Press, 1996.

Erber, Nancy. "The French Trials of Oscar Wilde," *Journal of the History of Sexuality*, 6 (1996), 549–88.

Ewing, Chatham. "American Wildes," *Reading Wilde, Querying Spaces: An Exhibition Commemorating the 100th Anniversary of the Trials of Oscar Wilde*. New York: Fales Library, 1995. 35–42.

Eynat-Confino, Irène. "Oscar Wilde and Dramatic Strategies," in *Rediscovering Oscar Wilde*, C. George Sandulescu, ed. Gerrards Cross: Colin Smythe, 1994. 127–36.

Faulkner, Peter, ed. *Oscar Wilde: The Picture of Dorian Gray*. London: Everyman, 1996.

Feltes, Norman. *Literary Capital and the Late Victorian Novel*. London: University of Wisconsin Press, 1993.

Finney, Gail. "Comparative Perspectives on Gender and Comedy: The Examples of Wilde, Hofmannsthal, and Ebner-Eschenbach," *Modern Drama*, 37 (1994), 638–50.

Foldy, Michael S. *The Trials of Oscar Wilde: Deviance, Morality, and Late-Victorian Society*. Hew Haven: Yale University Press, 1997.

Fong, Bobby, and Karl Beckson. "Wilde as Poet," in *The Cambridge Companion to Oscar Wilde*, Peter Raby, ed. Cambridge: Cambridge University Press, 1997. 57–68.

_____. eds. *The Complete Works of Oscar Wilde, Volume 1: Poems and Poems in Prose*. Oxford: Oxford University Press, 2000.

Foster, John Wilson. "Against Nature? Science and Oscar Wilde," *University of Texas Quarterly*, 63 (1993), 328–46.

_____. "Against Nature? Science and Oscar Wilde," in *Wilde the Irishman*, Jerusha McCormack, ed. New Haven: Yale University Press, 1998. 113–24.

Fothergill, Anthony, ed. *Oscar Wilde, Plays, Prose Writings and Poems*. London: Everyman, 1996.

Frankel, Nick. "'Ave Imperatrix': Oscar Wilde and the Poetry of Englishness," *Victorian Poetry*, 35 (1997), 117–37.

Frankel, Nicholas. *Oscar Wilde's Decorated Books*. Ann Arbor: University of Michigan Press, 2000.

Freedman, Jonathan. *Professions of Taste: Henry James, British Aestheticism, and Commodity Culture*. Stanford: Stanford University Press, 1990.

Fryer, Jonathan. *André and Oscar: Gide, Wilde, and the Gay Art of Living.* London: Constable, 1997.

_____. *Robbie Ross: Oscar Wilde's Last True Friend.* Forthcoming, 2000.

Gagnier, Regenia. *Idylls of the Marketplace: Oscar Wilde and the Victorian Public.* Stanford: Stanford University Press, 1986.

_____. "On the Insatiability of Human Wants: Economic and Aesthetic Man," *Victorian Studies*, 36 (1992), 125–53.

_____. "Aesthetics and Economics in *A Florentine Tragedy*," *Modern Drama*, 37 (1994), 71–83.

_____. "Is Market Society the *Fin* of History?," in *Cultural Politics at the Fin de Siècle*, Sally Ledger and Scott McCracken, eds. Cambridge: Cambridge University Press, 1995. 290–311.

_____. "Wilde and the Victorians," in *The Cambridge Companion to Oscar Wilde*, Peter Raby, ed. Cambridge: Cambridge University Press, 1997. 18–33.

_____. "The Law of Progress and the Ironies of Individualism in the Nineteenth Century," *New Literary History*, 31 (2000), 313–36.

_____. *The Insatiability of Human Wants: Economics and Aesthetics in Market Society.* Chicago: University of Chicago Press, 2000.

Gall, John. "The Pregnant Death of Dorian Gray," *Victorian Newsletter*, 82 (1992), 55–57.

Gallup-Diaz, Anjali. "The Author, his Friends, and *The Ballad of Reading Gaol*: Epistolary Acts," *Reading Wilde, Querying Spaces: An Exhibition Commemorating the 100th Anniversary of the Trials of Oscar Wilde.* New York: Fales Library, 1995. 77–89.

Garelick, Rhonda. *Rising Star: Dandyism, Gender and Performance in the Fin de Siècle.* Princeton, NJ: Princeton University Press, 1998.

Gates, Joanne E. *Elizabeth Robins, 1862–1952: Actress, Novelist, Feminist.* Tucaloosa: University of Alabama Press, 1994.

Gere, Charlotte with Lesley Hoskins. *The House Beautiful: Oscar Wilde and the Aesthetic Interior.* Aldershot: Lund Humphries, 2000.

Gide, André. *Oscar Wilde*. Forthcoming, 2000.

Gillespie, Michael Patrick. "Picturing Dorian Gray: Resistant Readings in Wilde's Novel," *English Literature in Transition*, 35 (1992), 7–25.

_____. "From Beau Brummell to Lady Bracknell: Reviewing the Dandy in *The Importance of Being Earnest*," *Victorian Institutes Journal*, 21 (1993), 119–42.

_____. "'What's in a Name?': Representing *The Picture of Dorian Gray*," *Bucknell Review*, 38 (1994), 44–60.

_____. "Ethics and Aesthetics in *The Picture of Dorian Gray*," in *Rediscovering Oscar Wilde*. C. George Sandulescu, ed. Gerrards Cross: Colin Smythe, 1994. 137–55.

_____. *The Picture of Dorian Gray: "What the World Thinks Me"*. Twayne Masterworks Series no 145. New York: Twayne, 1995.

_____. *Oscar Wilde and the Poetics of Ambiguity*. Gainesville: Gainesville University Press of Florida, 1996.

Gold, Barri J. "The Domination of *Dorian Gray*," *Victorian Newsletter*, 91 (1997), 27–30.

Golmitz, Lisa A. "The Artist's Studio," *Reading Wilde, Querying Spaces: An Exhibition Commemorating the 100th Anniversary of the Trials of Oscar Wilde*. New York: Fales Library, 1995. 43–51.

González, Antonio Ballesteros. "The Mirror of Narcissus in *The Picture of Dorian Gray*," in *Rediscovering Oscar Wilde*. C. George Sandulescu, ed. Gerrards Cross: Colin Smythe, 1994. 1–12.

Goodman, Jonathan. *The Oscar Wilde File*. 1989; London: Allison and Busby, 1996.

Goodman, Lawrence. "Narcissism and Oscar Wilde," *Imprimatur*, 1 (1995), 37–45.

Gordon, David J. "Shavian Comedy and the Shadow of Wilde," in *The Cambridge Companion to George Bernard Shaw*. Christopher Innes, ed. Cambridge: Cambridge University Press, 1998. 124–43.

Gordon, Robert. "Wilde's 'Plays of Modern Life' on the Contemporary British Stage," in *Rediscovering Oscar Wilde*. C. George Sandulescu, ed. Gerrards Cross: Colin Smythe, 1994. 156–66.

Gould, Warwick. "'The Crucifixion of the Outcasts': Yeats and Wilde in the Nineties," in *Rediscovering Oscar Wilde*. C. George Sandulescu, ed. Gerrards Cross: Colin Smythe, 1994. 167–92.

Green, Stephanie. "Oscar Wilde's *The Woman's World*," *Victorian Periodicals Review*, 30 (1997), 102–18.

Guy, Josephine M. "Aesthetics, Economics and Commodity Culture: Theorizing Value in late Nineteenth-Century Britain," *English Literature in Transition*, 42 (1999), 143–71.

_____. "An Allusion in Wilde's 'The Canterville Ghost,'" *Notes and Queries*, ns 45 (1998), 224–26.

_____. "Self-Plagiarism, Creativity and Craftsmanship in Oscar Wilde," *English Literature in Transition*, 41 (1998), 6–23.

Guy, Josephine M. and Ian Small. "How Many 'Bags of Red Gold'?: The Extent of Wilde's Success as a Dramatist," *English Literature in Transition*, 42 (1999), 283–97.

_____. *Oscar Wilde's Profession: Writing and the Culture Industry in the Late Nineteenth Century*. Oxford: Oxford University Press, 2000.

Harris, Frank. *Oscar Wilde: Including "My Memories of Oscar Wilde" by George Bernard Shaw*. Intro. Merlin Holland. New York: Carroll, 1997.

Harrison, S. J. "Prunes and Prism: Wilde and Dickens," *Notes and Queries*, ns 44 (1997), 351–52.

Harrison, William M. "Ada Leverson's Wild(e) *Yellow Book* Stories," *Victorian Newsletter*, 96 (1999), 21–28.

Hasseler, Terri A. "The Physiological Determinism Debate in Oscar Wilde's *The Picture of Dorian Gray*," *Victorian Newsletter*, 84 (1993), 31–35.

Havoc, James, ed. *Oscar Wilde, Salome and Aubrey Beardsley, Under the Hill*. London: Creation Books, 1996.

Heaney, Seamus. "Oscar Wilde Dedication: Westminster Abbey, 14 February 1995," in *Wilde the Irishman*. Jerusha McCormack, ed. New Haven: Yale University Press, 1998. 174–76.

Hicks, Malcolm, ed. *Oscar Wilde: Selected Poems*. Manchester: Carcanet, 1992.

Hoare, Philip. *Wilde's Last Stand: Decadence, Conspiracy and the First World War*. London: Duckworth, 1997.

Holland, Merlin, ed. *The Complete Works of Oscar Wilde*. Glasgow: Harper-Collins, 1994.

_____. "Plagiarist, or Pioneer?," in *Rediscovering Oscar Wilde*. C. George Sandulescu, ed. Gerrards Cross: Colin Smythe, 1994. 193–213.

Holland, Merlin, et al. *Album Oscar Wilde: Iconographie choisie et commentée par Jean Gattégno et Merlin Holland*. Bibliothèque de la Pléiade. Paris: Editions Gallimard, 1996.

Holland, Merlin. "Comments on Susan Balée's Review of *Oscar Wilde: A Long and Lovely Suicide*, by Melissa Knox," *Victorian Studies*, 39 (1996), 539–41.

_____. "Biography and the Art of Lying," in *The Cambridge Companion to Oscar Wilde*. Peter Raby, ed. Cambridge: Cambridge University Press, 1997. 3–17.

_____. *The Wilde Album*. London: Fourth Estate, 1997.

_____. ed. *The Oscar Wilde Anthology*. Glasgow: HarperCollins, 2000.

Holland, Merlin, and Rupert Hart-Davis, eds. *The Complete Letters of Oscar Wilde*. London: Fourth Estate; New York: Henry Holt, 2000.

Holland, Vyvyan. *Oscar Wilde*. 1966; London: Thames and Hudson, 1997.

_____. *Son of Oscar Wilde*. London: Rupert Hart-Davis, 1954; revised by Merlin Holland, London: Robinson, 1999.

Holloway, C. Robert. *The Unauthorized Letters of Oscar Wilde*. Princeton, NJ: Xlibris Corp, 1997.

Horan, Patrick M. *The Importance of Being Paradoxical: Maternal Presence in the Works of Oscar Wilde*. London: Associated University Presses, 1997.

Hyde, H. Montgomery Hyde. *The Trials of Oscar Wilde*. 1962; revised edn. 1973; repr. New York: Dover Publications, nd.

Jackson, Russell, ed. *Oscar Wilde: An Ideal Husband*. London: Ernest Benn, 1983; 2nd and revised edn. London: A. & C. Black, 1993.

_____. "Oscar Wilde's Contract for a New Play," *Theatre Notebook*, 50 (1996), 113–15.

_____. "The Importance of Being Earnest," in *The Cambridge Companion to Oscar Wilde*. Peter Raby, ed. Cambridge: Cambridge University Press, 1997. 161–77.

Jackson, Russell and Ian Small. "Oscar Wilde: A 'Writerly' Life," *Modern Drama*, 37 (1994), 3–11.

Jenkyns, Richard. *The Victorians and Ancient Greece*. Oxford: Blackwell, 1980.

John, Angela V. *Elizabeth Robins: Staging a Life, 1862–1952*. New York: Routledge, 1995.

Kaplan, Joel H. "A Puppet's Power: George Alexander, Clement Scott, and the Replotting of *Lady Windermere's Fan*," *Theatre Notebook*, 46 (1992), 59–73.

_____. "Oscar Wilde's Contract for *A Woman of No Importance*," *Theatre Notebook*, 48 (1994), 46–48.

_____. "Staging Wilde's Society Plays: A Conversation with Philip Prowse (Glasgow Citizens Theatre)," *Modern Drama*, 37 (1994), 192–205.

_____. "Wilde in the Gorbals: Society Drama and Citizens Theatre," in *Rediscovering Oscar Wilde*. C. George Sandulescu, ed. Gerrards Cross: Colin Smythe, 1994. 214–23.

_____. ed. *Modern Drama: Special Issue on Wilde*, 37 (1994).

_____. "Wilde on the stage," in *The Cambridge Companion to Oscar Wilde*. Peter Raby, ed. Cambridge: Cambridge University Press, 1997. 249–75.

Kellogg-Dennis, Patricia. "Oscar Wilde's *Salome*: Symbolist Princess," in *Rediscovering Oscar Wilde*. C. George Sandulescu, ed. Gerrards Cross: Colin Smythe, 1994. 224–31.

Kettle, Michael. *Salomé's Last Veil: The Libel Case of the Century*. London: Hart-Davis MacGibbon, 1977.

Kiberd, Declan. "Wilde and the English Question," *Times Literary Supplement* (16 December 1994), 13–15.

_____. "Oscar Wilde: the resurgence of lying," in *The Cambridge Companion to Oscar Wilde*. Peter Raby, ed. Cambridge: Cambridge University Press, 1997. 276–94.

_____. "Oscar Wilde: The Artist as Irishman," in *Wilde the Irishman*. Jerusha McCormack, ed. New Haven: Yale University Press, 1998. 9–23.

Kilroy, Thomas. "The Secret Fall of Constance Wilde (An Excerpt from a New Play)," in *Wilde the Irishman*. Jerusha McCormack, ed. New Haven: Yale University Press, 1998. 166–72.

_____. *The Secret Fall of Constance Wilde*. County Meath: The Gallery Press, 1997.

Kirschner, Paul. "Wilde's Shadow in Conrad's 'The Return,'" *Notes and Queries*, ns 40 (1993), 495–96.

Knox, Melissa. "Losing One's Head: Wilde's Confession in *Salome*," in *Rediscovering Oscar Wilde*. C. George Sandulescu, ed. Gerrards Cross: Colin Smythe, 1994. 232–43.

_____. *Oscar Wilde: A Long and Lovely Suicide*. New Haven: Yale University Press, 1994.

Ksinan, Catherine. "Wilde as Editor of *Woman's World*: Fighting a Dull Slumber in Stale Certitudes," *English Literature in Transition*, 41 (1998), 408–26.

Lambert, Angela. *Unquiet Souls*. London: Macmillan, 1984.

Lange, Robert J. G. "The Provenance of Oscar Wilde's *The Portrait of Mr W. H.*: An Oversight?," *Notes and Queries*, ns 42 (1995), 202–203.

Langlade, Jacques de. "Oscar Wilde as a Modern Dramatist and Actor," in *Rediscovering Oscar Wilde*. C. George Sandulescu, ed. Gerrards Cross: Colin Smythe, 1994. 244–48.

Langtrie, Lillie [Lady de Bathe]. *The Days I Knew*. London: n. d. [1925].

Lawler, Donald. "The Gothic Wilde," in *Rediscovering Oscar Wilde*. C. George Sandulescu, ed. Gerrards Cross: Colin Smythe, 1994. 249–68.

Lesjak, Carolyn. "Utopia, Use, and the Everyday: Oscar Wilde and a New Economy of Pleasure," *English Literary History*, 67 (2000), 179–204.

Losey, Jay. "The Aesthetics of Exile: Wilde Transforming Dante in *Intentions* and *De Profundis*," *English Literature in Transition*, 36 (1993), 429–50.

Mackie, W. Craven. "Bunbury Pure and Simple," *Modern Drama*, 41 (1998), 327–30.

Maguire, J. Robert. "Oscar Wilde and the Dreyfus Affair, *Victorian Studies*, 41 (1997), 1–29.

Mahaffey, Vicki. *States of Desire: Wilde, Yeats, Joyce, and the Irish Experiment*. New York: Oxford University Press, 1998.

Mahon, Derek. "Ellmann's Wilde," in *Wilde the Irishman*. Jerusha McCormack, ed. New Haven: Yale University Press, 1998. 146–51.

Marez, Curtis. "The Other Addict: Reflections on Colonialism and Oscar Wilde's Smoke Screen, *English Literary History*, 64 (1997), 257–87.

Mason, Jeremy, ed. *Oscar Wilde and "The Grave of Shelley"*. Edinburgh: Tragara Press, 1992.

McCollister, Deborah. "Wilde's *The Picture of Dorian Gray*," *The Explicator*, 54 (1996), 17–20.

McCormack, Jerusha. "The Once and Future Dandy," in *Rediscovering Oscar Wilde*. C. George Sandulescu, ed. Gerrards Cross: Colin Smythe, 1994. 269–73.

_____. "Wilde's fiction(s)," in *The Cambridge Companion to Oscar Wilde*. Peter Raby, ed. Cambridge: Cambridge University Press, 1997. 96–117.

_____. "The Wilde Irishman: Oscar as Aesthete and Anarchist," in *Wilde the Irishman*. Jerusha McCormack, ed. New Haven: Yale University Press, 1998. 82–94.

_____. *Wilde the Irishman*. London: Yale University Press, 1998.

McCormack, W. J. "Wilde and Parnell," in *Wilde the Irishman*. Jerusha McCormack, ed. New Haven: Yale University Press, 1998. 95–102.

McGuinness, Frank. "The Spirit of Play in *De Profundis*," in *Wilde the Irishman*. Jerusha McCormack, ed. New Haven: Yale University Press, 1998. 140–45.

Meisel, Martin. "The World, The Flesh, and Oscar Wilde: Bodily Politics in *Salome* and *Dorian Gray*," *Nineteenth Century Contexts*, 16 (1992), 121–34.

Melville, Joy. *Mother of Oscar: The Life of Francesca Jane Wilde*. London: John Murray, 1994.

Mikolyzk, Thomas A. *Oscar Wilde: An Annotated Bibliography*. Bibliographies and Indexes in World Literature no 38. Westport, CT: Greenwood Press, 1993.

Mitchell, Jason, P. "A Source Victorian or Biblical?: The Integration of Biblical Diction and Symbolism in Oscar Wilde's *Salomé*," *Victorian Newsletter*, 89 (1996), 14–18.

Mitchell, Julian (with an introduction by Stephen Fry). *Wilde*. London: Orion, 1997.

Moore-Gilbert, Bart. "From Miss Prism to Misprision: Oscar Wilde and Contemporary Theory," in *Rediscovering Oscar Wilde*. C. George Sandulescu, ed. Gerrards Cross: Colin Smythe, 1994. 274–82.

Morley, Sheridan. *Oscar Wilde*. 1976; London: Pavilion, 1997.

Murphy, Margueritte S. *A Tradition of Subversion: The Prose Poem in English from Wilde to Ashberry*. Amherst, MA: University of Massachusetts Press, 1992.

Murphy, Paula. "The Quare on the Square: A Statue of Oscar Wilde for Dublin," in *Wilde the Irishman*. Jerusha McCormack, ed. New Haven: Yale University Press, 1998. 127–39.

Murray, Isobel. "Oscar Wilde in his Literary Element: Yet Another Source for *Dorian Gray?*," in *Rediscovering Oscar Wilde*. C. George Sandulescu, ed. Gerrards Cross: Colin Smythe, 1994. 283–96.

Murray, Douglas. *Bosie: A Biography of Lord Alfred Douglas*. London: Hodder and Stoughton, 2000.

Murray, Isobel, ed. *Oscar Wilde: Complete Poetry*. The World's Classics. Oxford: Oxford University Press, 1997.

_____. ed. *Oscar Wilde: The Major Works*. The World's Classics. Oxford: Oxford University Press, 2000.

Musolf, Peter. "Bunburying and the Art of Kabuki: or, Wilde, Mishima and the Importance of Being a Sardine Seller," *New Theatre Quarterly*, 12 (1996), 333–39.

Nassaar, Christopher S. "Wilde's *The Ballad of Reading Gaol*," *Explicator*, 53 (1995), 158–60.

_____. "Andersen's 'The Shadow' and Wilde's 'The Fisherman and His Soul': A Case of Influence," *Nineteenth Century Literature*, 50 (1995), 217–24.

_____. "Wilde's *The Picture of Dorian Gray* and *Salome*," *Explicator*, 53 (1995), 217–20.

_____. "Wilde's *The Picture of Dorian Gray* and *Lady Windermere's Fan*," *Explicator*, 54 (1996), 20–24.

_____. "Andersen's 'The Ugly Duckling' and Wilde's 'The Birthday of the Infanta,'" *Explicator*, 55 (1997), 83–85.

_____. "Wilde's *La Sainte Courtisane*," *Explicator*, 56 (1997), 28–30.

_____. "Wilde's *Lady Windermere's Fan* and Shaw's *Mrs Warren's Profession*," *Explicator*, 56 (1998), 137–38.

_____. "Wilde's *The Picture of Dorian Gray* and *Salome*," *Explicator*, 57 (1998), 33–35.

_____. "Wilde's *Salome*," *Explicator*, 57 (1999), 89–90.

_____. "Wilde's *The Picture of Dorian Gray*," *Explicator*, 57 (1999), 216–17.

_____. "Wilde's *The Importance of Being Earnest* and Stoppard's *Rosencrantz and Guildenstern are Dead,*" *Explicator*, 58 (2000), 91–92.

Nilsen, Don. *Humor in Irish literature: A Reference Guide*. Westport, CT: Greenwood Press, 1996.

Nin, Anais, et al. *Going Down: Lip Service from Great Writers*. San Francisco: Chronicle Books, 1998.

Nixon, Nicola. "The Reading Gaol of Henry James's *In the Cage,*" *English Literary History*, 66 (1999), 179–201.

Noon, Gareth. "Wilde's Gracious Enclosures: A Brief Tour," *Victorian Newsletter*, 91 (1997), 17–20.

Nunokawa, Jeff. *The Afterlife of Property*. Princeton, NJ: Princeton University Press, 1994.

_____. *Oscar Wilde*. New York: Chelsea House, 1994.

_____. "Oscar Wilde in Japan: Aestheticism, Orientalism, and the Derealization of the Homosexual," in *Privileging Positions: The Site of Asian American Studies*, Gary Okihiro et al., eds. Pullman: Washington State University Press, 1995. 287–95.

_____. "The Importance Of Being Bored: The Dividends of Ennui in *The Picture of Dorian Gray,*" *Studies in the Novel*, 28 (1996), 357–71.

O'Donoghue, Bernard. "The Journey to Reading Gaol: Sacrifice and Scapegoats in Irish Literature," in *Wilde the Irishman*, Jerusha McCormack, ed. New Haven: Yale University Press, 1998. 103–12.

O'Gorman, Francis. "Ruskin, Wilde, and Lillie Langtry," *Notes and Queries*, ns 44 (1997), 349–50.

O'Toole, Fintan. "Venus in Blue Jeans: Oscar Wilde, Jesse James, Crime and Fame," in *Wilde the Irishman*, Jerusha McCormack, ed. New Haven: Yale University Press, 1998. 71–81.

Ostermann, Sylvia. "Eros and Thanatos in *The Picture of Dorian Gray,*" in *Rediscovering Oscar Wilde*, C. George Sandulescu, ed. Gerrards Cross: Colin Smythe, 1994. 297–304.

Page, Norman. "Decoding *The Ballad of Reading Gaol*," in *Rediscovering Oscar Wilde*, C. George Sandulescu, ed. Gerrards Cross: Colin Smythe, 1994. 305–11.

_____. ed. *Oscar Wilde: The Picture of Dorian Gray*. Peterborough, Ontario: Broadview Press, 1998.

Pearce, Joseph. *The Unmasking of Oscar Wilde*. London: HarperCollins, 2000.

Pease, Allison. "Oscar Wilde Plays on Two Stages: The Club and The Home," *Reading Wilde, Querying Spaces: An Exhibition Commemorating the 100th Anniversary of the Trials of Oscar Wilde*. New York: Fales Library, 1995. 53–64.

Pestka, Dariusz. "A Typology of Oscar Wilde's Comic Devices," *Studia Anglia Posnaniensia*, 22 (1989), 175–93.

_____. *Oscar Wilde: Between Aestheticism and Anticipation of Modernism*. Toruń: Uniwersytetu Mikołaja Kopernika, 1999.

Pine, Richard. *The Thief of Reason: Oscar Wilde and Modern Ireland*. Dublin: Gill and Macmillan, 1995.

Pollard, Patrick. *André Gide: Homosexual Moralist*. New Haven: Yale University Press, 1991.

Powell, Kerry. "'Oscar Wilde: An Appreciation': An Unpublished Memoir by Elizabeth Robins," *Nineteenth Century Theatre*, 21 (1993), 101–13.

_____. "Oscar Wilde, Elizabeth Robins, and the Theatre of the Future," *Modern Drama*, 37 (1994), 220–37.

_____. "Wilde and Two Women: Unpublished Accounts by Elizabeth Robins and Blanche Crackanthorpe," in *Rediscovering Oscar Wilde*, C. George Sandulescu, ed. Gerrards Cross: Colin Smythe, 1994. 312–18.

_____. *Women and the Victorian Theatre*. Cambridge: Cambridge University Press, 1997.

_____. "A Verdict of death: Oscar Wilde, actresses and Victorian Women," in *The Cambridge Companion to Oscar Wilde*, Peter Raby, ed. Cambridge: Cambridge University Press, 1997. 181–94.

Price, Jody. *"A Map of Utopia": Oscar Wilde's Theory for Social Transformation*. New York: Peter Lang, 1996.

Pulido, María Pilar. "Lady Wilde 'Speranza': A Woman of Great Importance," in *Rediscovering Oscar Wilde*. C. George Sandulescu, ed. Gerrards Cross: Colin Smythe, 1994. 319–27.

Pykett, Lyn, ed. *Reading Fin de Siècle Fictions*. London: Longman, 1996.

Quigley, Austin E. "Realism and Symbolism in Oscar Wilde's *Salomé*," *Modern Drama*, 37 (1994), 104–19.

Raby, Peter. "The Origins of *The Importance of Being Earnest*," *Modern Drama*, 37 (1994), 139–47.

_____. "Wilde and European Theatre," in *Rediscovering Oscar Wilde*, C. George Sandulescu, ed. Gerrards Cross: Colin Smythe, 1994. 328–37.

_____. ed. *Oscar Wilde: The Importance of Being Earnest and Other Plays.* The World's Classics. Oxford: Oxford University Press, 1995.

_____. *The Importance of Being Earnest: A Reader's Companion*. New York: Twayne, 1995.

_____. "'The Persons of the Play': Some Reflections on Wilde's Choice of Names in *The Importance of Being Earnest*," *Nineteenth Century Theatre*, 23 (1995), 67–75.

_____. "Wilde's comedies of Society," in *The Cambridge Companion to Oscar Wilde*, Peter Raby, ed. Cambridge: Cambridge University Press, 1997. 143–60.

_____. ed. *The Cambridge Companion to Oscar Wilde*. Cambridge: Cambridge University Press, 1997.

Raeside, James. "The Spirit is Willing but the Flesh is Strong: Mishima Yukio's *Kinjiki* and Oscar Wilde," *Comparative Literature Studies*, 36 (1999), 1–24.

Rashkin, Esther. "Art as Symptom: A Portrait of Child Abuse in *The Picture of Dorian Gray*," *Modern Philology*, 95 (1997), 68–80.

Reed, Jeremy. *Dorian: A Sequel to Dorian Gray*. Forthcoming, 2000.

Robbins, Ruth. "'A very curious construction': Masculinity and the Poetry of A. E. Housman and Oscar Wilde," in *Cultural Politics at the Fin de Siècle,* Sally Ledger and Scott McCracken, eds. Cambridge: Cambridge University Press, 1995. 137–59.

Roden, Frederick S. "The Scarlet Woman," *Reading Wilde, Querying Spaces: An Exhibition Commemorating the 100th Anniversary of the Trials of Oscar Wilde.* New York: Fales Library, 1995. 21–25.

Rohmann, Gerd. "Re-Discovering Wilde in Travesties by Joyce and Stoppard," in *Rediscovering Oscar Wilde,* C. George Sandulescu, ed. Gerrards Cross: Colin Smythe, 1994. 338–47.

Rosenstein, Roy. "Re(Dis)covering Wilde for Latin America: Martí, Darío, Borges, Lispector," in *Rediscovering Oscar Wilde,* C. George Sandulescu, ed. Gerrards Cross: Colin Smythe, 1994. 348–61.

Rosenstock, Gabriel. "Bás Wilde Mar a Tharla (The Real Death of Wilde)," trans. Noel Griffin, in *Wilde the Irishman,* Jerusha McCormack, ed. New Haven: Yale University Press, 1998. 173.

Rowell, George. 'The Truth About *Vera*,' *Nineteenth Century Theatre,* 21 (1993), 94–100.

Rudnicki, Stefan. *Wilde: the Novel of the Screenplay of Julian Mitchell.* London: Orion Publishing, 2000.

Sammells, Neil. "Rediscovering the Irish Wilde," in *Rediscovering Oscar Wilde,* C. George Sandulescu, ed. Gerrards Cross: Colin Smythe, 1994. 362–70.

_____. *Wilde Style: The Plays and Prose of Oscar Wilde.* Studies in Eighteenth- and Nineteenth-Century Literature. London: Longman, 2000.

Sandulescu, C. George, ed. *Rediscovering Oscar Wilde.* Gerrards Cross, Bucks: Colin Smythe, 1994.

Satzinger, Christa. *The French Influences on Oscar Wilde's "The Picture of Dorian Gray" and "Salome".* Lewiston, New York: Mellon Press, 1994.

Scarry, John. "A Correction for Richard Ellmann's *Oscar Wilde*," *Notes and Queries,* ns 40 (1993), 58.

Schaffer, Talia. "Fashioning Aestheticism by Aestheticizing Fashion: Wilde, Beerbohm and the Male Aesthetes' Sartorial Codes," *Victorian Literature and Culture*, 28 (2000), 39–54.

Schaffer, Talia. *The Forgotten Female Aesthetes: Literary Culture in Late Victorian England*. Charlottesville: University Press of Virginia, 2000.

Schenkar, Joan. *Truly Wilde: The Unsettling Story of Dolly Wilde, Oscar's Unusual Niece*. New York: Basic Books, 2000.

Schmidgall, Gary. *The Stranger Wilde: Interpreting Wilde*. London: Abacus, 1994.

Schroeder, Horst. *Oscar Wilde, "The Portrait of Mr W. H."—Its Composition, Publication and Reception*. Braunschweig: Technische Universität Braunschweig, 1984.

Schroeder, Horst. "ΕΡΩΣ ΤΩΝ ΑΔΥΝΑΤΩΝ—*L'Amour de l'Impossible*: A Graeco-French Collocation in 'The Critic As Artist,'" *Notes and Queries*, ns 40 (1993), 52–53.

_____. "Wilde's Commonplace Book and Symonds's *Studies of the Greek Poets*," *Notes and Queries*, 40 ns (1993), 53–54.

_____. "Pausanias and 'The Critic As Artist,'" *Notes and Queries*, ns 40 (1993), 55–56.

_____. "Bimetallism: A Topical Reference in Oscar Wilde," *Notes and Queries*, ns 40 (1993), 56–58.

_____. *Alice in Wildeland*. Braunschweig: privately printed, 1994.

_____. "Matthew Arnold and Oscar Wilde's Commonplace Book," *Notes and Queries*, ns 41 (1994), 359–60.

_____. "A Homeric Epithet in 'The Critic as Artist,'" *Notes and Queries*, ns 41 (1994), 362–63.

_____. "A Source for 'Pen, Pencil and Poison,'" *Notes and Queries*, ns 41 (1994), 363.

_____. "A Printing Error in 'The Soul of Man Under Socialism,'" *Notes and Queries*, ns 43 (1996), 49–51.

_____. "An Unacknowledged Quotation in 'Pen, Pencil and Poison,'" *Notes and Queries*, ns 43 (1996), 51–52.

_____. "Wilde, Wainewright, and Fuseli," *Notes and Queries*, ns 43 (1996), 433–34.

_____. "The Reference to Mantegna in 'The Critic as Artist,'" *Notes and Queries*, ns 44 (1997), 350–51.

_____. "Another Swipe at W. P. Frith by Oscar Wilde," *Notes and Queries*, ns 45 (1998), 224.

Schuchard, Ronald. "Wilde's Dark Angel and the Spell of Decadent Catholicism," in *Rediscovering Oscar Wilde*, C. George Sandulescu, ed. Gerrards Cross: Colin Smythe, 1994. 371–96.

Schulz, David. "Redressing Oscar: Performance and the Trial of Oscar Wilde," *Drama Review*, 40 (1996), 37–49.

Schweik, Robert. "Congruous Incongruities: The Wilde-Beardsley 'Collaboration,'" *English Literature in Transition*, 37 (1994), 9–26.

Sedgwick, Eve Kosofsky. "Tales of the Avunculate: Queer Tutelage in *The Importance of Being Earnest*," in *Professions of Desire: Lesbian and Gay Studies in Literature*, George E. Haggerty and Bonnie Zimmerman, eds. New York: Modern Language Association, 1995. 191–209.

Sheridan, Alan. *André Gide: A Life in the Present*. London: Hamish Hamilton, 1998.

Siegel, Sandra. "Oscar Wilde's Gift and Oxford's "Coarse Impertinence," in *Ideology and Ireland in the Nineteenth Century*, Tadhg Foley and Seán Ryder, eds. Dublin: Four Courts Press, 1998. 69–78.

Silver, Carole G. *Strange and Secret Peoples: Fairies and the Victorian Consciousness*. New York: Oxford University Press, 1999.

Sinfield, Alan. "'Effeminacy' and 'Femininity': Sexual Politics in Wilde's Comedies," *Modern Drama*, 37 (1994), 34–52.

_____. *The Wilde Century*. London: Cassell, 1994.

Small, Ian. "Oscar Wilde as a Professional Writer," *Library Chronicle of the University of Texas*, 23 (1993), 33–49.

_____. ed. *Oscar Wilde: A Woman of No Importance*. London: Ernest Benn: 1983; 2nd and revised. edn. London: A. and C. Black, 1993.

_____. ed. *Oscar Wilde: Complete Short Fiction*. Harmondsworth, Penguin, 1994.

Small, Ian. "The Economies of Taste: Literary Markets and Literary Value in Late Nineteenth Century," *English Literature in Transition*, 39 (1996), 7–18.

_____. "Some Unpublished Wilde Letters," *English Literature in Transition*, 41 (1998), 58–64.

_____. ed. *Oscar Wilde: Lady Windermere's Fan*. London: Ernest Benn, 1980; 2nd and revised edition, London: A. and C. Black, 1999.

Small, Ian, and R. K. R. Thornton, eds. *Oscar Wilde: Poems, 1892*. Oxford: Woodstock, 1995.

_____. eds. *Oscar Wilde: The Ballad of Reading Gaol, 1898*. Oxford: Woodstock, 1995.

Snider, Clifton. "Eros and Logos in Some Fairy Stories by Oscar Wilde: A Jungian Interpretation," *Victorian Newsletter*, 84 (1993), 1–8.

Stanford, Alan. "Acting Wilde," in *Wilde the Irishman*, Jerusha McCormack, ed. New Haven: Yale University Press, 1998. 152–57.

Stanley, Michael. *Famous Dubliners: W. B. Yeats, James Joyce, Jonathan Swift, Wolfe Tone, Oscar Wilde, Edward Carson*. Dublin: Wolfhound Press, 1996.

Stephens, John Russell. *The Profession of the Playwright: British Theatre 1800–1900*. Cambridge: Cambridge University Press, 1992.

Stokes, John. "Wilde Shot," *London Review of Books*, 27 February, 1992, 4.

_____. "Wilde Interpretations," *Modern Drama*, 37 (1994), 156–74.

_____. *Myths, Miracles, and Imitations*. Cambridge: Cambridge University Press, 1996.

_____. "Wilde the Journalist," in *The Cambridge Companion to Oscar Wilde*, Peter Raby, ed. Cambridge: Cambridge University Press, 1997. 69–79.

Stowell, Sheila and Joel Kaplan. *Theatre and Fashion: Oscar Wilde to the Suffragettes.* Cambridge: Cambridge University Press, 1994.

Summers, Claude J. *Gay Fictions, Wilde to Stonewall: Studies in a Male Homosexual Literary Tradition.* New York: Continuum, 1990.

Sweetman, David. *Explosive Acts: Toulouse-Lautrec, Oscar Wilde, Félix Fénéon, and the Art and Anarchy of the Fin de Siècle.* New York: Simon and Schuster, 2000.

Symonds, John Addington. *Renaissance in Italy: The Fine Arts.* London, 1877.

Tanitch, Robert. *Oscar Wilde on Stage and Screen.* London: Methuen, 1999.

Taylor, Michael, ed. *Oscar Wilde: Trial and Punishment 1895–1897.* London: Public Records Office, 1999.

Theoharis, Theoharis Constantine. "Will to Power, Poetic Justice, and Mimesis in *The Picture of Dorian Gray*," in *Rediscovering Oscar Wilde*, C. George Sandulescu, ed. Gerrards Cross: Colin Smythe, 1994. 397–404.

Toomey, Deirdre. "The Story-teller at Fault," in *Rediscovering Oscar Wilde*, C. George Sandulescu, ed. Gerrards Cross: Colin Smythe, 1994. 405–20.

Toomey, Deirdre. "The Story-Teller at Fault: Oscar Wilde and Irish Orality," in *Wilde the Irishman*, Jerusha McCormack, ed. New Haven: Yale University Press, 1998. 24–35.

Tydeman, William, and Steven Price, eds. *Wilde: Salome. Plays in Production.* Cambridge: Cambridge University Press, 1996.

Upchurch, David A. *Wilde's Use of Irish Celtic Elements in "The Picture of Dorian Gray".* New York: Lang, 1992.

Varty, Ann. *A Preface to Oscar Wilde.* Harlow: Longman, 1988.

Vernadakis, Emmanuel. "Wilde's Reading of Clemens Alexandrinus," in *Rediscovering Oscar Wilde*, C. George Sandulescu, ed. Gerrards Cross: Colin Smythe, 1994. 421–31.

Wearing, J. P. "Women in Victorian Theatre," *English Literature in Transition*, 42 (1999), 229–32.

Wellens, Oskar, "A Hitherto Unnoticed Review by Wilde," *Notes and Queries*, ns 41 (1994), 364.

White, Leslie. "Wilde, Browning and the 'New Obscurity,'" *English Literature in Transition*, 42, (1999), 4–22.

White, Victoria. "Women of No Importance: Misogyny in the Work of Oscar Wilde," in *Wilde the Irishman*, Jerusha McCormack, ed. New Haven: Yale University Press, 1998. 158–65.

[Wilde, Oscar]. *Nothing . . . Except My Genius*. Compiled by Alastair Rolfe. Introductory essay by Stephen Fry. Harmondsworth: Penguin, 1997.

Wilde, Oscar. *The Picture of Dorian Gray: The Lippincott Edition*. London: Creation Books, 2000.

Wisenthal, J. L. "Wilde, Shaw, and the Play of Conversation," *Modern Drama*, 37 (1994), 206–19.

Woodcock, George. *Oscar Wilde: The Double Image*. Montréal: Black Rose Books Ltd., 1989.

Wright, Thomas. *The Table Talk of Oscar Wilde*. Forthcoming, 2000.

Xiaoyi, Zhou. "Oscar Wilde's Orientalism and late Nineteenth-Century European Consumer Culture," *A Review of International English Literature*, 28 (1997), 49–71.

Zatlin, Linda Gertner. "Aubrey Beardsley's 'Japanese' Grotesques," *Victorian Literature and Culture*, 25 (1997), 87–108.

_____. *Beardsley, Japonisme and the Perversion of the Victorian Ideal*. Cambridge: Cambridge University Press, 1997.

Zeender, Marie-Noëlle. "John Melmoth and Dorian Gray: The Two-Faced Mirror," in *Rediscovering Oscar Wilde*, C. George Sandulescu, ed. Gerrards Cross: Colin Smythe, 1994. 432–40.

8. ii. Research Indexed to Wilde's Work

Letters

FOR EDITIONS AND NEW TEXTS OF WILDE'S LETTERS

Merlin Holland, ed. *The Letters of Oscar Wilde*. London: Fourth Estate, 2000.

Ian Small. "Some Unpublished Wilde Letters," *English Literature in Transition*, 41 (1998), 58–64.

FOR RELATED MATERIAL

Anya Clayworth. "Notes on Oscar Wilde: Two Unpublished Letters from the National Library of Scotland," *Notes and Queries*, ns 45 (1998), 221–24.

Poems
(including *The Ballad of Reading Gaol* and *The Sphinx*)

FOR EDITIONS OF WILDE'S POEMS

Karl Beckson and Bobby Fong. "A Newly Discovered Lyric by Oscar Wilde," *Times Literary Supplement*, 17 February 1995, 9.

Bobby Fong and Karl Beckson, eds. *The Complete Works of Oscar Wilde, Volume 1: Poems and Poems in Prose*. Oxford: Oxford University Press, 2000.

Malcolm Hicks, ed. *Oscar Wilde: Selected Poems*. Manchester: Carcanet, 1992.

Merlin Holland, ed. *The Complete Works of Oscar Wilde*. Glasgow: Harper-Collins, 1994.

Jeremy Mason, ed. *Oscar Wilde and "The Grave of Shelley"*. Edinburgh: Tragara Press, 1992.

Isobel Murray, ed. *Oscar Wilde: Complete Poetry*. The World's Classics. Oxford: Oxford University Press, 1997.

Ian Small and R. K. R. Thornton, eds. *Oscar Wilde: Poems, 1892*. Oxford: Woodstock, 1995.

_____. eds. *Oscar Wilde: The Ballad of Reading Gaol, 1898*. Oxford: Woodstock, 1995.

The Oscar Wilde Collection (of the William Andrews Clark Memorial Library Wilde holdings). Primary Source Media (Gale Group).

FOR CRITICAL DISCUSSION OF THE POEMS

Karen Alkalay-Gut. "The Thing He Loves: Murder as Aesthetic Experience in _The Ballad of Reading Gaol,_" _Victorian Poetry,_ 35 (1997), 349–66.

Karl Beckson. _The Oscar Wilde Encyclopedia._ New York: AMS Press, 1998; poems are discussed individually and identified by title as well as by the volume in which they appear.

Bobby Fong and Karl Beckson. "Wilde as Poet," in _The Cambridge Companion to Oscar Wilde,_ Peter Raby, ed. Cambridge: Cambridge University Press, 1997. 57–68.

Anjali Gallup-Diaz. "The Author, his Friends, and _The Ballad of Reading Gaol_: Epistolary Acts," _Reading Wilde, Querying Spaces: An Exhibition Commemorating the 100th Anniversary of the Trials of Oscar Wilde._ New York: Fales Library, 1995. 77–89.

Nick Frankel. "'Ave Imperatrix': Oscar Wilde and the Poetry of Englishness," _Victorian Poetry,_ 35 (1997), 117–37.

Donald Lawler. "The Gothic Wilde," in _Rediscovering Oscar Wilde,_ C. George Sandulescu, ed. Gerrards Cross: Colin Smythe, 1994. 249–68.

Jay Losey. "The Aesthetics of Exile: Wilde Transforming Dante in _Intentions_ and _De Profundis,_" _English Literature in Transition,_ 36 (1993), 429–50.

Margueritte S. Murphy. _A Tradition of Subversion: The Prose Poem in English from Wilde to Ashberry._ Amherst, MA: University of Massachusetts Press, 1992.

Christopher S. Nassaar. "Wilde's _The Ballad of Reading Gaol,_" _Explicator,_ 53 (1995), 158–60.

Nicola Nixon. "The Reading Gaol of Henry James's _In the Cage,_" _English Literary History,_ 66 (1999), 179–201.

Bernard O'Donoghue. "The Journey to Reading Gaol: Sacrifice and Scapegoats in Irish Literature," in _Wilde the Irishman,_ Jerusha McCormack, ed. New Haven: Yale University Press, 1998. 103–12.

Norman Page. "Decoding *The Ballad of Reading Gaol*," in *Rediscovering Oscar Wilde*, C. George Sandulescu, ed. Gerrards Cross: Colin Smythe, 1994. 305–11.

Sandra Siegel. "Oscar Wilde's Gift and Oxford's "Coarse Impertinence," in *Ideology and Ireland in the Nineteenth Century*, Tadhg Foley and Seán Ryder, eds. Dublin: Four Courts Press, 1998. 69–78.

The Fiction

FOR GENERAL DISCUSSION OF THE FICTION

Gareth Noon. "Wilde's Gracious Enclosures: A Brief Tour," *Victorian Newsletter*, 91 (1997), 17–20.

Claude J. Summers. *Gay Fictions, Wilde to Stonewall: Studies in a Male Homosexual Literary Tradition*. New York: Continuum, 1990.

Short Fiction

FOR EDITIONS OF THE SHORT FICTION

Isobel Murray, ed. *Oscar Wilde: The Complete Shorter Fiction*. The World's Classics. Oxford: Oxford University Press, 1979.

Ian Small, ed. *Oscar Wilde: Complete Short Fiction*. Harmondsworth, Penguin, 1994.

FOR CRITICAL DISCUSSION OF THE SHORT FICTION

Josephine M. Guy. "An Allusion in Wilde's 'The Canterville Ghost,'" *Notes and Queries*, ns 45 (1998), 224–26.

Christopher S. Nassaar. "Andersen's 'The Shadow' and Wilde's 'The Fisherman and His Soul': A Case of Influence," *Nineteenth Century Literature*, 50 (1995), 217–24.

_____. "Andersen's 'The Ugly Duckling' and Wilde's 'The Birthday of the Infanta,'" *Explicator*, 55 (1997), 83–85.

Clifton Snider. "Eros and Logos in Some Fairy Stories by Oscar Wilde: A Jungian Interpretation," *Victorian Newsletter*, 84 (1993), 1–8.

The Picture of Dorian Gray

FOR EDITIONS OF *THE PICTURE OF DORIAN GRAY*

Peter Faulkner, ed. *Oscar Wilde: The Picture of Dorian Gray.* London: Everyman, 1996.

Norman Page, ed. *Oscar Wilde: The Picture of Dorian Gray.* Peterborough, Ontario: Broadview Press, 1998.

The Picture of Dorian Gray: The Lippincott Edition. London: Creation Books, 2000.

FOR CRITICAL DISCUSSION OF *THE PICTURE OF DORIAN GRAY*

Antonio Ballesteros González. "The Mirror of Narcissus in *The Picture of Dorian Gray,*" in *Rediscovering Oscar Wilde,* C. George Sandulescu, ed. Gerrards Cross: Colin Smythe, 1994. 1–12.

Pia Brînzeu, "Dorian Gray's Rooms and Cyberspace," in *Rediscovering Oscar Wilde,* C. George Sandulescu, ed. Gerrards Cross: Colin Smythe, 1994. 21–29.

Joseph Bristow, "'A complex multiform creature': Wilde's sexual identities," in *The Cambridge Companion to Oscar Wilde,* Peter Raby, ed. Cambridge: Cambridge University Press, 1997. 195–218.

Timothy L. Carens. "Restyling the Secret of the Opium Den," *Reading Wilde, Querying Spaces: An Exhibition Commemorating the 100th Anniversary of the Trials of Oscar Wilde.* New York: Fales Library, 1995. 65–75.

Peter Allan Dale. "Oscar Wilde: Crime and the 'Glorious Shapes of Art,'" *Victorian Newsletter,* 88 (1995), 1–5.

Jean M. Ellis D'Alessandro. "Intellectual Wordplay in Wilde's Characterization of Henry Wotton," in *Rediscovering Oscar Wilde,* C. George Sandulescu, ed. Gerrards Cross: Colin Smythe, 1994. 62–75.

Lawrence Danson. "'Each Man Kills the Thing he Loves': The Impermanence of Personality in Oscar Wilde," in *Rediscovering Oscar Wilde,* C. George Sandulescu, ed. Gerrards Cross: Colin Smythe, 1994. 82–93.

John Wilson Foster. "Against Nature? Science and Oscar Wilde," in *Wilde the Irishman*, Jerusha McCormack, ed. New Haven: Yale University Press, 1998. 113–24.

John Gall. "The Pregnant Death of Dorian Gray," *Victorian Newsletter*, 82 (1992), 55–57.

Michael Patrick Gillespie. "Picturing Dorian Gray: Resistant Readings in Wilde's Novel," *English Literature in Transition*, 35 (1992), 7–25.

_____. "'What's in a Name?': Representing *The Picture of Dorian Gray*," *Bucknell Review*, 38 (1994), 44–60.

_____. "Ethics and Aesthetics in *The Picture of Dorian Gray*," in *Rediscovering Oscar Wilde*, C. George Sandulescu, ed. Gerrards Cross: Colin Smythe, 1994. 137–55.

_____. *The Picture of Dorian Gray: "What the World Thinks Me"*. New York: Twayne, 1995.

Barri J. Gold. "The Domination of *Dorian Gray*," *Victorian Newsletter*, 91 (1997), 27–30.

Terri A. Hasseler. "The Physiological Determinism Debate in Oscar Wilde's *The Picture of Dorian Gray*," *Victorian Newsletter*, 84 (1993), 31–35.

Deborah McCollister. "Wilde's *The Picture of Dorian Gray*," *Explicator*, 54 (1995), 17–20.

Donald Lawler. "The Gothic Wilde," in *Rediscovering Oscar Wilde*, C. George Sandulescu, ed. Gerrards Cross: Colin Smythe, 1994. 249–68.

Curtis Marez. "The Other Addict: Reflections on Colonialism and Oscar Wilde's Smoke Screen, *English Literary History*, 64 (1997), 257–87.

Martin Meisel. "The World, The Flesh, and Oscar Wilde: Bodily Politics in *Salome* and *Dorian Gray*," *Nineteenth Century Contexts*, 16 (1992), 121–34.

Isobel Murray. "Oscar Wilde in his Literary Element: Yet Another Source for *Dorian Gray?*" in *Rediscovering Oscar Wilde*, C. George Sandulescu, ed. Gerrards Cross: Colin Smythe, 1994. 283–96.

Christopher S. Nassaar. "Wilde's *The Picture of Dorian Gray* and *Salome*," *Explicator*, 53 (1995), 217–20.

_____. "Wilde's *The Picture of Dorian Gray* and *Lady Windermere's Fan*," *Explicator*, 54 (1996), 20–24.

_____. "Wilde's *The Picture of Dorian Gray* and *Salome*," *Explicator*, 57 (1998), 33–35.

_____. "Wilde's *The Picture of Dorian Gray*," *Explicator*, 57 (1999), 216–17.

Jeff Nunokawa. "The Importance of Being Bored: The Dividends of Ennui in *The Picture of Dorian Gray*," *Studies in the Novel*, 28 (1996), 357–71.

Sylvia Ostermann. "Eros and Thanatos in *The Picture of Dorian Gray*," in *Rediscovering Oscar Wilde*, C. George Sandulescu, ed. Gerrards Cross: Colin Smythe, 1994. 297–304.

James Raeside. "The Spirit is Willing but the Flesh is Strong: Mishima Yukio's *Kinjiki* and Oscar Wilde," *Comparative Literature Studies*, 36 (1999), 1–24.

Esther Rashkin. "Art as Symptom: A Portrait of Child Abuse in *The Picture of Dorian Gray*," *Modern Philology*, 95 (1997), 68–80.

Theoharis Constantine Theoharis. "Will to Power, Poetic Justice, and Mimesis in *The Picture of Dorian Gray*," in *Rediscovering Oscar Wilde*, C. George Sandulescu, ed. Gerrards Cross: Colin Smythe, 1994. 397–404.

David A. Upchurch. *Wilde's Use of Irish Celtic Elements in "The Picture of Dorian Gray"*. New York: Lang, 1992.

Marie-Noëlle Zeender. "John Melmoth and Dorian Gray: The Two-Faced Mirror," in *Rediscovering Oscar Wilde*, C. George Sandulescu, ed. Gerrards Cross: Colin Smythe, 1994. 432–40.

Non–Fictional Prose

Intentions, Criticism, *De Profundis*, Journalism,
"The Portrait of Mr W. H.," *The Soul of Man*, Commonplace Books

FOR CRITICAL ACCOUNTS OF WILDE'S CRITICISM AND *INTENTIONS*

Julia Prewitt Brown. *Cosmopolitan Criticism: Oscar Wilde's Philosophy of Art*. Charlottesville: University of Virginia Press, 1997.

Lawrence Danson. *Wilde's Intentions: The Artist in his Criticism*. Oxford: Clarendon Press, 1997.

_____. "Wilde as critic and theorist," in *The Cambridge Companion to Oscar Wilde*, Peter Raby, ed. Cambridge: Cambridge University Press, 1997. 80–95.

Jay Losey. "The Aesthetics of Exile: Wilde Transforming Dante in *Intentions* and *De Profundis*," *English Literature in Transition*, 36 (1993), 429–50.

Horst Schroeder, "ΕΡΩΣ ΤΩΝ ΑΔΥΝΑΤΩΝ—*L'Amour de l'Impossible*: A Graeco-French Collocation in 'The Critic As Artist,'" *Notes and Queries*, ns 40 (1993), 52–53.

_____. "Wilde's Commonplace Book and Symonds's *Studies of the Greek Poets*," *Notes and Queries*, ns 40 (1993), 53–54.

_____. "Pausanias and 'The Critic As Artist,'" *Notes and Queries*, ns 40 (1993), 55–56.

_____. "Matthew Arnold and Oscar Wilde's Commonplace Book," *Notes and Queries*, ns 41 (1994), 359–60.

_____. "A Source for 'Pen, Pencil and Poison,'" *Notes and Queries*, ns 41 (1994), 362–63.

_____. "A Homeric Epithet in 'The Critic as Artist,'" *Notes and Queries*, ns 41 (1994), 363.

_____. "A Printing Error in 'The Soul of Man Under Socialism,'" *Notes and Queries*, ns 43 (1996), 49–51.

_____. "An Unacknowledged Quotation in 'Pen, Pencil and Poison,'" *Notes and Queries*, ns 43 (1996), 51–52.

_____. "Wilde, Wainewright, and Fuseli," *Notes and Queries*, ns 43 (1996), 433–34.

_____. "The Reference to Mantegna in 'The Critic as Artist,'" *Notes and Queries*, ns 44 (1997), 350–51.

_____. "Another Swipe at W. P. Frith by Oscar Wilde," *Notes and Queries*, ns 45 (1998), 224.

Deirdre Toomey. "The Story-Teller at Fault: Oscar Wilde and Irish Orality," in *Wilde the Irishman*, Jerusha McCormack, ed. New Haven: Yale University Press, 1998. 24–35.

De Profundis

FOR EDITIONS OF *DE PROFUNDIS*

Merlin Holland, ed. *The Letters of Oscar Wilde*. London: Fourth Estate, 2000.

FOR CRITICAL DISCUSSION OF *DE PROFUNDIS*

Julia Prewitt Brown. *Cosmopolitan Criticism: Oscar Wilde's Philosophy of Art*. Charlottesville: University of Virginia Press, 1997.

Timothy D'Arch Smith and Horst Schroeder. "Feasting with Panthers," *Notes and Queries*, ns 42 (1995), 201–202.

Peter Allan Dale. "Oscar Wilde: Crime and the 'Glorious Shapes of Art,'" *Victorian Newsletter*, 88 (1995), 1–5.

Michael R. Doylen. "Oscar Wilde's *De Profundis*: Homosexual Self-Fashioning on the Other Side of Scandal," *Victorian Literature and Culture*, 27 (1999), 547–66.

Jay Losey. "The Aesthetics of Exile: Wilde Transforming Dante in *Intentions* and *De Profundis*," *English Literature in Transition*, 36 (1993), 429–50.

Frank McGuinness. "The Spirit of Play in *De Profundis*," in *Wilde the Irishman*, Jerusha McCormack, ed. New Haven: Yale University Press, 1998. 140–45.

Journalism

FOR ACCOUNTS OF WILDE'S CAREER AS A JOURNALIST

Anya Clayworth. "*The Woman's World*: Oscar Wilde as Editor," *Victorian Periodicals Review*, 30 (1997), 84–101.

Stephanie Green. "Oscar Wilde's *The Woman's World*," *Victorian Periodicals Review*, 30 (1997), 102–18.

Catherine Ksinan. "Wilde as Editor of *Woman's World*: Fighting a Dull Slumber in Stale Certitudes," *English Literature in Transition*, 41 (1998), 408–26.

John Stokes. "Wilde the Journalist," in *The Cambridge Companion to Oscar Wilde*, Peter Raby, ed. Cambridge: Cambridge University Press, 1997. 69–79.

Oskar Wellens. "A Hitherto Unnoticed Review by Wilde," *Notes and Queries*, ns 41 (1994), 364.

"The Portrait of Mr W. H."

FOR CRITICAL DISCUSSION OF "THE PORTRAIT OF MR W. H."

Joseph Bristow. "'A complex multiform creature': Wilde's sexual identities," in *The Cambridge Companion to Oscar Wilde*, Peter Raby, ed. Cambridge: Cambridge University Press, 1997. 195–218.

Robert J. G. Lange. "The Provenance of Oscar Wilde's *The Portrait of Mr W. H.*: An Oversight? *Notes and Queries*, ns 42 (1995), 202–203.

W. J. McCormack, "Wilde and Parnell," in *Wilde the Irishman*, Jerusha McCormack, ed. London: Yale University Press, 1998. 95–102.

Horst Schroeder. *Oscar Wilde, "The Portrait of Mr W. H."—Its Composition, Publication and Reception*. Braunschweig: Technische Universität Braunschweig, 1984.

Drama

FOR GENERAL DISCUSSIONS OF THE DRAMA

Joseph Bristow. "Dowdies and Dandies: Oscar Wilde's Refashioning of Society Comedy," *Modern Drama*, 37 (1994), 53–70.

Richard Allen Cave. "Wilde Designs: Some Thoughts about Recent British Productions of His Plays," *Modern Drama*, 37 (1994), 175–81.

_____. "Power Structuring: The Presentation of Outsider Figures in Wilde's Plays," in *Rediscovering Oscar Wilde*, C. George Sandulescu, ed. Gerrards Cross: Colin Smythe, 1994. 37–50.

_____. "Wilde's Plays: Some Lines of Influence," in *The Cambridge Companion to Oscar Wilde*, Peter Raby, ed. Cambridge: Cambridge University Press, 1997. 219–48.

_____. "Introduction," in *The Importance of Being Earnest and Other Plays,* Richard Allen Cave, ed. Harmondsworth: Penguin, 2000.

Francesca Coppa. "I Seem to Recognize a Device that Has Done Duty in Bygone Plays: Oscar Wilde and the Theatre of Epigram," *Reading Wilde, Querying Spaces: An Exhibition Commemorating the 100th Anniversary of the Trials of Oscar Wilde.* New York: Fales Library, 1995. 11–19.

Joseph Donohue. "Wilde and the Idea of a Theatre," in *Rediscovering Oscar Wilde,* C. George Sandulescu, ed. Gerrards Cross: Colin Smythe, 1994. 118–26.

Terry Eagleton. "Oscar and George," *Nineteenth Century Contexts,* 18 (1994), 205–23.

Sos Eltis. *Revising Wilde: Society and Subversion in the Plays of Oscar Wilde.* Oxford: Clarendon Press, 1996.

David J. Gordon. "Shavian Comedy and the Shadow of Wilde," in *The Cambridge Companion to George Bernard Shaw,* Christopher Innes, ed. Cambridge: Cambridge University Press, 1998. 124–43.

Robert Gordon. "Wilde's 'Plays of Modern Life' on the Contemporary British Stage," in *Rediscovering Oscar Wilde,* C. George Sandulescu, ed. Gerrards Cross: Colin Smythe, 1994. 156–66.

Russell Jackson. "Oscar Wilde's Contract for a New Play," *Theatre Notebook,* 50 (1996), 113–15.

Joel H. Kaplan. "Staging Wilde's Society Plays: A Conversation with Philip Prowse (Glasgow Citizens Theatre)," *Modern Drama,* 37 (1994), 192–205.

_____. "Wilde in the Gorbals: Society Drama and Citizens Theatre," in *Rediscovering Oscar Wilde,* C. George Sandulescu, ed. Gerrards Cross: Colin Smythe, 1994. 214–23.

_____. ed. Special Issue on Wilde, *Modern Drama,* 37 (1994).

_____. "Wilde on the stage," in *The Cambridge Companion to Oscar Wilde,* Peter Raby, ed. Cambridge: Cambridge University Press, 1997. 249–75.

Jacques de Langlade. "Oscar Wilde as a Modern Dramatist and Actor," in *Rediscovering Oscar Wilde*, C. George Sandulescu, ed. Gerrards Cross: Colin Smythe, 1994. 244–48.

Kerry Powell. "Oscar Wilde, Elizabeth Robins, and the Theatre of the Future," *Modern Drama*, 37 (1994), 220–37.

_____. *Women and the Victorian Theatre.* Cambridge: Cambridge University Press, 1997.

Peter Raby. "Wilde and European Theatre," in *Rediscovering Oscar Wilde*, C. George Sandulescu, ed. Gerrards Cross: Colin Smythe, 1994. 328–37.

_____. "Wilde's comedies of Society," in *The Cambridge Companion to Oscar Wilde*, Peter Raby, ed. Cambridge: Cambridge University Press, 1997. 143–60.

Alan Stanford. "Acting Wilde," in *Wilde the Irishman*, Jerusha McCormack, ed. New Haven: Yale University Press, 1998. 152–57.

Vera; or, The Nihilists

FOR CRITICAL DISCUSSION OF *VERA; OR, THE NIHILISTS*

George Rowell. 'The Truth About *Vera*,' *Nineteenth Century Theatre*, 21 (1993), 94–100.

A Florentine Tragedy

FOR CRITICAL DISCUSSION OF *A FLORENTINE TRAGEDY*

Regenia Gagnier. "Aesthetics and Economics in *A Florentine Tragedy*," *Modern Drama*, 37 (1994), 71–83.

La Sainte Courtisane

FOR CRITICAL DISCUSSION OF *LA SAINTE COURTISANE*

Christopher S. Nassaar. "Wilde's *La Sainte Courtisane*," *Explicator*, 56 (1997), 28–30.

Lady Windermere's Fan

FOR EDITIONS OF *LADY WINDERMERE'S FAN*

Ian Small, ed. *Oscar Wilde: Lady Windermere's Fan*. London: Ernest Benn, 1980; 2nd and revised edition, London: A. & C. Black, 1999.

FOR CRITICAL DISCUSSION OF *LADY WINDERMERE'S FAN*

Karl Beckson. "Narcissistic Reflections in a Wilde Mirror," *Modern Drama*, 37 (1994), 148–55.

Richard Allen Cave. "Wilde Designs: Some Thoughts about Recent British Productions of His Plays," *Modern Drama*, 37 (1994), 175–81.

Joel H. Kaplan. "A Puppet's Power: George Alexander, Clement Scott, and the Replotting of *Lady Windermere's Fan*," *Theatre Notebook*, 46 (1992), 59–73.

_____. "Staging Wilde's Society Plays: A Conversation with Philip Prowse (Glasgow Citizens Theatre)," *Modern Drama*, 37 (1994), 192–205.

_____. "Wilde on the stage," in *The Cambridge Companion to Oscar Wilde*, Peter Raby, ed. Cambridge: Cambridge University Press, 1997. 249–75.

Paul Kirschner. "Wilde's Shadow in Conrad's 'The Return,'" *Notes and Queries*, ns 40 (1993), 495–96.

Christopher S. Nassaar. "Wilde's *The Picture of Dorian Gray* and *Lady Windermere's Fan*," *Explicator*, 54 (1995), 20–24.

_____. "Wilde's *Lady Windermere's Fan* and Shaw's *Mrs Warren's Profession*," *Explicator*, 56 (1998), 137–38.

Salome and Salomé

FOR EDITIONS OF *SALOME* AND *SALOMÉ*

James Havoc, ed. *Oscar Wilde, Salome and Aubrey Beardsley, Under the Hill*. London: Creation Books, 1996.

Pascal Aquien, ed. *Salomé. With English version by Lord Alfred Douglas*. Paris: Falammarion, 1993.

FOR CRITICAL DISCUSSION OF *SALOME*

Karl Beckson. "Narcissistic Reflections in a Wilde Mirror," *Modern Drama*, 37 (1994), 148–55.

Brad Bucknell. "On 'Seeing' Salome," *English Literary History*, 60 (1993), 503–26.

Edward Burns. "Salome: Wilde's Radical Tragedy" in *Rediscovering Oscar Wilde*, C. George Sandulescu, ed. Gerrards Cross: Colin Smythe, 1994. 30–36.

Joseph Donohue. "*Salome* and the Wildean Art of Symbolist Theatre," *Modern Drama*, 37 (1994), 84–103.

_____. "Distance, death and desire in *Salome*," in *The Cambridge Companion to Oscar Wilde*, Peter Raby, ed. Cambridge: Cambridge University Press, 1997. 118–42.

Irène Eynat-Confino. "Oscar Wilde and Dramatic Strategies," in *Rediscovering Oscar Wilde*, C. George Sandulescu, ed. Gerrards Cross: Colin Smythe, 1994. 127–36.

Rhonda Garelick. *Rising Star: Dandyism, Gender and Performance in the Fin de Siècle*. Princeton, NJ: Princeton University Press, 1998.

Patricia Kellogg-Dennis. "Oscar Wilde's *Salome*: Symbolist Princess," in *Rediscovering Oscar Wilde*, C. George Sandulescu, ed. Gerrards Cross: Colin Smythe, 1994. 224–31.

Donald Lawler. "The Gothic Wilde," in *Rediscovering Oscar Wilde*, C. George Sandulescu, ed. Gerrards Cross: Colin Smythe, 1994. 249–68.

Melissa Knox. "Losing One's Head: Wilde's Confession in *Salome*," in *Rediscovering Oscar Wilde*, C. George Sandulescu, ed. Gerrards Cross: Colin Smythe, 1994. 232–43.

Martin Meisel. "The World, The Flesh, and Oscar Wilde: Bodily Politics in *Salome* and *Dorian Gray*," *Nineteenth Century Contexts*, 16 (1992), 121–34.

Jason P. Mitchell. "A Source Victorian or Biblical?: The Integration of Biblical Diction and Symbolism in Oscar Wilde's *Salomé*," *Victorian Newsletter*, 89 (1996), 14–18.

_____. "Wilde's *The Picture of Dorian Gray* and *Salome*," *Explicator*, 53 (1995), 217–20.

_____. "Wilde's *The Picture of Dorian Gray* and *Salome*," *Explicator*, 57 (1998), 33–35.

_____. "Wilde's *Salome*," *Explicator*, 57 (1999), 89–90.

Austin E. Quigley. "Realism and Symbolism in Oscar Wilde's *Salomé*," *Modern Drama*, 37 (1994), 104–19.

Robert Schweik. "Congruous Incongruities: The Wilde-Beardsley 'Collaboration,'" *English Literature in Transition*, 37 (1994), 9–26.

William Tydeman and Steven Price, eds. *Wilde: Salome. Plays in Production*. Cambridge: Cambridge University Press, 1996.

A Woman of No Importance

FOR EDITIONS OF *A WOMAN OF NO IMPORTANCE*

Ian Small, ed. *Oscar Wilde: A Woman of No Importance*. London: Ernest Benn, 1983; 2nd and revised edn. London: A. & C. Black, 1993.

FOR CRITICAL DISCUSSION OF *A WOMAN OF NO IMPORTANCE*

Karl Beckson. "Narcissistic Reflections in a Wilde Mirror," *Modern Drama*, 37 (1994), 148–55.

Anya Clayworth. "Notes on Oscar Wilde: Two Unpublished Letters from the National Library of Scotland," *Notes and Queries*, ns 45 (1998), 221–24.

Joel H. Kaplan. "Staging Wilde's Society Plays: A Conversation with Philip Prowse (Glasgow Citizens Theatre)," *Modern Drama*, 37 (1994), 192–205.

_____. "Oscar Wilde's Contract for *A Woman of No Importance*," *Theatre Notebook*, 48 (1994), 46–48.

An Ideal Husband

FOR EDITIONS OF *AN IDEAL HUSBAND*

Jackson, Russell, ed. *Oscar Wilde: An Ideal Husband*. London: Ernest Benn, 1983; 2nd and revised edn. London: A. & C. Black, 1993.

FOR CRITICAL DISCUSSION OF *AN IDEAL HUSBAND*

Richard Dellamora. "Oscar Wilde, Social Purity, and *An Ideal Husband*," *Modern Drama*, 37 (1994), 120–13.

Joel H. Kaplan. "Staging Wilde's Society Plays: A Conversation with Philip Prowse (Glasgow Citizens Theatre)," *Modern Drama*, 37 (1994), 192–205.

Jerusha McCormack. "The Wilde Irishman: Oscar as Aesthete and Anarchist," in *Wilde the Irishman*, Jerusha McCormack, ed. New Haven: Yale University Press, 1998. 82–94.

Peter Raby. "The Origins of *The Importance of Being Earnest*," *Modern Drama*, 37 (1994), 139–47.

John Stokes. "Wilde Interpretations," *Modern Drama*, 37 (1994), 156–74.

J. L. Wisenthal, "Wilde, Shaw, and the Play of Conversation," *Modern Drama*, 37 (1994), 206–19.

The Importance of Being Earnest

FOR EDITIONS OF *THE IMPORTANCE OF BEING EARNEST*

Joseph Donohue (with Ruth Berggren), ed. *Oscar Wilde's The Importance of Being Earnest: A Reconstructive Critical Edition of the Text of the First Production, St James's Theatre, London, 1895.* The Princess Grace Irish Library, 10. Gerrards Cross, Bucks: Colin Smythe, 1995.

FOR CRITICAL DISCUSSION OF *THE IMPORTANCE OF BEING EARNEST*

Christopher Craft. *Another Kind of Love: Male Homosexual Desire in English Discourse, 1850–1920.* London: University of California Press, 1994.

Gail Finney. "Comparative Perspectives on Gender and Comedy: The Examples of Wilde, Hofmannsthal, and Ebner–Eschenbach," *Modern Drama*, 37 (1994), 638–50.

S. J. Harrison. "Prunes and Prism: Wilde and Dickens," *Notes and Queries*, ns 44 (1997), 351–52.

Russell Jackson. "The Importance of Being Earnest," in *The Cambridge Companion to Oscar Wilde*, Peter Raby, ed. Cambridge: Cambridge University Press, 1997. 161–77.

W. Craven Mackie. "Bunbury Pure and Simple," *Modern Drama*, 41 (1998), 327–30.

W. J. McCormack. "Wilde and Parnell," in *Wilde the Irishman*, Jerusha McCormack, ed. New Haven: Yale University Press, 1998. 95–102.

Peter Musolf. "Bunburying and the Art of Kabuki: or, Wilde, Mishima and the Importance of Being a Sardine Seller," *New Theatre Quarterly*, 12 (1996), 333–39.

Christopher S. Nassaar. "Wilde's *The Importance of Being Earnest* and Stoppard's *Rosencrantz and Guildenstern are Dead*," *Explicator*, 58 (2000), 91–92.

Peter Raby. "The Origins of *The Importance of Being Earnest*," *Modern Drama*, 37 (1994), 139–47.

_____. *The Importance of Being Earnest: A Reader's Companion*. New York: Twayne, 1995.

_____. "'The Persons of the Play': Some Reflections on Wilde's Choice of Names in *The Importance of Being Earnest*," *Nineteenth Century Theatre*, 23 (1995), 67–75.

Horst Schroeder. "Bimetallism: A Topical Reference in Oscar Wilde," *Notes and Queries*, 40 (1993), 56–58.

Eve Kosofsky Sedgwick. "Tales of the Avunculate: Queer Tutelage in *The Importance of Being Earnest*," in *Professions of Desire: Lesbian and Gay Studies in Literature*, George E. Haggerty and Bonnie Zimmerman, eds. New York: Modern Language Association, 1995. 191–209.

John Stokes. "Wilde Interpretations," *Modern Drama*, 37 (1994), 156–74.

Index of Critics